Dorothy Evelyn
Deacon
Princess
Radziwill and
later Countess
Palffy (1891 - 1960)

GLADYS

DUCHESS OF MARLBOROUGH

Hugo Vickers

HOLT, RINEHART AND WINSTON
New York

First published in the United States in 1980 by
Holt, Rinehart and Winston, 383 Madison Avenue,
New York, New York 10017.

Library of Congress Cataloging in Publication Data
Vickers, Hugo.
Gladys, Duchess of Marlborough.
Bibliography: p.
Includes index.
1. Marlborough, Gladys Spencer-Churchill, Duchess of,
1881-1977.   2. England—Nobility—Biography.
I. Title.
DA566.9.M365V52   1980   942.082′092′4   [B]   79-925
ISBN 0-03-044751-8

Printed in the United States of America
1 3 5 7 9 10 8 6 4 2

Contents

Illustrations

Acknowledgements

The author wishes to express thanks to the following for assistance with this biography:

Mr and Mrs Austen T. Gray, whose help and encouragement over the past four years has been enormous; Mr Andrei Kwiatkowsky, who was Gladys's only servant and friend in the last years of her life; the Administrators of the Estate, Miss Joan M. Rees and Mr Victor Hadley; Mr N. H. Turner, Official Solicitor to the Supreme Court; Mr & Mrs Jan Tomaszewski, Count Palffy; Mrs John R. Chapin; Mrs Alison Gray; and the staff of St Andrew's Hospital, Northampton, in particular Sister June Dillon, Mrs F. E. Newton, Dr K. L. Trick and the nurses in O'Connell Ward.

In the United Kingdom: the Countess of Avon, Mr Alan Bishop, Mr & Mrs David Brown of Chacombe Grange, the Earl of Carnarvon, Mr & Mrs Peregrine S. Churchill, Mrs Ralph Cobbold, Helen Lady Dashwood, Mr Patrick Davies (Christie's), Mrs Sandra Dobson Jarroch, Lady Epstein, the late Miss Eve Fairfax, Mr Wynne Godley, Mr David Green, Mr Miron Grindea (Editor of ADAM), Mrs Barbara Halpern, Mr Peter Hartley, Mrs May Hobbs, Mr Philip Howard, Mr H. Montgomery Hyde, Lady Serena James, Mr R. A. Joscelyne, Anita Leslie, Lady Leslie, Mr Seymour Leslie, the Countess of Longford, Mrs Margaret MacDonald (University of Glasgow), Father John V. F. Maunsell, M Paul Maze, Mr Alan Pryce-Jones, Mr John & Lady Sophia Schilizzi, the late Mr R. B. Sharp, Mr Richard Allenby Shore, Mr & Mrs Simon Speed, Mr Julian Trevelyan, Mr & Mrs Igor Vinogradoff, Mrs Anne Wall, and the late Mrs Violet Wyndham.

In the United States of America: Mr Joseph W. Alsop, Donna Brambilla, Mr Edward Burns, Dr Francis de Marneffe (Director of McLean Hospital, Belmont, Mass.), Ellen S. Dunlap (Research Librarian, Humanities Research Center, The University of Texas at Austin), Mr Donald Gallup & Mr Peter Dzwonkoski (The Beinecke Rare Book and Manuscript Library, Yale), Dr R. M. Kenin, Professor Philip Kolb, Professor R. W. B. Lewis, Mr David McKibbin (Athenaeum, Boston), Mr Paul Padgette, Mrs Roland Redmond, Professor Ernest Samuels, and Meryle Secrest.

In France: M Bernard Cagnat (directeur, Hotel Splendide, Cannes), Mme Berthe Cleyrergue, M Jacques de Lacratelle, La Duchesse de La Rochefoucauld, Mr David Garnett, Comte Louis Gautier-Vignal, the late M Philippe Jullian, Mme Monique Laurent (Le Conservateur, Musée Rodin), the late Paul Morand, and Mr Stuart Preston.

In Italy & elsewhere: Dr Cecil Anrep, Sir Harold Acton, the late Don Salvador de Madariaga, Professor Leon Edel, Dr Fiorella Superbi Gioffredi (Villa I Tatti), Mr Ian Greenlees, Mrs G. Neumann, and Dr Joachim Storck.

Gladys's letters and diaries are quoted by kind permission of the heirs of her estate. The author also wishes to thank the following copyright owners: Captain Alexander Ramsay of Mar (HRH The Duke of Connaught), Mrs Barbara Halpern (Mary Berenson), The University of Texas at Austin (Lady Ottoline Morrell), and His Grace the Duke of Marlborough (9th Duke of Marlborough and Consuelo Vanderbilt). Bernard Berenson's letters are the copyright of Dr Cecil Anrep. While every effort has been made to trace all the copyright owners, the author apologizes to anyone whom he has failed to contact. Due acknowledgement will, of course, be made in any future reprint.

Finally to: Verena Vickers for translating letters from German, Hugh Montgomery-Massingberd for his constant advice, my aunt Margaret Vickers for help at the beginning and the end, Gillon Aitken, Victoria Glendinning, Tara Heinemann, Ione Harris, Andrew Barrow, Will Jaffray for an important clue, and Chloë Reed for typing the manuscript.

Hugo Vickers
December 1978

Illustration Acknowledgements

The author and publishers would like to thank the following for kind permission to reproduce the photographs: Florence, Berenson Archives, reproduced by permission of the President and Fellows of Harvard College, 5; Radio Times Hulton Picture Library, 12; Mr B. Gerald Cantor, 14; Mrs Austen T. Gray (Gladys's niece), 15, 19; Jane, Lady Abdy, 18; London Express News Service, 40. Photos Nos 7, 9, 24, 39 and 41 are in the possession of the author. The remaining photographs are in Gladys's papers, and many of them were taken by Gladys herself.

Introduction

Gladys Deacon was an American of outstanding beauty, personality and intelligence, who dazzled society in Paris, Rome and London. In 1902 she was so well known that cardboard dolls named 'Miss Deacon' were on sale to the general public. By 1967, however, the name had faded into obscurity; Gladys, Duchess of Marlborough, still appeared in *Kelly's Handbook* but no address was shown, and very few people knew anything about her.

In 1968 I chanced upon an astonishing reference in *Chips: The Diaries of Sir Henry Channon*. Chips described her in 1943 and contrasted her with her former self:

> I saw an extraordinary marionette of a woman – or was it a man? It wore grey flannel trousers, a wide leather belt, masculine overcoat, and a man's brown felt hat, and had a really frightening appearance, but the hair was golden dyed and long: what is wrongly known as platinum; the mouth was a scarlet scar. Bundi began to growl, and as I secretly examined this terrifying apparition, I recognized Gladys Marlborough, once the world's most beautiful woman ... the toast of Paris, the love of Proust, the *belle amie* of Anatole France.[1]

Never one to miss the chance to greet a Duchess, Chips went over to re-introduce himself. 'She looked at me, stared vacantly with those famous turquoise eyes that once drove men insane with desire and muttered: "Je n'ai jamais entendu ce nom-là", she flung down a ruby clip she was examining and bolted from the shop. . . .'

This story fascinated me, largely because I mistrusted it. I surmised that the vacant stare was hiding something and I

1

wanted to know more about this Miss Deacon, who had changed from 'the world's most beautiful woman' to a 'terrifying apparition'. It is hard to explain why one character fires the imagination while another can pass by without leaving an impression. I think she appealed to me in rather the same way as three figures of fiction which I had encountered as a child. These were Charlotte Brontë's first Mrs Rochester, enclosed in Thornfield Hall, Daphne du Maurier's unseen Rebecca and Charles Dickens's Miss Havisham. All of them had once had opportunities and all of them had come to grief. Yet their mysterious presences still had influence on the lives of others. None could be successfully brushed under the carpet as Gladys Deacon seemed to have been. Again, the contrast between the young and beautiful Gladys and this witchlike creature was intriguing. I wanted to know how and why this metamorphosis had taken place.

Curiosity overcame me at the age of sixteen after I had read *Chips*; I wrote the Duchess a letter, directing it to Chacombe, near Banbury, her last known address. I find this note in my diary of 22 March 1968:

> After breakfast my letter to Gladys, Duchess of Marlborough, was returned by the Official Returned Postal Packet service and the reason given was she had 'gone away'. This puzzles me a lot though it is not surprising in the circumstances. Throughout the day I was fascinated by her....

I remember wondering if she had taken to the road, was wandering unknown in some far-off country, or lay buried in an unmarked grave. Resolved to explore further, I prevailed upon an understanding aunt to drive me to Blenheim to make enquiries there. A sympathetic though slightly surprised guide told us that the Duchess was a very old lady living in a small village in Oxfordshire under the name of Mrs Spencer. The Marlboroughs supported her financially, but had nothing else to do with her. She was surrounded by dogs, which she walked late at night, carrying a small lamp. The guide also said that on bank holidays an old lady arrived at the palace swathed in furs and announced that years ago she had been Duchess there. She wondered if this was Mrs Spencer.

I thought it more than probable that my letter had arrived safely but that the old lady had rejected it because of the Marlborough name. I promised myself that when I was old enough to drive a car I would go to Chacombe and discover the truth. Meanwhile I made an abortive attempt to start this book, but my material only stretched to two pages.

Years passed until I was inspired to make my journey by a conversation in February 1975, which suddenly turned to the Duchess. I set off to Oxfordshire, located the house and peered nervously over the wall. Then I visited the pub, which was very small and quite unaccustomed to receiving visits from outsiders. I enquired if Mrs Spencer still lived at the Grange. The publican looked oddly at me, evidently confused by my interest. I found this hard to justify but muttered that she had once been a very beautiful and intelligent person and rather famous. He then replied, 'No, she's been gone a long time now.' I assumed that he meant dead, and my heart sank accordingly, but he continued, 'She's gone to a hospital up Northampton way.' He had not heard of her death, but reckoned she would be a great age if still alive. I tried to persuade myself that my curiosity was satisfied and returned to London. Then I chanced to relate the story of my day to someone, who, I felt sure, would not be at all interested. Yet this friend responded by relating a story he had once heard of a Duchess of Marlborough being evicted from Blenheim. I checked the dates and realized that it had to be Gladys Deacon.

This was too much. I declared then and there that I would write her life. My enthusiasm never waned, and though I started with slender knowledge, I was able to follow up a few clues, and each time I started to dig a hidden gem emerged from the undergrowth of time. Very soon it became clear that no part of this woman's life had been normal. Nor would she have been so interesting, I suspect, had she married Marlborough at twenty-one and retired gracefully to the Dower House after his death. My task was to lift the veil that for some reason had fallen over her and unmask the truth.

The most terrifying question concerned her present whereabouts. If she was still alive, how old was she? Where was she? Was she *compos mentis*? Would I ever be allowed into her presence? I was extremely pessimistic.

Several people told me that there was a well-known hospital in Northampton, but for a long time nobody that I consulted could recall its name. Then one day the name 'St Andrew's' was mentioned. On 9 May I telephoned the secretary and said, 'I have reason to believe that the Duchess of Marlborough is a patient at the hospital. What do I have to do to ask for permission to come and see her to tell her I want to write her biography?' He neither confirmed nor denied her presence there, but suggested I put my request in writing. This I did and by the end of the month I was excited to learn that she was still alive and that my application was being considered. Furthermore I received a letter from her nephew, Count Palffy, in which he said, 'The purpose of your letter has indeed retained my fullest attention and interest. . . .' He suggested a meeting.

Wasting no further time I made my way to Lausanne, nervously considering how to convince this nephew that Gladys Deacon had a life interesting enough for a book. However, he was thoroughly aware of the scope of her life and gave me a number of further clues and introductions. If anything, he was surprised why one so young should wish to undertake the task. He warned me that before visiting his aunt, I would do well to brush up on my Keyserling and Hofmannsthal. 'She's as cute as a cat', he said. 'She'll look right through you.'

The first visit to the Duchess was delayed until July 1975. In the mounting anticipation, I became very nervous, and further terror was instilled in me by the warnings I was given: 'Be careful of her'; 'Don't underestimate her'; and the questioning look of the solicitor who armed me with an introduction to the hospital – a look that asked 'Can anyone want to go and visit her?' The terror had its first outlet in a vivid nightmare three nights before the visit in which I came face to face with the Duchess in hospital, a fragile invalid yet restored to her youth and beauty. I found myself being observed by eyes, which sometimes showed anger and sometimes deceived; all of which left me more frightened.

The actual visit took place on the afternoon of Sunday 6 July. I drove to Northampton in trepidation, feeling less than confident. My appointment was for two o'clock. Punctually I drove in through the gates and up to the front door of the impressive building. Presently the Chief Nursing Officer, Mrs Newton, took charge of me and we began the long walk to O'Connell Ward. We passed patients playing cards, reading or wandering about as though they were in a large country hotel. Some made polite greetings, others were silent. The occasional hostile face glared from its bedroom, angry to see us pass. I had never been in a

4

psychiatric hospital before and was not at my ease. Nor did my confidence increase when Mrs Newton warned me, 'You'll find her very ugly, but she has beautiful eyes.' I asked if the Duchess was expecting me. 'I thought it better not to tell her', she replied. 'She's very temperamental, the Duchess. She may tell you she's dead. You may have had a completely wasted journey.'

Having travelled a long and winding route, which involved the unlocking and re-locking of several doors, we arrived in the stark, clinical corridor of O'Connell Ward, a psycho-geriatric ward on the first floor of the hospital. A chirpy Japanese nurse informed us 'The Duchess is in the Green Room'. Only one or two patients were indoors; the rest were out in the sun.

The Duchess was seated in her chair by the door with a white linen cloth over her face, her feet resting on a stool. All I could see of her was her white hair, and I was surprised at how small she was. Mrs Newton roused her and I knelt down beside her.

The first thing that happened was that she began to raise the cloth. I saw her jaw which was very distorted, partly due to wax injections and partly to old age. As the cloth was lifted higher, I found myself being stared at by those eyes which were so blue that any description of them would be inadequate. She gazed at me for a few moments, then cried out 'Later, later, later', dropped the veil and returned to sleep. Sister Dillon then arrived and said they would put her to bed and we could try again in half an hour. Meanwhile I wandered in the garden where I met a clergyman who thought I was a patient, or a patient who thought he was a clergyman, or a genuine clergyman who was also a patient, I still do not know. We had a brief conversation which did nothing to improve the state of my nerves.

The second visit took place three-quarters of an hour after the first. We retraced the long journey through the hospital's corridors and this time went to the Duchess's bedroom. Mrs Newton ushered me into the small rectangular room and left me there while she went to find the Sister. From another room there emerged a maniacal scream reminiscent of all film versions of *Jane Eyre*, while I came face to face with Gladys Deacon.

She was in bed, dressed in a pink nightgown and wide awake. I went over to her and gave her some photographs I had taken of her sphinx at Blenheim. She took them, looked at them, and handed them back with the words 'I don't like them'. Then Sister Dillon came in and sat down on the bed. She gave her the message that I was going to write about her, but this got no response. Then she showed her another photograph I had brought, one of her eye painted in the portico of Blenheim. Gladys looked at it and suddenly began to laugh. Then she asked for some doughnuts, which were to have jam and sugar in them. 'Tell me what I'm going to dream about tonight?' she asked, and then, 'How's the Mississippi?' After a while she dismissed the Sister, adding 'Take him with you, will you.'

My first conclusion was that she was quite senile, and I left feeling rather hollow inside. Only later did I wonder if she had not been taking in rather more than she liked to let on. I resolved to visit her again.

My second visit signified something of a breakthrough. Gladys was sitting in a corner of the 'lounge' with her hair in a bun. She was wearing a white dress with black spots, stockings and slippers and a blue shawl. There were flowers on the table and she was surrounded by nurses. In their midst, Sister Dillon was telling her that a visitor was on his way, a Mr Vickers, who was going to write a book about her. I entered the room just as Gladys was saying, 'But I don't see why I should be disturbed by Mr Vickers.' I sat down beside her. Her head turned to look at me and she continued slowly in a different tone: 'And he doesn't think so either.' 'He's come to see you', said the Sister. 'Well I don't like this story', she said.

Then I produced a bundle of photographs to show her – of Hofmannsthal, David Garnett, Freud, Harold Nicolson, Proust and Consuelo Vanderbilt. She had great fun denying that she had ever seen any of them before. She laughed at the picture of Proust, and enquired 'Is that you?' She liked the dress in the picture of Consuelo, so we tried it again. This is how the conversation went:

Vickers: Shall we show her this one again? She liked the dress.
Sister: Yes, she liked the dress of that one.
Vickers: She was a friend of yours, this one.
Gladys: No, I told you, I've never heard of her.

Then we wrote the name, which gave her the chance to score a point.

Sister: Look, read it.
Gladys: Consuelo, never heard. . . .
Sister: You have.
Gladys: She's a consul, she's a consul. Consuelo. Where have
           I seen her face? Never seen. . . . No! Let him see it!

She beckoned to one of the male nurses and asked him if he had ever seen the lady in the photograph. Prompted by me, he replied, 'It's Consuelo.' With much laughter she continued:

Gladys: Did you ever see a consul dressed like that? No!
           That's a very fine consul. I'm not smart enough to
           hobnob with consuls!
Sister: Oh! You were!
Gladys: What?
Sister: You were!
Gladys: No, no! I've never seen a consul in my life.[2]

Then Gladys pointed to the picture of Proust and addressed a young nurse: 'When you want to get married, you go to a fellow like that!' Soon afterwards she gave me back the picture and said, 'Thank you very much. You've given me a better laugh than I've had since I came here.' She offered me a cup of tea, asked me to stay with her and we began the slow process of making friends.

Because I brought pictures, she referred to me in those early days as 'the photographer'. Three visits later she recognized me and gave me a huge greeting. My visits began to extend to three hours at a time and she invited me to keep coming to see her. In January 1976, she started to *tutoyer* me when speaking French, and just before I went to America in March she took my hands, put them to her forehead and declared, 'Friends for ever.' All in all I visited Gladys sixty-five times.

Never for a moment did I dream that she would lift her ban on discussing the past. Yet that February I showed her a book on d'Annunzio and told her I was reading it. She suddenly told me she used to know him in Rome and asked me what I thought of him. I almost jumped in the air. She continued:

> He had spark, but not fire. In this respect he was like Winston Churchill. Winston. . . . he was not a great man. . . . He had weight, yes, but he was not a gentleman. I knew him well enough. He used to come to that place where we were. He liked to lay down the law!

Hitler, however, she thought was a great man. 'He had a telling personality. When you think how hard it is to create a rising in a small village, well, he had the whole world up in arms. He was larger than Winston. Winston couldn't have done that!' She went on to describe insanity as 'a disease of the brain, like a lock'. Then she urged me to take over the hospital. 'Hoof them out', she said. I pointed at some young nurses. 'Not them, they're small fry!'³

Once a little light had been shed on the past I learnt that she would respond to books, liked looking at pictures and discussing the different characters. Because she was quite deaf, she often missed oral questions, but her eyesight was phenomenal and she read without spectacles. By writing on a piece of paper I could put questions to her which she would read slowly and then reply to swiftly. Gradually I worked my way through the artists and writers and society figures of the day, a process mutually enjoyed and with numerous tangents and diversions. We looked at pictures of works of art and cities; everything was of interest. At the end of a meeting which sometimes lasted as long as four hours, it was invariably myself who was tired and not Gladys.

Only one subject remained taboo unless she mentioned it, and that was her own life. She was never to be directly associated with her past life. She might say, 'Rodin liked to precipitate himself on every woman he met. You know, hands all over you.' But if you then said 'Ah! You knew him then?' she would either shut up like a clam, or say 'I never met him, but a close woman friend of mine told me.' And when I asked her once, 'Where is Gladys Deacon?', she looked at me with a twinkle in her eye and said slowly:

'Gladys Deacon? . . . She never existed.'⁴

PART ONE

Early Days

Chapter One

A REMARKABLE YOUNG PERSON

Gladys Deacon was born in Paris at the Hotel Brighton in the rue de Rivoli, opposite the Tuilerie Gardens, on Monday 7 February 1881. Her mother, Florence Deacon, was twenty-one years old and thrilled at the sight of the baby with its arms outstretched and its little hands opening and closing. In 1914 she recalled to Gladys 'the rapture I felt these many years ago when first I held you in my arms. I can never think of it without emotion.' The date of Gladys's birth was a closely guarded secret all her life and she took elaborate and very feminine precautions to ensure that it remained so. On her marriage certificate in 1921 her age is given as thirty-five, not forty, while her passport bore the conflicting date 1890. On her ninety-fifth birthday in 1976 she sat unwillingly at the head of a long table and gazed in wonder at the cake with its handful of candles. Earlier she had pretended she had forgotten when her birthday was. 'How could I know? I couldn't say "Here I am!"' She dismissed the matter with an alternative theory: 'I was not born. I happened.'

Edward Parker Deacon and his wife Florence were smart Americans, who had chosen to live in Europe. In the last decades of the nineteenth century, Paris was enjoying that phase now known as 'La Belle Epoque'. It was an era of respectable idleness and security, before economic and political pressures halted the glamorous way of life of those few who could afford to be elegant, extravagant and do exactly as they pleased. 'Le gratin', or the upper crust, existed stylishly in the world of salons and smart restaurants, of magnificent balls, exclusive clubs and strolls in the Bois de Boulogne. It lived in the Faubourg Saint-Germain and included such characters as the flamboyant Count Robert de Montesquiou-Fezensac and the rakish

Count Boni de Castellane. The Deacons were accepted in the highest circles. They led the same unquestioning life as 'Le gratin' and would travel, according to the season, to Cannes, Nice or Trouville. They might visit Genoa or Homburg, Geneva or St Moritz. From time to time they crossed the Atlantic for the season at Newport.

Gladys was the most beautiful and the most brilliant of the four Deacon sisters, all of them endowed with good looks and intelligence, and each one destined to glitter in European or American society. Next in line was Audrey, born in Paris in November 1885. She was very close to Gladys and frequently covered up for her mischievous elder sister. Her beauty was more regal than Gladys's, and she had brilliant dark eyes and a classic brow. Audrey was very tall and was teased by her sisters with the persistent question 'What's it like up there in the Heavens?' Edith was born on 16 February 1887 in Cannes, where the Deacons habitually spent the winter season. Her devotion to her mother was total and in later life she could scarcely mention her name without tears in her eyes. She disliked Gladys, who was a superb mimic, and did not fail to include her mother in her extensive repertoire. The youngest sister, Dorothy, was not born until 1891; there was a brother too, Edward Parker, who was born in Paris in 1883 but died before he was four years old.

Gladys's first home was 14 rue Pierre-Charron, just off the Champs-Elysées. She began life in most respects as a little French girl. During her early years in France she liked to call herself Marie-Gladys, the names by which she was baptized in the Episcopal Church of the Holy Trinity on 20 March 1881. Later she swopped the names round and settled for Gladys on its own, which she pronounced 'Glaydus' in the style of Americans such as Gladys Vanderbilt Szechenyi. The children were brought up in a mixture of French and English, so much so that when Edith settled in America she had to struggle with her English for a time.

Though American by birth, Gladys was European by environment. She played down her American origins and in old age vigorously denied any connexion with the United States. She was, however, thoroughly American by blood and a varied mixture of it flowed through her veins. The Deacons originated in Burlington, New Jersey, with her great-grandfather, David

Deacon, who became a captain in the United States Navy and served with distinction under the once legendary figure, Commodore Edward Preble. David Deacon was one of 'Preble's boys' and took part in the Tripoli campaign against Barbary pirates in 1804. He was later imprisoned by the British in the War of 1812 and interned at Little York. He named his second son Edward Preble after the Commodore and bequeathed to him 'the farm near Erie commonly called Kent Farm on Walnut Creek by purchase from the estate at a fair valuation'. David Deacon showed sound judgment in the distribution of his assets, insisting that 'my sons receive as good an education as the property I leave them will afford – being more desirous that they should be well educated, than that the money should be reserved to spend after they are of age'.[1]

Edward Preble Deacon, Gladys's grandfather, had a varied career, climbing several rungs of the American social ladder in his short life of thirty-eight years. In the late 1830s he had a whaleboat business with his brother Adolphe. But on an excursion at Port Sheldon, Adolphe was the victim of over-exposure, 'uttered a groan, fell violently on the deck in convulsions'[2] and presently expired. Edward Preble Deacon was then engaged in lumbering in Michigan, and later took up the post of attaché to the United States Legation in Boston under General Lewis Cass.

Arriving in that city he exuded an aura of mystery. One rumour had it that he was a Frenchman because he had travelled abroad, but Mrs Charles Pelham Curtis described him as 'a handsome man, but without visible property . . . coming from one of the Middle States'.[3] In November 1841 he made a most advantageous marriage with Sarahann Parker, daughter of Peter Parker, a rich merchant, residing at 46 Beacon Street, and a member of the well-known family of Boston Parkers.* Hence their son, who was Gladys's father, liked to call himself Edward Parker Deacon because it sounded smart, and the youngest Deacon girl, Dorothy, went a step further and hyphenated the names.

Peter Parker decided that his daughter and son-in-law should live in a magnificent dwelling. He was prepared to finance this. Thus Deacon House was built on the corner of Washington

---

* The Parkers descend from Nathaniel Parker, born in Dedham, Massachusetts, in 1670, the son of Samuel Parker, of English birth.

Street, between Worcester and East Concord Streets in Boston's South End. The house was designed by James Lemoulnier and is an early example of French architecture in Boston, which had until then looked to England for inspiration.

Edward Preble Deacon had acquired avant-garde tastes in the course of his many travels in France, with the result that fabulous furnishings were shipped over and earned the house its reputation as 'a wonder of the mid-century'. Amongst the more spectacular embellishments were a large square piece of Gobelin tapestry representing 'Victory', which hung by the oak staircase in the hall, and four large oil-paintings by Fragonard on the 'History of Love'. From the salon with its mirrors, gilded panels and candelabra, great parlours extended one beyond another in a glorious vista. Yet the treasures were amply contrasted with dismal curiosities, for the house had more than its share of dingy green velvet draperies, and ancient breastplates and shields surrounded by divers diabolical weapons. Mrs Curtis recalled a beautiful ball at the house and 'some charming small dances, ending in a supper, announced to us by tall French foot-men in livery'.[4]

Sarahann Parker brought social status and wealth to the Deacons. She and her husband would have been splendid characters in an early Henry James novel – Sarahann, a dull, rich, unattractive bride, the victim of Edward Preble Deacon, a dashing profiteer. They produced two sons and a daughter; one of the sons was Gladys's father, born on 2 October 1844. Their marriage lasted a mere ten years, for Edward Preble Deacon, remembered as 'the chief attraction'[5] of Deacon House, died of consumption in Savannah, Georgia, on 1 March 1851. Gladys's father was left in the care of his mother and his rich Parker grandparents and lived on in Deacon House until 1861.

Thereafter things went rapidly from bad to worse. Sarahann was rumoured to be suffering from a nervous disease. Her eccentricities became a source of embarrassment to Boston society. She apparently insisted on being addressed as 'Mrs de Konn', would scream at people in the street and had a curious predilection for sliding on the icy gutter in Sumner Street, obliging her footman to await her arrival feet first at the end of the slide, and catch her in his arms.

But her troubles were more serious than that. She was an epileptic. In 1861 she took her family to Europe with her, and eventually made her way to England. After years of epilepsy and eighteen months of diabetes mellitus, she died on 18 May 1900 at an institution called Wyke House in Middlesex, where nobody knew or cared who she was. She was the first of three generations of Deacons to end their lives in a sanitorium, all for different reasons, and at the time of her death her son was already eking out his days in the McLean Hospital in Boston.

Deacon House itself fared little better. It sank into a state of decrepitude and ghostly stories grew up about it. One nocturnal visitor told a mysterious tale of a tall lady, dressed in rich, flowered brocade, who swept through the empty rooms at dead of night holding high a tiny lamp which glimmered above her head. The willowy shade did not appreciate being disturbed. Turning her eyes full on to the intruder, she raised her hand with a commanding gesture towards the door.

The contents of the house fell to an auctioneer's hammer in February 1871 and raised $27,250. But the house still stands and can be seen today looming up behind garish shop-fronts, as deserted and forgotten as the family who once lived in it.

Edward Parker Deacon, dark and intelligent, had the straight eyebrows and bright, powerful eyes which his daughter inherited. In his youth he served in the 2nd United States Colored Cavalry and spent some time in Virginia and North Carolina. Having profited from the sale of Deacon House and still owning property in Boston, he led the leisurely life of a rich gentleman, was a member of Boston's famous Somerset Club and travelled widely abroad. On his travels he met sixteen-year-old Florence Baldwin, and nobody was particularly pleased when he led her to a specially constructed altar at the Fifth Avenue home of her father and made her his wife on 29 April 1879.

In contrast to the adventurous Deacons and the fashionable Parkers, the Baldwins were a very grand New England family with a considerable fortune, her share of which Florence succeeded in squandering by 1918. They came from Aston Clinton in Buckinghamshire in the early 1600s and had been Americans since 1638. Florence's father was Rear-Admiral Charles H. Baldwin, whose grandfather, Captain Daniel Baldwin, had been a Captain of the Revolution, a close ally of George Washington and a founder member of the Society of the Cincinnati. The Admiral's naval career was determined when as a lad building toy castles at home in New York he chanced on the tales of the British novelist, Captain Frederick Marryat. These books kindled in him an ambition to be a sailor, and led to a successful career in the American Navy. Thus Gladys had naval ancestors on both sides, and appropriately a love of the sea was passed down to her. Her inspiration was Joseph Conrad, and when reminded of him she threw up her hands and cried, 'Oh! I used to revel in his books. I wanted to take to the sea at once!'[6]

The Admiral was by no means a modest man. In his later years at Snug Harbor on Bellevue Avenue, Newport, Rhode Island, he enjoyed relating tales of his naval career:

> After six weeks of beating against the trade wind, which is constant all summer, we reached Monterey, capital of California, several hours ahead of the English. I was ordered ashore with a boat's crew, and raised the American flag over the Cuartel. Next day the squadron sailed for Yerba Buena [now San Francisco] and I was left behind in command of a hundred sailors. That act of raising the American flag brought into the Union the territory between British Columbia, the Rocky Mountains, and what is now Mexico – about the size of the whole of Europe, if you leave Russia out![7]

In 1854 Baldwin resigned from the Navy and was given command of one of the Vanderbilt Nicaraguan steamers which plied between New York and the Pacific Ocean. A warm friendship grew between Baldwin and 'Commodore' Vanderbilt, a friendship which was to be echoed by the fondness of their respective progeny, Gladys and Consuelo, who both married the same Duke. While Admiral Baldwin was deeply grateful to the Commodore and warmly disposed towards him, he could not help looking down on the Vanderbilts as a clan. It is reported that he once chopped off Florence's hair for the crime of having danced with a Vanderbilt at a party. The Admiral later commanded SS *Vanderbilt* in the Civil War at the express wish of the Commodore.

The Admiral passed some years in California as Fleet Captain of the Northern Pacific Squadron and was a special partner in the commission firm of Edward L. G. Steele & Co. He became a Rear-Admiral in 1879 and due to his large fortune earned a reputation as a generous host. Alas, the genial disposition adopted by the Admiral at his table deserted him when he took to sea. He became a stern disciplinarian and it was unwise to transgress aboard one of his ships. No man sent for court martial was ever reprieved and the sentences meted out were an ugly deterrent to future offenders. For assaulting an officer of police, a wretched First Class Fireman was sentenced 'to be confined for thirty days in double irons on bread and water with full rations every fifth day; to lose one month's pay, amounting to thirty-five dollars; and to perform extra duty and be deprived of liberty for three months'. Approving the sentence, the Admiral felt compelled to add: 'I consider the punishment awarded as exceedingly light for the offence which the accused has committed.'[8]

The climax of the Admiral's career inspired from him behaviour less than worthy of his rank. Because he was the most distinguished American in the vicinity he was appointed to attend the coronation of Czar Alexander III of Russia in 1883 and to 'indicate the friendship of the United States for the Czar and the Russian people'. The Admiral sailed to Kronstadt and progressed to Moscow. The night before the ceremony he began to get anxious as his invitation had not arrived. In a report to the Secretary of the Navy he gave his version of what occurred:

No invitations having come at midnight, I notified the minister; and at seven o'clock the next morning I received from him cards of admission to the Tribune which was said to be opposite to the Church in which the Emperor was to be crowned, and which was occupied by Attachés of Legations, Russian Officers, etc., etc. (I may here state that the ceremony was to begin at 8 o'clock, and we were required to be in full dress and were two miles from the Kremlin.) Of course I could not attend in such an inferior position. Although the Church in which the Coronation took place was small, accommodating about three hundred people, still, all the Ambassadors, Foreign Ministers, their wives, daughters, Secretaries of Legations, and all Military Attachés were invited; – consequently I have the mortification to report that I was not able to be present at this great and most important ceremony.[9]

Then the representative of the United States Legation at St

Petersburg gave his account, describing the Admiral's conduct as having been in most questionable taste:

> From this office I drove to the Admiral's house, though it was then 2 a.m., when he had doubtless retired, and arousing him, gave him my message with the assurance in the name of the Chamberlain that he would be taken to his place at the ceremony. The Admiral replied that 'he would accept no invitation given at the 11th hour; that he preferred taking his coffee comfortably at home', and nothing I could say had any influence on his decision.[10]

His boycott of the ceremony did not prevent the Admiral from expressing his opinions about it. A few weeks afterwards, he told Mrs Mary King Waddington, the American wife of a French diplomat, that he thought it was 'all show (not much of one) and hollow'. They entered into heated discussion and Mrs Waddington concluded, 'I fancy he always takes the opposite side on principle.'[11] Soon after this the Admiral retired to Newport with his second wife, Marraine*, who was a devoted step-mother to Florence and adored the Deacon children.

Gladys's forebears were not comparable in wealth or enterprise to families such as the Astors, the Vanderbilts, the Morgans or the Goulds. Nevertheless both the Baldwins and the Parkers provided Gladys with a family tree proven back eight generations. They gave her a place in society and her mother the wealth to pursue social ambitions on behalf of herself and her daughters. Gladys's background gave her the confidence that she was of high birth and permitted her to cast aspersions on the origins of less well-connected Americans. A favourite insult in later life was to describe someone as 'middle class'.

From her mother she inherited great beauty and from her father a sense of adventure and a bizarre intelligence. From their union there emerged a remarkable young person, endowed with charm, high spirits and a keen sense of humour. Gladys herself was not too modest to comment: 'I was a miracle. Differential Calculus was too low for me!'[12]

---

* His first wife, Pamelia Tolfree, mother of Charlie and Florence, had died in 1872. Marraine was formerly Mrs Mary Morgan Reade.

Chapter Two

THE DEACONS IN THE BELLE EPOQUE

'Nul n'est Abeille, s'il n'a un aiguillon.'[1]

Mrs Deacon was not an intelligent woman, but she was cultured and immensely beautiful. When she entered a Paris ballroom, the reaction was as stunning as if a crystal chandelier had fallen to the floor. People gasped at her beauty and were transfixed by her gracefulness and luxurious clothes. She felt her beauty needed fine adornment and her extravagance knew no bounds. She was a good customer at all the famous Paris shops and salons and, like Eleanora Duse and some of Proust's heroines, she loved the serpentine pleated dresses of Fortuny. She worshipped beauty and beautiful things. On one occasion she bought an entire dressing table set in vermeil despite the fact that she possessed three at home already.

Her wealth and beauty did not fail to inspire considerable jealousy. Agnes de Stoekl recalled that at a ball at the Cercle Nautique in Cannes at which the Prince of Wales was present, Mrs Deacon was dressed in black and wore a long necklace from which huge pearls hung at intervals. The size of the pearls and their obvious value attracted a lot of comment, so that when Mrs Deacon retired to the ladies room and accidentally lost a pearl to the depths of the plumbing system, a good number of the ladies found it hard to control their delight. However, a plumber retrieved the pearl and their smiles faded accordingly.

As she grew older, Mrs Deacon became increasingly formidable, her fine features o'er-topped by an immaculate pile of mahogany-coloured hair. Boldini's portrait of her in 1906 admirably captures the quality of this handsome and stylish woman. She was still noticed when she entered a room, but now the effect was more like a battleship sailing gloriously in. It is easy to pour scorn on her for her values, ambitions and aspirations are hard to admire. Yet she survived many grave crises and disasters which would have driven a lesser woman to take the veil. Not only an ardent lover of high society, Florence Deacon also sought the company of a number of artists, musicians and writers, such as Auguste Rodin, Bernard Berenson and Maurice Lobre. A particular friend was Robert de Montesquiou, who remembered her as a likeable, worthy enough woman. It was through her mother that Gladys met many of her artistic friends, but in the early years she knew well the frustration of being presented in the drawing room and then spirited away to the nursery by Irma, while the grown-ups continued their conversations for each other's benefit. Gladys would have liked to stay and join in.

Unfortunately Gladys and her sisters did not have a happy childhood. Their parents had widely differing tastes. Whereas Mrs Deacon was fond of fashionable society, Mr Deacon preferred the less austere company of his own countrymen. Due to the immense amount of publicity the Deacon family were to receive in the 1890s there is no dearth of 'authoritative statements' about their way of life, related by their friends to eager journalists.

Troubles began early in their married life. About a month after the wedding in 1879 Mr Deacon is reported to have knocked his wife down because he did not like the way her hair was arranged. In the hotels in which they stayed, he forbade the servants to wait on her and would not even allow a basket of wood to be brought to her room without written instructions from him. In the winter of 1884, which they spent in Paris, Mrs Deacon was about to leave for a ball when she found that one of the children's nurses had gone off duty without permission. Mr Deacon insisted that his wife should go on her own, promising to join her later. When he had failed to appear by one o'clock she returned home to find him barricaded in their apartment. When at last an entrance was effected, Mr Deacon was found 'rushing about undressed, in a state of frenzy'.

In May 1887 sorrow fell on their house when their only son died. Mr Deacon was not in the least bit sympathetic when he found his wife alone weeping. He reproached her for her tears and then beat her so cruelly that she was marked for days. He was also accused by Mrs Deacon's friends of intemperance and cruelty to the children. Gladys used to relate to villagers at Chacombe that he was very tough to all the sisters and frequently thrashed them.

At noon on 17 November 1888 in the midst of these troubles Mrs Deacon's father died. Death came to Admiral Baldwin at 590 Fifth Avenue, New York, at the age of sixty-eight. Mrs Deacon hastened to New York on the steamship *La Bourgogne* to attend the obsequies. The funeral was a magnificent spectacle. Five hundred marines escorted the oak coffin with its silver handles, draped in the American flag, from the Admiral's residence to St Thomas's Church, Fifth Avenue. Mrs Deacon, Charlie Baldwin, and her step-mother Marraine led the mourners. The pall-bearers were selected from the leading men of the day, Rear-Admiral Gherardi, General W. T. Sherman, General George W. Cullam, John W. Hammersley, Hon Levi P. Morton, D. Ogden Mills, Rear-Admiral Rhind and W. H. Tillinghast. The Society of the Cincinnati was represented by a delegation including William Waldorf Astor. After the service, the hearse proceeded to St Mark's cemetery, where a military salute was fired. The Admiral was then lowered into the family vault of St Mark's-in-the-Bowery, the second oldest building and oldest site of worship in New York City and the resting place of Peter Stuyvesant, the Dutch Governor of New York.

One of the effects of Admiral Baldwin's death was that Mrs Deacon now inherited one million dollars, a third share of the immense fortune which the Admiral had divided between his widow, Charlie and Florence in a will dated 13 January 1888. From that moment on, it was said that Mr Deacon resolutely refused to contribute one cent towards the household expenses or the support of his family.

Further drama followed. Mrs Deacon's friends alleged that in 1889 Deacon attempted to choke her on the way home from the theatre, forcing her to leap from the carriage and tread the last mile home through the snow, that he struck her a blow on the way to a ball because she asked him to close the window of their coupé, and that after a dinner party the Deacons gave for friends in a suburban restaurant outside Paris in 1890, he continuously insulted his wife, fell to the floor as he rose from the table and had to be carried out by one of his guests.

Such were the allegations levelled at Mr Deacon. However

exaggerated they may be, the picture is not a happy one. Mrs Deacon is said to have hoped by forbearance to subdue his temper which bordered at times on insanity. Throughout their subsequent troubles, the couple were united on one thing only : they were anxious that their children should be well cared for. Mrs Deacon was also desperate to avoid any scandal that might threaten her place in society. Somehow there was no scandal, and even Mr Deacon conceded that until 1888 his wife's behaviour was exemplary. Only much later did he accuse her of improper conduct with a number of men unknown to him; but foremost in the list of lovers was a man with whom he was only too well acquainted.

Emile François Abeille, who met the Deacons at Villers-sur-Mer in 1888, played a considerable and unenviable role in their family life. Abeille was described in 1892 as a young French attaché of about thirty, the same age as Florence Deacon, the implication being that Edward Parker Deacon's problems with his wife stemmed from the fact that he was fifteen years older than she. Yet Abeille, born in Paris on 3 January 1845, was forty-seven in February 1892, a bachelor who had long indulged in high life and, coincidentally, a mere three months younger than Deacon himself. An intelligent man, Abeille had nevertheless given up the diplomatic service in favour of a life of travel, sport, summer resorts and lovely ladies, one of whom, the Comtesse du Bari, was to assist in his undoing.

According to Gladys, the Abeilles had Jewish blood. The presiding judge at the Nice court of Assizes referred to the Abeilles as 'a Parisian family most justly respected and esteemed'. Emile's father had worked with Georges Haussmann, who rebuilt so much of Paris, and then amassed a considerable fortune in the laying down of the Suez Canal. His mother was a Parisian, well known for her parsimony. She shared with Mrs Deacon the dubious honour of being satirized by Montesquiou in *Les Quarante Bergères*. Emile was not the only Abeille to come to grief. A subtle distinction between those Abeilles who came to sticky ends and those who lived their full span of years can be seen on the family tomb in the cemetery at Passy. 'Mort à Paris' denotes tragedy, 'décédé à Paris' signifies a natural death.

Emile Abeille wasted no time in becoming a close friend of

both Mr and Mrs Deacon and a regular visitor to their home. He paid assiduous attention to Mrs Deacon. As she stated later, 'My husband was quite aware of the frequency of his visits at Paris as well as at Cannes. He was always received at our house as an intimate friend.'[2] In Paris at that time there were certain people who, for lack of more constructive entertainment, were in the habit of writing anonymous letters to husbands warning them of the dangers, inherent in Paris life, into which their wives might be lured. Mr Deacon received his share of these, but when he questioned his wife, she reproached him bitterly for not understanding the 'Parisian flirt'. Having successfully disposed of his suspicions, the couple set off for Newport in 1889.

All would no doubt have been well but for the fact that Mrs Deacon foolishly left a letter in her secretaire which began 'Ma cherie, pourquoi avez-vous rompu avec moi?' Her husband was able to identify this conclusively as having come from Abeille, but once more Florence Deacon succeeded in appeasing her husband by stating that it was impertinent of Abeille to have written to her, but what could she do? The following summer the Deacon family were again at Newport, where they hoped in due course to buy a cottage for use on their vacations.

In March 1891 the Deacons moved to an apartment at 142 rue de Grenelle in the heart of the Faubourg Saint-Germain. This fine block stands at the end of the Boulevard des Invalides on the corner opposite the Ministère du Travail. The adjoining apartment was occupied by the Comte and Comtesse de Castries: this is known because in one of his not infrequent rages, Mr Deacon once knocked down their front door. Here, on 12 April 1891, Mrs Deacon's youngest child Dorothy* was born. Gladys was ill at the time, and Mr Deacon found the domesticity too much for him. He promptly left for a hotel for a fortnight.

A month after Dorothy's birth a *facture de lingerie* reminded Mr Deacon of Abeille's threatening presence. One evening at about ten o'clock, he came home from a Rothschild party to find Abeille hidden behind the curtain as tradition and a desire for self-preservation demand. Mrs Deacon was again able to pull the wool over her husband's eyes: 'My friend, Monsieur Abeille, knew I was unwell. He came to leave his visiting card,

---

* Dorothy Evelyn Deacon (1891–1960) was married first to Prince Antoni Albrych Radziwill, and then, after an annulment, became the second wife of Count Palffy ab Erdoed.

so I asked him to come up. Your brusque arrival worried him, your unjust suspicions of earlier times came to mind, but I assure you there is nothing between us.' Feeling her case was growing weaker, she enlisted the help of her brother and step-mother, who pointed out to Deacon that he did not understand the etiquette of Paris life, that everything was perfectly inno-cent and that he had better be careful not to further alienate his wife's affections by his persistent jealousy. Mr Deacon was duly humbled.

Abeille became more zealous in his attention. He engaged chambers in the rue d'Anjou under the pseudonym of Adam. Here Mrs Deacon visited him. One of her friends was Kate Moore, a jolly American, and a noted social climber with a loose tongue. Mrs Deacon unwisely confessed to her that she used to swing quite naked on a swing in his apartment for Abeille's greater enjoyment. In 1908 Bernard Berenson heard an account which supports the evidence against her from a lawyer friend in St Moritz. This lawyer had been employed by one of the Astors to shadow a Frenchman (not Abeille as it happened), and he had discovered some correspondence between the French-man and Mrs Deacon. Berenson reported that the letters 'left no doubt that their relations were all that they could be'.[3]

Neither of the Deacons was in good health. Mrs Deacon's doctor recommended a change of air, and accordingly des-patched her to St Moritz with her baby Dorothy. Mr Deacon's doctor diagnosed an inflammation of the stomach, so he left for Homburg with Gladys, Audrey and Edith. This period of separa-tion should have brought peace to both parties, but Deacon was still fired with jealousy, continually rekindled by fresh rumours about Abeille. The paramour's former mistress, the Comtesse du Bari, wrote to Deacon several times. The letters were found in his papers after his death. In happier days she had received a regular allowance from Abeille, but this had ceased when Abeille took up with Mrs Deacon. Now she took her revenge.

Mr Deacon heard no news from his wife and became increas-ingly anxious. Finally he telegraphed her demanding that she break with Abeille or divorce. He promised to be the best and most loving of husbands. After two weeks Mrs Deacon replied that he was a tyrant and, knowing he had business there, urged him to go to America and leave her alone. She added that it would be better if they communicated through their solicitors in future. Deacon's reaction to this was to announce that she would be receiving a visit from him at St Moritz. Mrs Deacon cabled at once that she was leaving the next day and proceeding to the Italian lakes with the Gramonts.

Mr Deacon accepted this, but, feeling no better physically, came to Geneva to consult a specialist. There he learned from a friend Mr Scheffer that Abeille had been ensconced in St Moritz. By telegraphing the hotel, he established that the Gramonts had left a fortnight before Mrs Deacon. Knowing that she would stop at the Hotel Promontorio in Grisons, Switzerland, he sent an ingenious despatch enquiring whether or not 'Monsieur et Madame Abeille' had left yet. The reply came back 'Left for Bellagio'. Years of suspicion now culminated in certain knowledge. According to Mrs Deacon, though hotly denied by her husband, she received from him at this time an ironic telegram : 'Amusez-vous bien avec votre Abeille.'

Mr Scheffer then intervened and told Deacon that it was ridiculous to suggest that Abeille and his wife were having an affair. They were both far too well known in society. It would have been impossible. Mr Deacon was forever willing to think the best of his wife, and in the confusion vacillated from a state of fury to one of contrition. He wrote to his wife apologizing for his actions. Some days later Mrs Deacon came down from the Villa Serbelloni to Geneva and explained that a series of coincidences had been the cause of the misunderstandings. There was something of a reunion and the family spent some days together in Aix-en-Provence.

For Gladys, this was the last tranquil time she spent in the company of both parents, but it was short-lived. At the age of ten she was acutely aware of the instability of her home. All her life, to think of her parents together was to be reminded of endless quarrelling.

Soon it was time for Mr Deacon to depart for the United States. As he embarked on a steamer at Le Havre, he clutched a friendly telegram from his wife signed 'Love from All'. In the middle of October 1891 he returned to Paris. Once more he found Abeille a regular visitor to his house. The question of divorce raised its head again. He employed detectives from the Agence Tricoche to try and catch Mrs Deacon at 12 rue de Penthièvre where Abeille had an entresol, but his plan was rumbled by an agent in the pay of Mrs Deacon who put his men off the scent. Mr Deacon never had enough evidence for legal action, and in these circumstances let Mrs Deacon and the children set off for the South of France for the winter season, while he remained in Paris deciding what to do next.

Chapter Three

A TRAGEDY AT CANNES

Edward Parker Deacon advanced into the room, his eyes darting from side to side in a cursory examination that was interrupted when his wife, her composure regained for the moment, blew out the candle.

'Permit me', said the hotel secretary in the background. 'I have another candle.' 'Thank you,' said Edward Deacon, 'we'll see how good the hunting is in the sitting room.'

He found his quarry cowering behind a couch. Three shots signalled the end of a two-year chase and Edward Deacon re-appeared in the doorway, a smoking pistol in his right hand.

'I suggest', he said to the hotel secretary, 'that you summon the gendarmes. M. Emile Abeille seems to be dead.'

Heartbreaks of Society[1]

Mrs Deacon began her stay in the South of France at the Hotel de Noailles in Marseilles, but early in February 1892 she moved to Cannes, where she expected to spend the rest of the season. Travelling with her were her four daughters, her step-mother, and a small retinue of servants. A few paces behind was Emile Abeille.

It is no surprise to find Florence Deacon in Cannes, which had been transformed from a simple fishing village into a fashionable resort by the fortuitous arrival there of the distinguished English statesman, Lord Brougham, in 1831. Brougham was in the process of avoiding a British winter and, being prevented by a cholera epidemic from entering Italy, he gravitated towards the Gulf of Napoule where he bought an estate for five sous a metre. Gradually the fame of Cannes grew and it became famed as a winter resort not so much for the favourable climate found there but for the inclement weather avoided elsewhere.

French and Germans, but most of all English, flocked to Cannes in the late nineteenth century and spent their time playing bridge, flirting, or having tea at Rumplemayer's on the Boulevard de la Croisette. Next door, easily spotted due to a profusion of multi-coloured flags, stood the Cercle Nautique, a favourite haunt of Mr Deacon. Here the Prince of Wales played baccarat, here his younger brother, the Duke of Albany, a haemophiliac, fell down the club stairs with fatal results, and here the barman once counted seven Russian Grand Dukes forgathered at the same time. Powdered footmen in knee-breeches waited on the distinguished company which, though it admitted Edward Parker Deacon at twenty-five guineas a year, excluded Oscar Wilde from membership.

Mrs Deacon took rooms for her family at the Hotel Windsor, one of eight good hotels on the eastern side of the Boulevard du Cannet. It was a highly suspicious Mr Deacon who arrived there suddenly on Monday 15 February. He wasted no time in examining the hotel register and was not altogether surprised to spot the name of Abeille amongst the guests. At once he demanded that the family move elsewhere. Rooms were therefore engaged at the Hotel Splendide, opposite the yachting harbour, one of Cannes's oldest hotels and still flourishing today. Gladys's friend, Elisabeth de Gramont, recalled later that the hotel was flanked by palms and was a suitable theatre for a drama of jealousy 'because of its air of Italian opera'. Mrs Deacon chose a salon and bedroom for herself on the first floor but told her husband that there were no other rooms available there. So Mr Deacon, Marraine Baldwin and the children were lodged on the floor above.

Mrs Deacon's liaison with Abeille was long-standing, and the normal precautions taken by wife and paramour were gradually lapsing. But she still felt quite confident that she could pull the wool over her husband's eyes. Considering, however, that Deacon's suspicions were so thoroughly aroused, it is astonishing that Abeille once again had the temerity to instal himself in Mrs Deacon's hotel. It was not long before the bright eyes and dark brow of Edward Parker Deacon were poised intently over the Splendide's register. Again the name of Abeille leaped from the page. Deacon went directly to the hotel office where the management, obeying instructions, informed him that Abeille had departed. This was not the case. Abeille was hiding in a room on the other side of Mrs Deacon's salon. He would soon find more reasons than one for regretting the absence of a communicating door.

A cautious low profile was maintained for the next two days while Deacon prowled about, his mind alert for any clue leading to Abeille. Nothing happened on Tuesday night, and on Wednesday Mrs Deacon paid a visit to Comtesse Melanie de Pourtales, the most beautiful of the three ladies-in-waiting to Empress Eugénie of France in the famous Winterhalter portrait. She returned home feeling tired only to find her husband keen to discuss divorce again. This time his plan was that Mrs Deacon should not contest the action, thereby avoiding much of the scandal. But divorce meant ostracism from society and, apart from her children, society was Florence Deacon's dominant reason for living. Besides, except during the periodical bouts of curiosity and suspicion in which her husband indulged, Mrs Deacon was quite content with the present arrangement.

When Gladys and her sisters were safely in bed, both Deacons called on Marraine Baldwin. At ten o'clock Mr Deacon excused himself and left the hotel to attend a ball at the Cercle Nautique. A clear half-hour later, Abeille, attired in a smoking jacket, called on Mrs Deacon. At 10.45 Irma Deodat helped Mrs Deacon undress and left her in a white dressing-gown. A lady of the most professional silence, Irma neither saw nor heard any sign of Abeille.

Mr Deacon came back at about midnight and observed a light shining under his wife's door. He approached with stealth and recognized 'the rough voice of Abeille' within. He went up to his room, collected his revolver and went in search of M Baumann, the hotel secretary, who was at work in his office. Deacon ordered Baumann to accompany him and they proceeded in silence to Mrs Deacon's bedroom door, Baumann carrying a lighted candle. Exhorting the secretary to 'follow me with the light as soon as the door is opened', Deacon knocked loudly. The response was a quick shuffling sound.

There was a delay of two or three minutes before Mrs Deacon opened the door, during which some hurried decisions were made. Abeille had few options and little time for thought. He could not get through to his own room directly, but he could leave by the salon door into the passage. If he did this, however, he would come face to face with Mr Deacon. Another possibility was to leave by the window, putting his trust in a cornice of twenty centimetres which ran round the outside of the building. In the haste of the moment, his nerves on edge, that idea was discarded as too risky. Mrs Deacon claimed later that Abeille 'was reclining against the mantelpiece' as an innocent visitor might do, but knowing Mr Deacon's fiery temper, it is small wonder that what he actually did was to take sanctuary behind the sofa in the salon.

'Open the door at once!' cried Mr Deacon. 'If you do not open the door, I will burst it in.' Mrs Deacon opened the door, and as soon as she saw that her husband was armed she blew out the dressing-table candle, rushed back, and knocked the secretary's candle from his hand. Deacon had noticed that the salon door was open, and when a new light had been struck, he forced his way in and fired three shots at the figure lurking behind the sofa. One bullet lodged itself in the wall, another hit Abeille in the breast and the third entered his leg. Deacon then pushed the sofa aside, seized Abeille and addressed him in French: 'Vous êtes bien là! Je vous tiens!'

Abeille did not reply but just managed to get up and stagger into the passage, where he collapsed in a pool of blood. Deacon, who remained exceptionally cool during all these events, asked him if he was badly wounded. Abeille responded with a droop of the head. Then Florence seized her husband's hands, threw herself at his feet and implored him to spare her, to leave Abeille alone and to make no scandal for the children's sake. It was too late of course, because the shots had aroused the servants and other guests on the first floor. They all came running out until they saw Mr Deacon, whereupon they retreated quicker than they came. Mr Deacon pushed his wife away and replied: 'I will not shoot you for the sake of our children. I have caught you at last, and now leave you to give myself up.' True to his word he went at once to the Commissaire of Police and spent the remaining hours of the night at the Mairie.

Meanwhile the partially dressed victim, his clothes soaked in blood, was carried to his room and attended to by Irma. A local doctor, Dr Escarra, and Dr Vaudremer, a physician from Paris, came to examine him and pronounced his condition to be very serious. Both Montesquiou and Prince Poniatowski wrote that Abeille was fit enough to make a new will in favour of Mrs

Deacon, and the sum of 500,000 francs was mentioned. Montesquiou also recalled that Abeille constantly cried out somewhat unnecessarily, 'J'suis foutu!' Though everything possible was done to help him, Abeille, who had a weak constitution, lost consciousness at about eight o'clock in the morning and died soon afterwards.

Mr Deacon remained in custody. That afternoon he made a statement before Dr de Valcourt, the American Vice-Consul. He was given the chance to prosecute his wife for adultery but, when told this would mean that she would be taken into custody, he replied: 'No, I shall not lay a complaint for the sake of my children, nor did I intend to kill Mr Abeille. I only wished to mark him.' At all times he expressed consideration for his children to whom he was deeply attached, and his main concern was to obtain custody of them. Mr Deacon spent the night of the eighteenth at Dr de Valcourt's house. The next morning at ten o'clock he was conducted to Grasse by the Chief Commissaire where he was put in prison.

Florence Deacon began the day after the crime rather differently, by cancelling a luncheon engagement with the Princesse de Sagan. She was generally criticized for this, though Montesquiou, after parodying the incident in his poem 'Déa' in *Les Quarante Bergères*, enquired 'Does disaster preclude politeness?' He concluded that at this moment of social ruin, such a gesture was not in bad taste. A few days after the murder, Mrs Deacon was given permission to go to Paris to consult friends. The children remained with Marraine Baldwin. In her apartment at the rue de Grenelle, Mrs Deacon made a statement to the *Daily Telegraph* reporter:

> When I am at home I am accustomed to relinquish ceremony, and while I went into my bedroom to put on a dressing gown M Abeille remained in the salon. . . . The best proof that we had nothing to be ashamed of is that he remained where he was, and his appearance, as well as mine, shows that we were simply conversing together when he was attacked in such a cowardly manner. I am aware that it has been said that I took a great deal too long to open the door of my room but you must remember that I was in the salon, and it took me some little time to light the candle.[2]

News of the tragedy received widespread coverage in France,

England and the United States. Mr Deacon came under hostile attack in the French papers. That an American had shot a Frenchman engaged in the national sport was considered outrageous. Deacon was described as a 'cowardly assassin', and a change in the law relating to husbands who take life in such circumstances was demanded. On the other hand, the large American colony in Cannes tended to be sympathetic towards him. The American code of conduct in such matters is different from the French. Thus Mr Deacon received many messages of support. The *New York Times* correspondent in Cannes reported that 'many of the quieter class of people here considered the style of Mrs Deacon too pronounced, though she was popular on account of her great beauty'.[3] In Newport, where Peter Parker had been well known, the activities of his grandson caused 'quite a sensation'. For the next year or so the international press followed the case and subsequent family crises with the closest attention.

The tragedy also fired the imagination of Henry James, who had not forgotten that one summer afternoon shortly after their marriage the Deacons had visited him at his home in Bolton Street, London. Now he reached for his notebook:

> A very good little subject (for a short tale) would be the idea – suggested to me in a round-about way by the dreadful E.D. 'tragedy' in the South of France – of a frivolous young ass or snob of a man, rather rich, and withal rather proper and prim, who marries a very pretty girl and is pleased with the idea of getting her into society – I mean the world smart and fast, *où l'on s'amuse* – the sort of people whom it most flatters his vanity to be able to live with.[4]

James then outlined a characteristically complicated plot. Though he returned to the subject as late as 1901 and urged himself not to 'lose sight, by the way of the subject that I know – I've marked it somewhere, as the E. Deacon subject',[5] he never made use of it.

The long slow process of French law ground inexorably into action. Witnesses were examined, including the hotel secretary, M Baumann. On 27 February the Deacons were confronted in 'an exceedingly painful scene'. Mr Deacon was so affected by the ordeal that he had to go to bed immediately afterwards. Mrs

Deacon persisted in denying any impropriety between her and Abeille. On 4 May Mr Deacon altered his will to exclude his wife from it but establish a trust for his four daughters. This trust provided Gladys with an annual income all her life and was only wound up when she died.

The murder trial took place in the Assize Court of the Alpes Maritimes in Nice on 20 May. The day before the case was due to be heard, Alexandre Dumas *fils* made an unexpected declaration. He strongly believed that now the divorce law existed in France, the days of *crimes passionnelles* were over. He maintained that husbands 'have only the right to repudiate wives, and that if they shed blood they are liable to be dealt with as ordinary assassins'.[6]

The court-room was filled to capacity, the end gallery unusually colourful with a contingent of fashionable ladies in elegant bonnets come to see justice done. From early in the day the heat was stifling. Mrs Deacon herself was not in court, pleading illhealth, but a statement from her was read. Mr Deacon attempted to defend himself in French, but he was no linguist and the jury struggled to understand him. Presently he resumed his story in English. The lengthy proceedings had the occasional light moment, as when Mr Deacon spoke of Abeille: 'When I saw this little man wounded, I felt poignant regrets, for a man having some conscience must always regret killing another man.' A loud cheer went up from the spectators who conspicuously supported Deacon in his predicament. But Maître Demange, Deacon's counsel, privately regretted his words, feeling that he had prejudiced his case.

Despite an address in which Demange 'justified his reputation for forensic eloquence', the jury's verdict was that Deacon was guilty of unlawfully wounding Abeille, but without intent to cause death. In a barrage of hisses and groans the sentence of a year's imprisonment was passed. Mr Deacon's brother shook him by the hand and pronounced it 'a most unjust verdict and sentence'. Meanwhile Deacon 'moped the while in a somewhat grim style, repressing his feelings like a veritable stoic, yet really looking very near breaking down'.[7]

Thus Edward Parker Deacon left the court for a Nice prison cell. His last words were addressed to his brother: 'Take care of the children.'

Chapter Four

NO BREAD-AND-BUTTER MISSIS

Gladys passed her eleventh birthday in Cannes shortly before the startling events of 18 February 1892. When the lawyers took over she and her sisters remained in the care of their mother, and occasionally of their step-grandmother. But on 10 March the Public Prosecutor transferred custody of them to Mr Deacon, who promptly sent representatives to take them away. Mrs Deacon strongly opposed this decision and the girls left in a scene fraught with hysteria and emotion. Audrey and Edith went to Mr Deacon's brother, while Gladys and the baby Dorothy travelled to Genoa with Marraine Baldwin. A few weeks later both Gladys and Dorothy were sent to the Convent de l'Assomption at Auteuil in Paris. Dorothy became 'the pet of the community', living in the care of the sisters, while Gladys began her lessons.

'I so often think of you and wish you were here with me', wrote her father as he awaited trial at the Hotel Richemont in Cannes; but he explained that she was now a *demoiselle* and must be 'where you may learn all that will go towards making you a good intelligent honest woman'.[1] Mr Deacon clearly hoped that Gladys would not take after his wife.

On 2 April Gladys sent news of herself to her mother: 'One little line from Gladys to give you a thousand loves and kissis and tell you I am very good and busy preparing for the examins [which] begin on Wednesday.' The Sister sat beside Gladys as she wrote and gave a report on her. She was 'trying hard to be very good, her health and spirits are excellent'. Before the letter was finished Gladys's spirits got the better of her, to the extent that the poor Sister concluded: 'Have you ever had Gladys by you when you and she were occupied in correspondence? Not a sinecure – n'est-ce pas?'[2] Gladys remained in the convent during her father's trial and the further litigation of her parents.

In June T. Jefferson Coolidge, the United States Minister to France, responded to requests from the American Legation to get Mr Deacon released, by writing to the French Foreign Secretary to say it would give much pleasure to the Americans residing in Paris if Deacon was set free. On 22 September President Carnot granted a pardon in celebration of the centenary of the establishment of the first French Republic. In July Mrs Deacon applied in the courts to regain legal possession of her children. She failed, but it stirred Mr Deacon into prosecuting her for adultery to ensure that he always kept them.

His sole aim on leaving prison in September was to take the children to America and devote himself to their education. Immediately he was released he wrote to Gladys, who had been on holiday at the Hôtel des Réservoirs in Versailles, declaring 'I will do everything in my power that you shall be happy and not stay at the convent this winter but have a good home. I will see you very soon.'[3] The case for the possession of the children was settled in his favour before the Tribunal of the Seine in Paris on 3 November.

No sooner was the verdict granted than Mr Deacon made purposeful steps to the Convent de l'Assomption to find Gladys, but when he arrived the Lady Superior told him that Gladys was not there. The day before had been a holiday and Mrs Deacon had come to take Gladys out. Neither had returned. Mr Deacon summoned the police, who searched the convent and the Deacon home in the rue de Grenelle, but both the mother and the kidnapped child had disappeared, as the press put it, to 'some place beyond the reach of Mr Deacon'.

The illegal abduction of Gladys was part of a plan to prevent Mr Deacon from taking her to America. Mrs Deacon also hoped that if she obtained the guardianship of her children she would maintain some footing in society. She threatened that if her husband did not stop his criminal action against her, he would never see Gladys again. The Tribunal sat on 16 and 17 November and decreed that Gladys should be returned to the convent, where both parents would be allowed to visit her. But the case had been making headlines in the press, with the result that the abashed nuns refused to take her back.

A considerable number of lawsuits were now pending. In

Grasse, Mr Deacon had sued his wife on the grounds of criminal adultery. This case, if proved, could end in the imprisonment of Mrs Deacon. Mrs Deacon had appealed in Aix, and she had filed a divorce suit in Paris on the grounds of cruelty and demanded custody of the children. Finally, Mr Deacon had filed a divorce suit in New York, where they were married.

The moment an absolute divorce was granted in February 1893 and custody of the three eldest children had been confirmed to Mr Deacon, all the other suits were dropped. Florence Deacon reverted to being Florence Baldwin and remained in Paris with her youngest daughter Dorothy. Marraine Baldwin took Audrey and Edith to New York and Gladys was handed over to her father. Once more it was a time for farewells. When Mr Deacon and Gladys crossed the Channel to England, Gladys wrote to her mother: 'I cannot tell you how much I feel to leave you altho' I am sure it will be but for a time, as Papa tells me you are coming to see us all in America.'[4]

There is every reason to believe that Mr Deacon assured Gladys that she would soon see her mother again, but none to suppose he meant what he said. Indeed his major preoccupation from now on was to stave off the constant sallies of Gladys's mother to prise her children from him.

The excitement of London awaited Gladys. She and her father stayed at the Burlington Hotel in Cork Street and set off to explore the stores together. Mr Deacon bought Gladys a dress, an ulster and a hat for their forthcoming voyage. On their return to the hotel soldiers and police were keeping the crowd back because the Prince of Wales was holding a levée. 'How big and clean the English soldiers look', reported the twelve-year-old. Presently they set sail from Southampton on the steamship *Trave*. Gladys was delighted to have a huge cabin all to herself. They arrived at New York on 23 March where, inevitably, a *New York Times* reporter was lying in wait for the man who had caused so much sensation during the past year. Mr Deacon began by saying he was very tired. He continued:

And what a crowd the Abeilles are. One of the progeny of brothers produced in court a forged letter, purporting to come from me, which said that it was my intention to kill Cocoa Abeille as soon as I was released. I have come to America to stay, but if I hear of that man Cocoa defaming my character, I will cross the ocean again to have an interview with him.[5]

He went on to say that his divorced wife was a woman destitute of moral sense. He tapped his forehead and added: 'She has something wrong here.' Mr Deacon himself had suffered from his great ordeal. Deep furrows lined his brow and his hair was streaked with grey. Gladys and her father went at once to the Buckingham Hotel where she was reunited with her two sisters, who came rushing up to her, screaming 'Gladys, Gladys'. 'Then', noted Gladys, 'I received Edith's bear-hugs.'

The three girls remained in their father's custody for the next three years. They settled in Newport, where they had already spent several summers. Newport, formerly a nest of trading in rum, slaves and molasses, had transformed itself, like Cannes, into a resort famed for its climate, beautiful scenery and wide sandy beaches. It still retained much of the charm of an old New England seaport. By 1860 the habit of spending a summer there had become well established and was at its zenith at the time when Gladys knew it. Families with second-generation wealth built homes there, called cottages, some of which were of exceptional magnificence. Marraine Baldwin still occupied the Admiral's cottage, Snug Harbor, on Bellevue Avenue and, despite the family difficulties, had succeeded in maintaining good relations with Mr Deacon. He liked going to Newport because, as Gladys put it, he liked to hear the news.

Their first home was a small cottage at 83 Rhode Island Avenue. Several coloured servants were employed, and the food was excellent. Another resident of the house was Gladys's dog, Eden, who had travelled with her from New York. On the first lap of the journey Eden had been obliged to travel with the luggage, but between Boston and Newport Gladys succeeded in smuggling him in her cloak. In May domesticity was further assured when all the girls became the proud owners of kittens.

Gladys enjoyed riding in a dog-cart and taking picnics in a steam launch loaned to Mr Deacon. One fishing excursion was particularly successful, and Gladys was quick to inform her mother: 'I caught the most.' She spent Easter in Boston, where she heard Jean de Reszke as Faust at the Opera, and in June the family went for a driving tour in the White Mountains. One thing was made perfectly clear by Mr Deacon at all times. He intended to keep custody of the girls. He told Gladys: 'As long as I have a penny and life, no one shall part us.'[6]

Florence Baldwin came over to Newport from France in October 1893 to see her children and to try to regain custody of them. Inevitably the visit revived interest in the Deacons and rumours spread that there might even be a reconciliation. They were swiftly denied. To Mrs Deacon's delight her visit proved a social success and she was openly welcomed by the *grelot* of Newport society. Her life in Paris was quieter. Living at the rue de Grenelle with her aunt, Mrs Micheler, she devoted all her time to Dorothy. She was much annoyed the following year by an unfounded story that she was about to marry Comte Louis de Turenne, a diplomatist of the old school with a witty and encyclopaedic knowledge of the intrigues, digressions and personal histories of Europe's leading figures.

Gladys began her schooling in Newport with her sisters and secured excellent results in her first exams. But at twelve she was considered too old for the local school, so in November she began a three-year stint at Howard Seminary, West Bridgewater, Massachusetts. She pronounced it 'much nicer than I thought it would be', and gave her mother a full account:

> Each girl has her own room and they hang pretty pictures up and other things so that some of them have quite lovely rooms. The school building is built of red brick. It has two 'tourelles'. I really think it looks more like a museum. The letters here are not read.[7]

Gladys was always polite and dutiful in writing to her father, but her letters to him have none of the love and affection she reserved for her mother. She sent reams of affectionate prose to France, invariably expressing the heartfelt wish that they should be reunited: 'P.S. Chère Mamma, je t'aime, je t'aime et je t'aime et je crois que c'est presque sure que nous viendrons toutes ensemble cette été.' Gladys did much to boost her mother's morale; but Mrs Baldwin was still depressed about her lot in the world. Gladys quoted to her the cheery line 'après la pluie, le beau temps', but could almost see her mother shaking her head forlornly and replying: 'After the rain the good weather for everyone else, but the good weather of my life is over and after the fine days of winter the April rains must come.'[8]

No Bread-and-Butter Missis

On the day after her thirteenth birthday, Gladys examined her own situation, writing in her diary:

> I did annoy myself a little yesterday. I should have liked so much to have been at home in Paris with Mamma and to have a great and beautiful party I use [*sic*] to have when I was little. Mrs Willard tells me things of this world pass quickly and are but an introduction to the beauties of the next. But after [all] she has never seen her other world, neither have I. Neither has anybody and I [think] that this old Earth would be an awfully nice place for all people say, if there were not so many black sheep in the flock.
>
> I wonder if I really am worldly! I wonder if it's nice to be so. If I could only have someone to tell me, someone who would not preach to me, for I always feel as though I want to be bad and to shock the ones who preach so much.[9]

September 1894 found Mr Deacon and his daughter at Greenfield, Massachusetts, and news reached Newport that he and Gladys were in excellent health. Edith stayed at Greenfield, living with an Episcopalian minister and his wife. With surprising insight from one so young, Gladys reported that they 'worship Edith with all the pent up love of a childless couple'.

In October Gladys wrote to her mother complaining that she had had no news of her since the previous spring. Her letter also had a 'business part'. Gladys was anxious to draw Mrs Baldwin's attention to her need for a guitar. She claimed that her mother knew so much about music and that a better instrument could be found in Paris. The guitar was to be of the best quality, not too highly decorated, and to arrive as soon as possible, because Gladys was fed up with practising on one belonging to another girl. Her father agreed to pay for it, and so Mrs Baldwin obliged and despatched the cherished instrument. Gladys was entranced, and wrote to her aunt in New York: 'Sometimes, even often, I take it on my bed and play some sweet sad melody which seems somehow to belong more especially to that beautiful instrument.'

Gladys also played the mandolin and sang with a voice which developed from a 'high, clear soprano' into a 'very deep contralto'. She began to learn German and to take an interest in the theatre and opera. She entertained a secret fear that the great actress, Sarah Bernhardt, might not survive long enough for her to hear her. Soon, however, it was painting that became 'the only thing I care for'.

In April 1895 Gladys began to collect a library of beautiful books. It did not matter in which language they were written, but Gladys stipulated that they should be by good authors and well bound. She also took an interest in her clothes and confided in her mother 'a little secret' – that she would like a new gown:

> I would like to have it made of pale green silk with a sort of 'reflet' in it. I do not care how it is trimmed as long as it is very pretty. I feel as if I were asking too much but I feel I know you would like to see your little Gladys well dressed.[10]

In June 1895 Mrs Baldwin arrived in the United States. From New York she went at once to Boston but again failed to win her children back. In September Gladys joined the battle to escape from her father. Besides a natural yearning to be with her mother, she was lured by news of a beautiful new home in Sorrento. She told her mother that she was much comforted by being able to write her letters 'and not feel that the person who stands between us and our happiness should read them'. She reminded her mother that the lawyers had said it was only a question of time before she would be granted custody, 'and time you know heals all wounds even as it has Audrey's nose'. She urged her mother to press on with her negotiations and hoped that by Christmas 'they will give me up to you, my darling'. In the midst of all this she was particularly galled to read an account of herself in a Kansas newspaper which said she was to visit her mother. 'Oh those American newspapers, what will they say next?'

In September a batch of new girls arrived at the convent, but Gladys did not care for them: 'They are all very frumpy and slangy and not at all my style . . . but it can't be helped if they are common, it isn't their fault.'[11] Gladys was a diligent and successful pupil at Howard Seminary, and by and large she appeared to be a contented soul. Her only preoccupation concerned her parents and her longing to escape from her father, but she was optimistic that in due course she would have her way. She looked forward to enjoying to the full a house in Paris, the beauty of Sorrento in the Gulf of Naples, and the love of her mother, whom she saw so rarely.

The greatest opportunities for idle thought in life are presented in the early and late years. Just as in old age fears become exaggerated, so the teenager is susceptible to all kinds of impressions, some of which can be magnified out of all proportion. At school more than at any other time Gladys's alert mind was open to such impressions. Unfortunately an item she read in the newspapers caught her imagination to such an extent that it came to obsess her. This obsession became a crusade, and in time its power became so strong that it steered her on to a course quite unworthy of her.

Gladys was fourteen years old in October 1895 when the headlines caught her eye. This extract in a letter to her mother is full of portent:

> I suppose you have read about the engagement of the Duke of Marlborough.
>
> O dear me if I was only a little older I might 'catch' him yet! But Hélas! I am too young though mature in the arts of woman's witchcraft and what is the use of one without the other? And I will have to give up all chance to ever get Marlborough.
>
> But 'Oh Miss Gladys don't you cry your sweetheart'll come by and by. When he comes he'll dress in blue, what a sign his love is true!' You see what consolation there are in those simple lines![12]

To Gladys as to many American girls of her background, Consuelo Vanderbilt's engagement to the Duke of Marlborough was the ultimate in success. The union of her wealth and beauty with his dukedom and Blenheim conferred sudden respectability on the Vanderbilts, whose fortune of 200 million dollars had been acquired by means more foul than fair. The Duke of Marlborough was portrayed in the press as the most eligible bachelor ever to arrive on the East Coast of the United States. For reasons beyond her control Gladys had missed the chance of capturing him, but in her mind she was capable of doing as well if not better. Whatever happened she would outdo Consuelo. Not for a moment did she dream that she would ever meet Marlborough. She was too late, but the world was by no means void of dukes and princes.

It was unfortunate that Gladys did not know the true circumstances of Consuelo's match. Only later did the story of how

Consuelo was coerced into marriage turn that fairy-tale into a tragedy.

What is more strange is that only a few years later many people believed that Gladys was one of Consuelo's bridesmaids at her wedding in New York in November 1895. Flights of the imagination have even produced the ingenious theory that the Duke, an unwilling groom, turned to see his reluctant bride coming up the aisle, caught sight of Gladys and decided then and there to marry her one day instead. Alas, this is nonsense. Though Marble House, the eleven-million-dollar Newport home of the Vanderbilts, was directly opposite Marraine Baldwin's cottage, Gladys and Consuelo never met in America. There was a four-year age difference between them, and besides Consuelo was travelling abroad for much of the time between 1893 and 1895. Of her stays at Newport she wrote that she was a virtual prisoner with her mother and governess as warders. Gladys was neither a bridesmaid nor even a guest at the wedding. She was safely tucked away at Howard Seminary dreaming of the impossibility of it all.

There occurred another event which added weight to Gladys's dreams. At some time in her early life she visited a fortune-teller, whose prognostications had a considerable effect on her. Years later, on 25 October 1942, her friend Mrs Grylls wrote to her:

> Do you know I believe that all your life you have subconsciously been influenced by that wretched fortune-teller & that if it had not been for his wickedness in telling you all the things he did you would be a different woman – living a normal life in a normal way – Don't be furious with me for writing this – it is not meant to be impertinent – I just feel that this man is responsible for the ruin of your life – it makes me simply mad.

It is impossible to do more than guess what the fortune-teller said. Gladys seems only to have spoken about it to Mrs Grylls, and only once, in a brave moment, did Mrs Grylls make reference to it. Clearly, however, it was not without significance.

Gladys went to New York occasionally, but she dreaded it, because 'those frivolous old gossips . . . will clump around me to see the talked-about "daughter of those Deacons" '. She consoled herself that she was 'wise in worldly knowledge, not a bread-and-butter missis', and she told her mother: 'I can face those warriors of society armed with their gossip-loving tongues and well coated with rouge and powder'. Marraine Baldwin worried that Gladys was no longer a child and noted that her cheeks had taken on a bright glow of health. Gladys felt this glow compared well with Marraine's cheeks, the glow in which was encouraged by other than natural means.

In December Gladys was reunited with her sisters at the Buckingham Hotel. Her only disappointment was that there was still no sign of her mother. She was growing increasingly disenchanted with her poor father who, she reported, having delivered Audrey and Edith to the tender care of Marraine Baldwin, had 'retired to some other part of the city, I know nor care not where'.

1896 was Gladys's last year at Howard Seminary, and found her taking part in many gregarious activities. She was a member of the school dramatic and social club, of a dinner club that met every Saturday, and of a secret organization mysteriously known as 'S.N. of B.F.'; and she was president of a five-girl tea and chocolate party group which met regularly in her room. This involved a certain amount of unwelcome work:

> The care of dishwashing falls to the lot of both president and secretary. I have to wash all the tea cups while my unfortunate secretary has to wash the spoons and saucers.
>
> I always make the tea or chocolate whichever it may be and I assure you it is no small labor.[18]

On her fifteenth birthday Gladys returned to the Marlborough theme. A friend of hers had stayed in the same hotel as the Duke and Duchess in Cairo and wrote to Gladys that the Duchess wore 'the most beautiful gowns imaginable'. Gladys had but recently been commenting on the way all the Vanderbilts had been taking to matrimony. Consuelo's mother had finally married Perry Belmont, despite gossip which suggested she was out for a duke herself. Gertrude Vanderbilt had become engaged, and Gladys predicted correctly that Cornelius was about to be betrothed to Grace Wilson. She worried for 'poor ill Mrs Blight with her two daughters as yet unmarried and a third fast growing up'. It was Mrs Blight's avowed intent that one daughter at least should wed a Vanderbilt.

The lawyers had long said that it was only a matter of time

before Gladys, Audrey and Edith would be handed back to Mrs Baldwin. In the spring of 1896 there were sudden developments. Her father informed Gladys that she and Audrey could go to Mrs Baldwin for the Easter vacation. 'I know you will be pleased to hear this', he wrote. That was straightforward enough; but Mrs Baldwin still pressed for total custody. Thus Mr Deacon arrived at the Seminary one day and laid his terms before Gladys. If Mrs Baldwin did not accept his proposal of the Easter vacation, then he would indeed give her up completely. But in exchange Mrs Baldwin would have to relinquish all claims to the other children, Gladys would have to become a Baldwin and would have to renounce him as her father. Gladys was in a desperate dilemma:

> I feel my brain power giving way under this awful weight. Everything is a blur. I don't seem to realise, I can't understand, comprehend my position. I am not fit to decide anything either for myself or for the others .... I am crazy. I don't know what to do. My poor little sisters I may never see them again! That is for long years to come.[14]

Shortly afterwards, however, Mr Deacon's lawyer, W. P. Blake, swiftly settled the matter. He did so, according to Gladys, for fear that if Mrs Baldwin came to Boston to do battle with 'this peculiar man (Papa)' she would influence him to give her more than he intended. But Gladys was far from satisfied with the outcome and declared she would like to meet Blake, reckoning she was more than a match for him: 'I swear revenge.' The outcome of it all was that not long after this Gladys returned to live with her mother in France. In order not to interrupt their education Audrey and Edith stayed in America for a while longer.

Gladys never saw her father again, though she kept in touch with him and sent him regular presents. In receipt of a pair of braces, he replied: 'Of course anything worked by the hands of my handsome daughter would be prized by me.' Gladys also urged Audrey to write to him. Meanwhile he passed his time between Narragansett Pier, Newport, and the Hotel Bellevue in Boston, where the story is still told that one night he was at the Somerset Club when the assembled company fell to discussing *crimes passionelles*. A callow young man gave it as his opinion that they never happened any more. Whereupon Mr Deacon looked at him darkly and enquired: 'Young man, do you know who I am?'

An acquaintance from England followed what he called 'the varied drama' of Mr Deacon's life with interest and compassion. This was Henry James, who wrote to him on 6 June 1897 about

the drama that has restored you (for how long?) to your native land, and of which you give me an impression in your allusion to the part played in your existence by your daughters, by what you can do for them, and by all that they, I take for granted, are able to do for you.

Henry James's early interest in Mr Deacon was revived, and he longed to discuss his situation with him – that of a Europeanized alien restored to America. He hoped one day to meet Gladys and her sisters:

I wish I could see your girls. But I shall be sure to – the future is theirs and I shall hang on to it hard enough and long enough to be brushed by their wing. I give them meanwhile my blessing; and je vous serre bien la main – two lame ducks careful not to squeeze too hard.[15]

But Henry James and Gladys did not meet, though she was one of his keen admirers. In her old age she commented:

He was the English Flaubert . . . a rare product of America. He foresaw present-day problems and was a keen observer of characters which he then explored in his books. He was thoroughly honest. He had a brain as fine as silk.[16]

Henry James's hope that 'in some place of cool Atlantic airs' Mr Deacon was bearing 'the burden of flesh' was to be confounded. Alarming reports circulated about his mental condition. One stated that he had been expelled from the Newport Reading Room, America's oldest surviving club, 'because he persisted in taking ice from a water pitcher to cool his head'. For some time he had been accustomed to travel with a valet-cum-nurse, E. L. Peck. In 1897 his doctor diagnosed 'a form of insanity known as confusional mania; an exhaustion insanity'. The case was serious in a man with a naturally unstable nervous system and an inherited taint. The doctor advised that Mr Deacon should go to a quiet place where he could be watched, but still continue riding, walking and fishing. He warned that eventually he would go insane, and that if he did not get proper rest he could even become dangerous.

The worst happened on 22 August 1897 at the Hotel Bellevue in Boston. Mr Deacon had a fit and became almost uncontrollable. Mr Blake arranged for him to be sent to the McLean Hospital in nearby Belmont. Mr Deacon calmed down when he arrived there and was thoroughly aware that he was about to become an inmate of an insane asylum. A newspaper report described him:

> Mr Deacon looked haggard, worn and emaciated when he was admitted to the institution, and he did not have that commanding and dignified air for which he was once noted. He seemed but a shadow of his former self, and to be worn with troubles and age.[17]

A fortnight after his admission, the medical superintendent of the hospital forwarded Mr Blake a letter which Mr Deacon had written to Gladys. 'I send it to you because knowing the circumstances so well, you can tell better than I whether it should go as addressed.' Mr Deacon was more relaxed than had been anticipated but the other patients annoyed him. For this reason he was moved to a suite of rooms in Upham House at fifty dollars a week. Here is the hospital opinion of the case:

> It seems to us extremely probable that he has had a disease of the spinal cord for several years, that more recently the same disease has appeared in the brain, constituting what is known as general paralysis, and that he will never recover.
>
> It is quite possible that he may have a remission during which he may appear to be quite well and may even be able to live outside a hospital, but I expect that sooner or later he will grow worse again and that he will not live many years; he should live a very regular and quiet life under medical supervision.[18]

In his last quiet years he took comfort from the letters that Florence Baldwin wrote to him, enjoying news of their children. In March 1898 he was delighted to hear that she intended to visit him. He retained a sense of humour, as when speculating to her about his brother's wife: 'I wonder Mrs Harleston has no babies. Probably Harl is too serious for that ! ! !' And the man who had insisted so vehemently that his wife should renounce his name now addressed his envelope to 'Mrs Florence Deacon', and began 'My dearest Florence'.

On 5 July 1901 Edward Parker Deacon died at the hospital from pneumonia. Three days later he was buried next to his sister in Island Cemetery, high above Newport.

PART TWO

The Pursuit of
Pleasure

Chapter Five

THE MAENAD, THE POET
AND THE FAUN

Gladys returned to Europe for good. In the late 1890s Mrs Baldwin moved from the rue de Grenelle to 30 rue Jean-Goujon, four doors along from the Rothschild stable, and established a new home with her daughters, the nurse Irma and a few servants.

In the autumn of 1897 she took Gladys to England with the purpose of introducing her into London society. To each daughter, she gave the advice 'Tenez la dragée d'haute'. Others must learn to respect.

Here, to her enormous delight, Gladys came face to face with the man of her American dreams, the ninth Duke of Marlborough. Consuelo was recuperating from the birth of the heir, Lord Blandford, and so the Duke was alone. He was very taken with Gladys and he invited her to come to Blenheim. She met Consuelo, her invisible Newport neighbour, they became friends, and she formed the habit of spending part of the late summer at Blenheim. Consuelo gave a generous description of the young girl whom she now admitted to her world:

> Gladys Deacon was a beautiful girl endowed with a brilliant intellect. Possessed of exceptional powers of conversation, she could enlarge on any subject in an interesting and amusing manner. I was soon subjugated by the charm of her companionship and we began a friendship which only ended years later.[1]

The German phase of Gladys's education began in October 1897. In old age she recalled her dislike of it: 'I was at school in Bonn in a small house near the University. I had to learn by listening and that was no good .... It was a stupid place. I learnt nothing there.'[2] Gladys was more or less a beginner in German, though she had taken lessons in America and continued her studies in Paris with a German governess, who was very proud to be a 'von something or other'. Mrs Baldwin accompanied her to Bonn and was delighted to find that she was to be living with German girls. What she did not appreciate was that these girls were enthusiastically trying to learn English and French and spoke nothing but one of those languages. It was not long before Gladys was dismissing Bonn as 'this weary hole'.

She went to the Frölich School to attend all the German classes in the hope of hearing good German spoken. She explained her attitude to her mother:

> I am going to give this place a fair trial until Xmas and study hard, but if I don't speak then, I don't think it would be worth while to come back. I am in hope that the course at Frölich will help me, if they don't, then 'I hang up the hat' as the saying goes.[3]

Despite frequent supplications to be taken away over the ensuing months, Gladys stayed in Bonn until December 1898. She lodged at 10 Baumschulen-Allee, a house in a wide street in the centre of the town, from where she wrote in February 1898: 'the heating is so elementary that my hands are perishing with cold'. One delight was a regular painting lesson with an artist who spoke no French or English, so that while Gladys could understand his German he could not understand any of her questions. A solution to this problem was found when a German lodger who spoke French was found. The teacher 'came back literally dragging the poor frightened creature behind him who nevertheless served very well as interpreter'. Gladys also took Italian lessons; and by April she could play a waltz 'quite finely' at the piano. Her studies at the keyboard came to an end for two reasons. One day she sat beside an open window and heard someone else playing so beautifully that she knew she could never aspire to that standard. Also one of her sisters played at home, and she concluded that one person practising in a house was quite enough. Other recreations included taking photographs with a Kodak and working a tapestry.

While at Bonn, Gladys paid frequent visits to friends at Darmstadt, a place of which she was particularly fond. For a time her life was 'nothing but parties, coaching trips, etc., with some very charming people'. Gladys and her sister Audrey were naturally worried as to how they would be received in society after the publicity the family had suffered over the years. It did not seem to have an adverse effect. In Italy Gladys went to a ball with her friend Lily Kirk and made a court bow to the King and Queen. She reassured Audrey that she was full of confidence about her position in the world: 'I have had enough success to ensure it, so don't worry about yours.'

Gladys attended a course on Homer at the end of 1898 and was overjoyed that she could understand every word. She took up Latin by herself and dived enthusiastically into a book of Pliny, which she described as 'a wonder of elegance in its style'. Blessed with great application of mind she thoroughly enjoyed her work: 'This studying mania is getting stronger and stronger and I shall end as a professor before long.'

In her last term Gladys was the ring-leader in a school revolution, brought on by the 'ridiculous severity' of the teachers. They tried to win her over, but she proved more than a match for them: 'I did not give way at all but I let them think I was on the point of coming to their side, bringing with me the other ten girls and re-establishing peace at Baumschulen 10.' From that day on she held the whip. The teachers were all too aware that at a sign from her, hostilities would begin again. 'It is a delightful comedy', wrote Gladys, 'and I begin to enjoy the sweets of Divine Right!'[4]

The following year Gladys returned to Paris, where she studied mathematics with a tutor at Sacré Coeur, a method of learning that held more appeal for her than 'listening' at Bonn. She was able to make rapid progress. 'We discussed', recalled Gladys. 'I worked and he corrected .... Sometimes he saw it my way!'[5]

Gladys was fortunate to have a brain which could digest new information accurately at first reading. She also knew how to dispense to others what she had just learned to maximum advantage. A report in 1902 which concerned itself more with her beauty than with her brains had this to say of her:

She is a bright, lively girl, thoroughly well-bred and intelligent, and up-to-date both in literature and art, but full of fun, even witty at times .... She is quite at home in conversing either with young or old, and with the latter evinces a pretty deference which wins her golden opinions.[6]

F. Marion Crawford, the novelist, commented: 'She is clever, and has read a great mass of stuff without quite understanding it, but always meaning to understand and judge fairly of the values of things and people.'[7] After many years of friendship, Bernard Berenson became suspicious about Gladys's powers. He wrote: 'She did not really know how to "learn", but she would retain everything which would be useful to her in making an effect.'[8] Her tutor called her 'a brain genius' and Gladys suggested this was the reason why she was able to spend so much time totally alone. Then there is her own declaration: 'I was a miracle. Differential Calculus was too low for me!' She never attended university but was a keen advocate of a university education. 'It smooths life', she said in old age, and strongly recommended it to a young person, enquiring: 'Have all your talents been brought out of you?' She continued to study on her own or with tutors for some years to come and emerged with seven languages, a wide general knowledge, a fascination for mythology and a life-long love of art, literature and poetry. 'When I read poetry', she declared, 'I am up in Heaven.'

Gladys's power of conversation, her extraordinary use of the written word and her intriguing personality had an astonishing effect on nearly everyone she met in her long life. Combined with this was another gift, that of a quite remarkable beauty. Here is a contemporary description of it:

> Her manner is radiant, her smile equally so; in fact, she seems the embodiment of sunshine, with sunny brown hair, a wonderful rose-leaf complexion, with yet no tint of insipidity of colouring, and a bright winsomeness of manner which immediately takes you by storm. Her chief beauty, perhaps, lies in her large grey eyes, and the perfect moulding of her brow, and although by no means of a classical cast of feature, yet she attracts more than many with a perfect profile.[9]

A great lover of the classics, it would not be long before she aspired to acquire a 'perfect profile' by bizarre means. She possessed a good Hellenic profile, but for a small dip between the nose and the forehead, and this dip worried her to an inordinate extent.

The contemporary account described Gladys's eyes as grey. They were, in fact, large, bright blue, and set quite wide apart. With those enormous staring eyes she looked directly at the person she was talking to, and seemingly right into their soul. Many found this an alarming experience. Nor did she ever lose the flair for rolling her eyes provocatively.

In Paris Gladys was swept up into the world of Comte Robert de Montesquiou-Fezensac. Mrs Baldwin had long been a friend of Montesquiou, the most flamboyant of all aesthetes. Often mocked and derided by his contemporaries, he was both a nobleman and a poet, or, as Gladys would have it, 'a poet of sorts'. Proust drew on his character for Baron de Charlus, and Oscar Wilde, in some part, for Dorian Gray. He lived in considerable style and entertained lavishly, though for every party there were two lists, one for those to be invited and another for those to be excluded. Montesquiou derived considerably more pleasure from the latter.

He had a faithful secretary, Yturri, who had been raised in Buenos Aires before emigrating to Paris at the age of fifteen. Yturri had been poached by Montesquiou from his friend Baron Doasan in 1885 and died in the Count's service twenty years later. Gladys thought Yturri secretly hated Montesquiou, and so maligned was the poor Count that it was even said that Yturri composed his master's poems. Yturri made great friends with Gladys and one day she sent him a small present. She was thrilled with the success of her gift, which inspired in return 'such delicious verse'.

Montesquiou liked Mrs Baldwin, whom he found dignified in appearance. He had sympathy for her in her misfortunes and took her side over the Abeille drama. It was to him that she once said plaintively: 'I was not born to be ignored.' He liked her, too, because she was pretty and said pretty things. One day, wearing a hat festooned with ivy, she announced: 'I'm already wearing the head-dress of a ruin.' Montesquiou was delighted to welcome her daughter to his circle. Indeed Berenson said that he and Montesquiou between them launched Gladys into society, playing Svengali to her Trilby. The Count was genuinely impressed by Gladys and nicknamed her 'the marvel'. At dinner following one of his celebrated fêtes at Versailles he and

Yturri raved over the success of the afternoon to Elisabeth de Gramont: 'And Gladys Deacon was truly beautiful. She had the absolute appearance of an archangel.'[10]

Montesquiou was also one of the great chroniclers of his day. His papers, beautifully arranged by Yturri's successor, comprise some five hundred volumes. He was also the author of numerous books, some of which were privately printed. He was a patron of the arts and particularly of artists such as Helleu, Boldini and Jacques-Emile Blanche. Gladys was a natural subject for immortality on canvas, and Montesquiou could not wait to have her 'springlike profile' painted and sketched by Helleu. Thus Helleu set to work in the winter of 1901.

Montesquiou introduced Helleu to many of the beauties of the Faubourg Saint-Germain, and the charming and intelligent artist made his name with his drypoints and crayon portraits of the ladies. In time he sketched Gladys's sisters and the young Duchess of Marlborough until she discovered he was doing brisk business on the side selling the pastels, drawings and etchings, for which he refused to let her pay. He greatly delighted at the prospect of portraying Gladys and urged Montesquiou to let him know the moment she returned to Paris. He had to suppress himself for a while longer until Gladys recovered from a bout of 'flu, but at last his time came. He expressed his joy to Yturri:

You are fortunate to possess that one thing that I have adored for so many years! What luck you have! I saw Miss Deacon last night and she told me that she can come and pose here. You know I would be delighted to lunch with you and Montesquiou but there's not a minute to lose. And as she is happy about it, I prefer that she should come here and pose. You have no idea what a bore it is to leave after lunch, with a sketch under one's arm after the first sitting. For 1000 francs I will do many drawings of the adorable creature. What a nuisance that she is leaving! There are so many things I could have done of her this winter . . . .

Gladys kept Montesquiou informed of the progress of the portrait: 'the sittings continue every afternoon, but it was only yesterday after numerous trys that the master believed he had grasped the runaway spirit in the pose'.

Jacques-Emile Blanche also prepared to paint Gladys's portrait, but he hesitated before the magnitude of the task. He told her he had never seen anyone so beautiful, and suggested that she might come and spend the summer with himself and his wife at Offranville in Normandy. Life would be simple and a contrast to 'spending weeks after weeks in some disgusting Palace Hotel on the top of absurd mountains'. He hoped his proposal was not 'too daring and preposterous', but the idea of Offranville held no appeal for Gladys and so the portrait was not attempted. Curiously, Sargent did not paint Gladys either, though he was very much conscious of her existence.

On the other hand, Boldini was a great friend of Gladys's for a long time despite frequent quarrels. He sketched her in 1899, and many years later he painted a fine portrait of her. Giovanni Boldini came from Ferrara in Northern Italy and made a name for himself as a fashionable society portrait painter in Paris. Berenson knew him well and wrote of him: 'disagreeable, rather dandaical personality, looked as if he had a nasty taste in his mouth. As artist, ultra-chic, particularly when portraying elongated society ladies as if with translucent glass, very taking and with a certain dash and pep even.'[11]

Boldini had acquired what Consuelo Vanderbilt described as 'a salacious reputation with women' at an early age, finding it hard to resist plucking a fruit that came within his grasp. In his later years when a female head shared his pillow, he instructed his maid to rouse him at seven with an appropriate excuse. His companion then departed and he repaired cheerfully to his work. Consuelo had her portrait painted by Boldini and found that during the sittings 'it was difficult for him to restrain the sallies that his bohemian nature inspired'. He called her 'La Divina', and she took it as a compliment, little realizing that he gave the title to every woman he knew. Such was his reputation that Consuelo felt obliged to advise Gladys in October 1901 not to see too much of him. Elisabeth de Gramont also sat for a portrait but gave up the sittings realizing that she would have to pay 'one way or another'.

Boldini cut a dashing figure. He frequented cafés, was a splendid raconteur, rode elegantly and danced well. He played the piano and sang. He navigated one of the first huge bicycles, and was among the first of Paris's residents to own an automobile. But painting and drawing were more important to him than anything else, and Gertrude Stein went so far as to hail him as 'the initiator of modern painting' because of the simplicity of his designs.

Soon after he first met her, Montesquiou sent Gladys his photograph with a flattering note. She replied that she was 'very, very touched' by what he said about her 'little head', and promised him her photograph in due course. Later he offered her some poetry. 'I am in delicious anticipation of the verse you are going to dedicate to me', she wrote. 'Nothing could go to my heart more than such an honour and I thank you with true feeling.' The poem 'L'Eventail' (The Fan), published in *Les Paons* (The Peacocks) in 1901, described the gentle waving of a fan held in a pale hand, which sent out imperceptible ripples of air which reached the stars and the ocean and the forest and Heaven and far-off unknown universes beyond. Gladys read the poem at Versailles in 'a silence where battles are bemoaned' and was enchanted. She urged Montesquiou to explore 'the externalized soul of Aubrey Beardsley', the artist, who had recently died.

Whistler was another point of shared interest. Montesquiou had been fascinated by a recent contretemps in which Whistler and Sir William Eden* had been involved. Sir William had commissioned a portrait of his wife and before it was completed gave Whistler a Valentine's Day gift of 100 guineas for it, the lowest possible fee. Whistler then painted out Lady Eden's face and refused to hand over either the portrait or the 100 guineas. The artist gained much welcome publicity in the ensuing litigation. The story is told in *The Baronet and the Butterfly*, put out by Whistler in a small edition of 250 copies. Montesquiou urged Gladys to find a copy, but she discovered that most of them had been snapped up by friends of Sir William. Eventually to their mutual delight she secured copy number ten of the Paris edition. Her strong friendship with Montesquiou was forged through such collaborations.

Gladys first met Bernard Berenson in St Moritz in August 1899. Her mother regularly stayed at Sils near St Moritz and often visited Florence where Berenson was living in the late 1890s. Bernard Berenson – he was 'Bernhard' until the First World War – was a Lithuanian, born in Russia in 1865. His parents

---

* Father of the future Prime Minister, Anthony Eden.

emigrated to Boston when he was ten and he attended school there, but his real education did not begin until he discovered the Boston Public Library, where he soon became a self-confessed pest, drawing out more books than the attendants could possibly believe he ever read. His first aim was to devote himself to the study of *belles lettres* and to become a critic and literary historian. In the pursuit of this aim, Berenson was sent on a three-year educational tour of Europe, financed by certain members of the Harvard community and by Isabella Stewart Gardner. By concentrating on the field which he considered himself the weakest, he discovered art. He became a great connoisseur, and repaid Mrs Gardner by helping her form one of the most important collections in the United States.

He went into business with Joseph (later Lord) Duveen, who made an immense fortune selling works of art. Yet as Gladys explained: 'Duveen couldn't sell a picture without Berenson's endorsement, even if it was worth ten million dollars!'[12] Berenson duly took his cut of the profit, though it was something he did not much like discussing. Berenson is also remembered for introducing expressions such as 'life-enhancing' into the world of art, and extended the metaphor to his friends. People were judged either 'life-enhancing' or 'life-diminishing'.

Villa I Tatti at Settignano in the hills above Florence became Berenson's home in 1900. Here he collected a library which, he wrote, contained 'nearly everything, although not everything that my lust for knowledge required'.[13] He liked having the books close to him 'so as to be able to use them when one is piping hot with eagerness for them and malleably receptive to what one can get out of them'.[14] I Tatti itself became a haven of culture where 'B.B.' held court for nearly sixty years. Such a legend has grown up of life there that it is almost impossible to think of Berenson as ever having existed without it. Yet Gladys came into his life before I Tatti days, and survived well into the time when the villa had become the Harvard University Center for Italian Renaissance Studies, alive with blue-jeaned students on 'study programs'.

In the late 1890s Berenson was at work on *The Drawings of the Florentine Painters* which was published in two volumes in 1903. He met his future wife in 1890, and they fell in love at first sight. Marriage was impossible as Mary's husband Benjamin Costelloe was still alive and she had become a Roman Catholic.

Instead she left her children with her parents and travelled with B.B. as 'his pupil and secretary'. They were married in December 1900.

Mary Berenson* did not meet Gladys or her mother until 1901. At the end of that year, when her marriage with B.B. was going through a shaky period, she received a letter from him saying that he had loved Gladys very much and would dearly like to have married her. The letter was written in an atmosphere of recrimination, but it indicates how deeply the art critic felt for Gladys. Here is Mary's reply:

> I had no idea, dear, thee was so much in love with Gladys as that. I think thee did wrong not to follow that strong feeling, and try to marry her. There would have been some chance for thee to have at least a little real, satisfying joy, instead of the frugal fear of duty. However, thee did what thee thought right, and if it was a mistake, all we can do is to make the best of it.[15]

Mary, deeply distressed, wrote again the next day, saying she felt she was going to die and quite wished she could. She pursued the Gladys theme: 'But even if thee had had the bliss of marrying Gladys by now I am sure thee would be in Hell. And could thee be sure of making a good third choice?'[16]

Gladys's relationship with B.B. was steeped in the magic of mythology. She saw herself as a Maenad, a wild creature frenzied with wine. And B.B. was a Faun, a rustic god, a kind of Roman Pan, a prophet who spoke to men in their dreams, the guardian of herds and the patron of rural pursuits. From time to time the Maenad warned the Faun that her thyrsus was getting hot and she would soon be pursuing him over Florentine hills.

At one point in the relationship Gladys sent B.B. a thistle from Paris as 'a tiny souvenir of my pleasant character'. She explained: 'I fear alas that even this thistle is not enough to adequately express my prickly disposition. But search and you will find that within the spiky exterior there lies a heart capable of feelings of fondness and serenity.' Her point made, she

---

* Formerly Mary Pearsall Smith (1864–1945), sister of Logan Pearsall Smith. A Quaker from Pennsylvania, previously married to Benjamin Costelloe, by whom she had two daughters.

rushed to catch a train to Versailles begging him to accept 'the loving feelings of the Baccharista'.

When she was in Paris, she missed him and longed to see him. 'You are not a person to me', she declared, 'you are an état d'esprit et d'âme.' She found one of his publications in a local bookshop and made friends with the shop-man so as to be able to dip into it from time to time. Then occasionally Mrs Baldwin announced they would go to Florence, and Gladys was thrilled:

> B.B. we will make long walks, you will tell me everything. In the late afternoon we will come home bringing to your comfortable arm-chairs that slight weariness so exquisite at twilight and it will be a year before dinner is served.[17]

In 1899 Mrs Baldwin decided to take Gladys for a three-month visit to Charlie Baldwin at Beaulieu in California. Gladys found the departure very difficult, not only because it meant separation from B.B. but because of the seemingly endless visits to couturiers and milliners, parasites whose existence depended on woman's vanity. She wrote to B.B.:

> Every day until now I would ride in the enchanted forests, full of memories and ghosts. It's Marly, it's Versailles, it's Garches; but now I'm left with Paquin, with Doucet and with Worth.[18]

Gladys would have much preferred to remain in Paris, gathering cherries and weaving garlands. She regretted being condemned to a life of perpetual emigration. She had more romantic notions:

> I wish I could die so as to be buried in the earth and return in the shape of a beautiful tree with a slender and glorious silhouette, or rather to emerge from its branch as a delicate and beautiful flower which, no sooner picked, would wilt in order to return the next year more beautiful still. Why can't it be so?[19]

She was concerned that B.B., who was forever surrounded by beautiful women, would forget her during her absence but hoped he would come to Paris to celebrate her eighteenth birthday the following February. Meanwhile she begged him to accept the gift of her feelings as 'a discreet offering from the

Maenad to the Faun, who without a thought tramples on the wailing and burning hearts of mortals'.

Gladys and her mother then set off from Le Havre to the United States. Between New York and California their journey took a traumatic turn. Here is the account she gave of it to Berenson:

> The Fates presided over our destinies for the tedium of our journey was relieved by every disagreeable incident possible.
>
> Caught in a sandstorm in the yellow ghastly desert of Arizona, we were eight hours late and arrived in a state which baffles description.
>
> We found ourselves in the astounding whirlwind of carnival in New Orleans with one room for Mamma, myself and the maid! Then on the way through the swamps of Georgia, our train was nearly wrecked, the rails having been tampered with by some brigands.
>
> As it was our two engines were thrown right over, and the baggage car followed them with all our belongings.
>
> And there we remained all night on a tressel some thirty feet high with water at the average of ninety foot deep all around us. It was simply awful hanging between life and death for what seemed like all eternity. Some of the men were killed, and mortally wounded but the passengers were all saved, the horrid things. I went to see the worried firemen the next morning and hearing of their miserable *pecunerie* condition started out to wring some money out of my fellow passengers. Oh my dear friend, the awful time I had with these creatures for give they would not though these men had saved their lives in sacrificing their own.
>
> However I made some three hundred francs by my tenacity but the disgust I felt has left a deep scar in my breast.[20]

When Gladys returned to Paris she was relieved to hear that B.B. had not forgotten her and that she had not been 'relegated with the herd of past conquests'.

In the spring of 1900, Mrs Baldwin went alone to Biarritz while Gladys stayed in Paris. Without her mother to chaperone her, she did not go out much; instead she spent her time reading late into the night and succeeded in straining her eyes so badly that she had to spend ten days under a black bandage. But Gladys loved springtime in Paris and could not understand how

B.B. could have failed to fall victim to its 'omnipotent charms'. Spring brought visitors from overseas: 'such a relief to talk to other than those odious Frenchmen'. It also brought Gladys into the world of the Marchioness of Anglesey,* an American with fine porcelain features, who entertained at Versailles. Gladys referred to Mini Anglesey as 'Aunt Min'; the artist Romaine Brooks wrote of her conversation: 'With each slight puff of her breath, feathery thoughts were wafted from place to place . . . . A vocabulary was not necessary; mere chirping and twittering answered just as well.'[21]

Gladys enjoyed Mini Anglesey's receptions where she met a mixture of bohemians and *gens du monde*:

> This combination is a most happy one. The ones bring out their various talents to dazzle the others and these in turn make great show of 'grandes façons' so as to show these good people that a man with tradition shows off to a better advantage in a salon than any other however clever.[22]

A life of receptions and travelling continued. In the daytime Gladys might exhaust herself 'in contemplation of the wonders of the English Section' at the Louvre, and then in the evening dress up as a Hoppner with powdered hair and flowing robes to attend a ball. In the autumn of 1900 she prepared to spend the winter in Rome. Mrs Baldwin informed Berenson that 'she has promised to go and is delighted with Italians. She can talk of nothing else.' There was an early hint of instability in her character, to judge from Mrs Baldwin's added comment: 'She is much improved to my thinking, more *assise* and less *éballetine*.'[23]

Both Mrs Baldwin and Gladys hoped to meet Berenson in Blesio, but he had more important things to do. Benjamin Costelloe had died and he was on the point of marrying Mary. Shortly before the marriage B.B. sent Gladys some beautiful buttons, which, commented Mrs Baldwin, were 'too pretty to be out of a connoisseur's vitrine'. Gladys had known of Berenson's matrimonial plans since April, so she was not surprised. For a while, she told him, the whole family had been furious. So too was Prince Doria Pamphili, her mother's latest admirer.

---

* Mary Livingstone King, born in Georgia, married first to the Hon Henry Wodehouse. She became the third wife of the fourth Marquess of Anglesey and died in 1931.

Only when Carlo Placci, a leading figure in Florentine society, assured them that his future wife was a charmer, did they decide to forgive him. But change was inescapable:

> I am afraid your faun days are over and all that remains for your only Maenad is to follow your illustrious example. . . . And so, dear friend, goodbye. Forgive such a long silence from a beautiful woman who has a true and deep friendship for you.[24]

She signed her letter 'une pauvre Ménade délaissée' (a poor forsaken Maenad). But though Gladys believed their relationship was over, this was very far from the case.

Chapter Six

CORONATION SUMMER

In March 1901 Mrs Baldwin and Gladys went to stay with the Berensons at I Tatti. The new Mrs Berenson, meeting Gladys for the first time, was fascinated by her extraordinary personality. A fortnight later she and B.B. joined Gladys and her mother in Siena. B.B. took Mrs Baldwin for a tour around a picture gallery and came back very impressed by her intelligence and appreciation. He told Mary that he was surprised that such an apparently superficial woman should have so much taste and natural feeling for art. Alas, B.B. had been taken in, for Gladys later revealed that her mother collapsed on her bed in a state of exhaustion, exclaiming: 'What a delightful man he could be if only he would stop caring for those old *croûtes*!'[1]

Nevertheless a close friendship was forged between Mrs Baldwin, Gladys and the Berensons. It was to survive all manner of complications in the years to come. Shortly afterwards Mary Berenson went to England to see her children, something she did frequently, often resulting in long periods of separation from B.B. Mrs Baldwin clamoured for her address and B.B. urged Mary to make her journey home through Paris, staying at the rue Jean-Goujon. 'I do want to keep hold of Gladys', he wrote, 'even at the expense of her mother and I really am fond of her on her own account.'[2]

Mary spent two nights in Paris and Mrs Baldwin welcomed the chance to pour out her heart to her. She confessed she was desperately in love with the Marquis de Lubersac, who had nearly broken her heart by having an affair with the famous courtesan, La Belle Otéro. Mrs Baldwin also had an admirer in Prince Alfonso Doria Pamphili, whom she had met at least a year before – introduced by Gladys, according to some. Prince

Doria was often in Paris with his wife, formerly Lady Emily Pelham-Clinton, daughter of the sixth Duke of Newcastle.

Meanwhile Gladys was clamouring for some Greek marbles that B.B. had promised to her. Besides the marbles, the Berensons arranged a Greek tutor to come to her through the French archaeologist Salomon Reinach. Gladys did not see them again until the following year, though news of her still reached them from a variety of sources. By May poor B.B. was suffering from ennui. He was indifferent towards everything and everyone, except Mary, who wrote sadly: 'Even Gladys had faded out of his grasp.'[3]

In July 1901 Gladys's father died in America. This caused little more than a passing upset in the family, since all the sisters had been brainwashed by Mrs Baldwin into believing that Mr Deacon was but a sad victim of her own beauty. In later life all that the third sister, Edith, would say of him was: 'His insanity was a great tragedy.' Gladys remembered him well but Dorothy was too young and hardly ever saw him. Under the terms of his will, the four girls began to receive income from the Deacon Trust.

In August 1901 Mrs Baldwin enticed Lubersac away from La Belle Otéro and they set off together to Carlsbad. Mrs Baldwin was so pleased at this victory that she told Mary, who became convinced that they were lovers. Meanwhile Gladys crossed the Channel for a six-month stay at Blenheim with the Duke and Duchess of Marlborough. She arrived in their lives at a time when neither was particularly happy.

Charles Richard John Spencer-Churchill, ninth Duke of Marlborough, survived a gruelling childhood. He was born in Simla, India, on 13 November 1871. He was known all his life as 'Sunny', not for his 'sunny disposition', as Maurice Ashley has pointed out in his book, *Churchill as Historian*, but because the subsidiary title of his father which he used by courtesy was Earl of Sunderland. The sobriquet 'Sunny' gave pause to his cousin Winston Churchill, when he wrote to him from India in 1898:

> My dear – I hesitate how to begin. 'Sunny' though melodious sounds childish: 'Marlborough' is very formal; 'Duke' impossible between relations; and I don't suppose you answer to either 'Charles' or 'Richard'. If I must reflect, let it be Sunny.

But you must perceive in all this a strong case for the aboli-
tion of the House of Lords and all titles . . . .⁴

Once this hurdle was overcome Sunny and Winston became
lifelong friends. In 1901 Consuelo reported to Gladys: 'Sunny
is still devoutly attentive to Winston's every remark – a great
sign of friendship.'⁵ Consuelo was less enthusiastic: 'Winston
is still on the talk – never stops and really it becomes tiring.'⁶

The Duke's parents were divorced in 1883, following the
sensational elopement of his father Lord Blandford with the
Countess of Aylesford, a notorious *cause célèbre* with many
unfortunate ripples, not least the attempted blackmailing of the
Prince of Wales by Lord Randolph Churchill. Lady Aylesford
bore Lord Blandford a son in 1881. This boy, known as Bill
Spencer, spent much of his youth at Blenheim and was last
spotted by a member of the Churchill family walking alone in
Chelsea some time after the Second World War.

Sunny used to complain in later life that he had been bullied
by his father. Gladys confirmed this: 'He was wounded as a
child.'⁷ His aunt Maud, the Marchioness of Lansdowne, knew
Sunny well all his life and gave Gladys this impression of him:

> Up to ten years old he was one of the most charming boys I
> ever met & most joyous; after that his spirits seemed to have
> vanished & he quite changed, but I have always remained
> very fond of him.⁸

Duty was instilled into him by his formidable grandmother,
Frances (Anne), Duchess of Marlborough. Her husband had
been Viceroy of Ireland, and when they returned to England,
her services particularly as a fund-raiser were recognized in a
personal letter from Queen Victoria. She had the tiresome habit
of taking the letter out, showing it to Sunny and admonishing
him: 'You realize that in my life, I have been of some use to my
fellow subjects.'

In December 1891, Albertha Lady Blandford had to petition
her former husband for the upkeep of her son, but the court
decided that it could order no provision to be made. Sunny
nevertheless succeeded in completing his education at Win-
chester and Trinity College, Cambridge, before his father died
'somewhat suddenly' at Blenheim on 9 November 1892 at the
age of forty-eight. Thus, four days before his twenty-first birth-

day, Sunny became Duke of Marlborough and master of Blenheim.

When Marlborough married Consuelo Vanderbilt, $2,500,000 of capital stock of the Beech Creek Railway Company was transferred to two trustees for his benefit, and an annual income of 4 per cent was guaranteed to him by the New York Central Railroad Company until the day he died. Those who marry for money invariably earn it during their lifetime. Sunny had to relinquish a girl he loved in favour of the Vanderbilt fortune, which he needed to maintain Blenheim. Much has been written of Consuelo's reluctance to marry him. She had considered herself engaged to Winthrop Rutherford until her socially ambitious mother decided Marlborough would be a better catch. She and the Duke had nothing in common, and in her memoirs, *The Glitter and the Gold*, Consuelo painted a depressing picture of silent meals, frosty atmospheres, and of social activities generally rejected as 'tiring'.

Thus Gladys was welcomed equally by Sunny and Consuelo. Just as both Berensons delighted in her company, the Marlboroughs needed her to relieve the depression of their co-existence. Not only was the Duke dazzled by Gladys, but so too was Consuelo. She adored talking to Gladys late into the night, discussing art and books with her. Theirs was an intimate friendship, and in January 1901 Consuelo begged Gladys not to pass her many exams and get beyond 'your poor old Coon'. From the loneliness of Blenheim, Consuelo wrote to her new friend:

> Whenever I am depressed I imagine myself in Italy with you – not with the Italians – just reading, contemplating everything beautiful and breathing in the spirit of the universe in great deep breaths – uplifting and refreshing. Don't laugh at me! I think I should have liked to have been a Vestal Virgin & forever nourished the fire of life & rejoiced as such! or else Cleopatra – I hate the middle course.[9]

Gladys asked Consuelo for a lock of hair and Consuelo promised to send her 'a Coon ringlet'.

Similarly, by August 1901, the Duke's interest in Gladys was thoroughly engaged. A few days before the end of that month, he wrote to her from Harrogate, sending her his 'fond remembrances' and quoting La Rochefoucauld: 'L'absence diminue les médiocres passions et augmente les grandes, comme le vent éteint les bougies et allume le feu.'[10] The Duke cherished the 'fond illusion' that the candle had not yet been blown out, and lingered on thoughts of the fire 'and the possibility of its burning'. At this time he was reluctantly pessimistic about his chances.

Full of fun and mischief, Gladys arrived at Blenheim in the summer of 1901 in time for a large Unionist reception on 10 August. By the end of the month, that well-known purveyor of gossip, Kate Moore, had told Carlo Placci, who in turn told B.B., that Ivor Guest, Lord Wimborne's heir and a first cousin of Marlborough's, had fallen in love with Gladys. He imparted the news to Mary, who was disappointed:

> I almost wish Gladys would marry some nice Englishman, but I have heard that the Wimbornes are rather social climbers, and I suppose if she marries there, she will be lost to us. Well she was a radiant vision & with entrancing possibilities in her. The pity is that they will probably come to very little – from our point of view.[11]

While the Berensons speculated about Ivor Guest, an open landau drawn by four horses with outriders swept through the gates of Blenheim, and out stepped a shy young man, Crown Prince William of Prussia.

The Crown Prince was nineteen, just a year younger than Gladys, and had come over to England from the austere German court, still in mourning for the Empress Frederick. 'The Crown Prince', wrote Consuelo, 'was tall and slight, and gave one an impression of shyness and indecision. Very fair, with prominent blue eyes, and a silly expression that accentuated the degeneracy of appearance he nevertheless had charming manners and took infinite pains to please.'[12] The Crown Prince had acquired the reputation for being susceptible to a pretty face, though his family were not worried about this as he was susceptible to every pretty face, and they consoled themselves with the famous adage that there was safety in numbers. This time he fell badly.

No house-party gathered at Blenheim for the Crown Prince's stay. Apart from the Marlboroughs and Gladys, Viscount Churchill and his extraordinary wife Verena, there was only the German suite – Count Metternich, the German ambassador,

Count Mensdorff, Count Eulenburg and Colonel von Pritzelwitz. The visit was instigated by the Kaiser who had stayed at the Palace in 1899 and now asked the Marlboroughs to receive his son. As Consuelo wrote, 'we could but agree'.

According to a serial in *Le Matin* published in August 1902, love burgeoned between Gladys and the Crown Prince as the sun set on a perfect summer evening and a game of tennis drew to its close. The Crown Prince pledged his love with the ring his mother had given him for his first communion, and Gladys gave him her bracelet. Meanwhile Count Metternich did his best to keep a discreet if anxious eye on the progress of the flirtation, while Consuelo tried in vain to exert restraint on Gladys. The ambassador thought his trouble was over when the Crown Prince leaned over the Visitors Book and inscribed : 'I felt very much at home here'; but worse was to follow.

The Prince insisted on personally driving the Marlborough coach to Oxford. Metternich shook his head anxiously and protested to Consuelo that the love-lorn youth had never driven a coach in his life. Consuelo therefore sat next to the Prince in order to seize the reins in an emergency. Gladys was sandwiched in the back seat between Marlborough and Metternich, and the Crown Prince continually turned round to gaze at her to the consternation of the other passengers and the near apoplexy of the ambassador.

The day was spent in Oxford, affording the Crown Prince the chance to see several colleges and to inspect the relics of William of Wykeham, founder of New College. Shortly before six o'clock he left Oxford in one of the Great Western Railway's special saloons. Consuelo heaved a sigh of relief as she watched 'his silly face protruding from the window to catch a forlorn and parting glimpse of the lady he was leaving'.[13]

But this was not the end, for on his return to Germany the saga continued. The Kaiser noticed that the Crown Prince's ring was missing and sent a furious message via his chamberlain to Consuelo, demanding its immediate return. Gladys surrendered it somewhat reluctantly, and Colonel Pritzelwitz returned the bracelet. Inevitably there was gossip, but Consuelo protected Gladys as best she could by assuring the greatest talker she knew that there was no truth in the story and that Gladys had given back the ring, dismissing the incident as 'childish nonsense'.

In September, Gladys and Consuelo travelled to Germany to do some sightseeing. The visit instilled nervousness in the German court and the moment they arrived at their hotel in Berlin, an Imperial A.D.C. presented himself, on the Emperor's instructions, to show them round. It soon transpired that his real mission was to make certain that there was no tryst between the Crown Prince and Gladys. In contrast to Consuelo and Gladys, who revelled in exploring Sans Souci and the galleries, the A.D.C. presented a dour visage of enforced boredom. The Kaiser had taken no chances. Not only was the Crown Prince banished from Berlin, but the officer selected proved to be 'a man impervious to woman's charm', as Consuelo euphemistically described him. In Dresden they were released from his company and free to converse again about life, art and philosophy. They took steamers down the Elbe and went to the opera in the evenings. Their only point of dissent was the Germans, whom Gladys liked and Consuelo detested. It was a trip Consuelo remembered as a happy break from the tedium of Oxfordshire.

Gladys's romance with the Crown Prince left her unscathed. Shortly before the German trip Mrs Baldwin reported her as still at Blenheim and 'perfectly happy'. But for the Crown Prince there were numerous unfortunate repercussions. In October 1902 he confessed to Daisy, Princess of Pless, that he was furious at not being allowed to go to England or to attend Edward vii's Coronation, 'but papa would not let me go again because he says I flirted too much!'[14] Shortly before his death in 1951 he announced that there had once been a charming American that he would much have liked to marry. The Kaiser forbade the match because, according to the rules of the Royal House, his son could only marry a princess. (In her memoirs Consuelo compared the incident to the later case of Edward viii and Mrs Simpson.) Had the Kaiser permitted his son to marry Gladys, the course of twentieth-century history might have been very different. Might there have been a German-American alliance in the Great War? Though it is an interesting question for speculation, eventually nothing came of the romance but a successful libel writ, and that in 1920. Presently, on 6 June 1905, the Crown Prince married Princess Cecilie of Mecklenburg-Schwerin.

Not long after Gladys returned to Paris from Dresden, the

Duke of Marlborough came to see her. He found her in good spirits, and set off home bearing gifts from her for his two sons. Consuelo was enchanted with them:

> The nigger is especially amusing and ingenious and delighted M quite as much as the children. Blandford and Ivor send you kisses and many thanks. They remember you quite well.[15]

Gladys prepared for another visit to 'the fog of London' in an atmosphere heavy with gossip about her involvement with the Marlboroughs. On the point of departing, she revealed a restless spirit to B.B.:

> I am so tired of those self complacent English, of their talk of never-coming victory, of the new beauty & perhaps of a possible scandal of an impossible kind!
>   I had so much of it last summer I nearly had an attack of hydrophobia![16]

She was not disappointed in her expectations of London: 'It is cold. The ink stand is full of icycles and my head of blue devils. I wait in patience for a brilliant epistle from the "lady-killer of Settignano".'

In October 1901 a keen aspirant for Gladys's affections for nearly a year arrived in Paris, much encouraged by Mrs Baldwin. He was Lord Francis Pelham-Clinton-Hope, brother of Princess Doria. Francis Hope would not have been everybody's idea of the perfect match, even though he was destined to inherit the dukedom of Newcastle and already owned the Hope Diamond, a mighty stone of $44\frac{1}{4}$ carats. Lord Francis has been described as 'a fellow of abandoned habits whose genius for picking losers at Epsom and other race tracks was a legend in English sporting circles'. After a particularly calamitous season at Newmarket, he was declared a bankrupt. His first wife was an American actress called Mary Yohé, who used to sport the Hope Diamond amidst costume jewelry on the stage. They had separated and were divorced in 1902, so the future Duke was free to pursue Gladys, and being a future Duke stood him in good stead.

  In the late autumn, however, he was involved in a shooting accident. For some time the future of one foot was in the balance and eventually he lost it. Along with the foot he feared he would surely lose any chance of acquiring Gladys, but she continued to be very concerned and made enquiries about him through her actor friend, Norman Forbes. He encouraged Gladys to keep in touch with Lord Francis and was very glad when she did: 'I know now that you have a throbbing heart somewhere though it may be a tiny one!'[17] Lord Francis sustained his interest in Gladys for the next two years and even deserted a fiancée on her account, but ultimately all was in vain.

Gladys spent the Christmas of 1901 in Paris. It was at this time that B.B. revealed to Mary his desire to have married Gladys. Mary kept a categorized list of special friends, and Gladys was promptly relegated to class two and crossed out. Festive greetings from Gladys arrived at I Tatti with the first of many mischievous messages for Mary: 'And please give my love to Isolde.' B.B. was in a state of depression, and replied rather dramatically that he was 'tired, over-worked and ill' but wished Gladys 'happiness this year and every year till the happy end'.[18] She responded once more by wishing him 'luck and pluck for the coming year'. Like many who lead full and adventurous lives most of the year she found the Christmas season oppressive, but she was full of advice for her learned friend:

> Why instead of being plummeted by a masseuse every morning don't you ride? It is so delicious to gallop in the deserted woods and fancy all the sprites, ghouls, leprechauns, manes, fays and elves, hiding in the underbush.
>
> Don't live with too many sages but associate with these, the gay and gracious.[19]

Gladys went shopping in the boulevards, but Paris was full of crowds. She found it a strain and concluded that her respect for political institutions was growing: 'I could not but wonder how it was that so many people could live in one town, under one law and with comparative unison and contentment.' One of her friends at this time was Leo Stein, brother of Gertrude. Leo was a tall balding man with an undernourished red beard. He was full of bizarre gestures and eccentric ideas. For instance, to comply with some quirk of his digestion he sometimes sat down and rested his feet on a book-case somewhat above the level of his head. Gladys liked him for his appreciation of art and his good collection of modern pictures. She commented: 'He is too nice really, quite elemental, by which I mean partaking of the irrepressible nature of the wind & sea etc.'[20] In old age she added: 'He was the ugliest man I ever saw, but my goodness he was clever!'[21]

Mary Berenson thought that by February 1902, when Gladys was twenty-one, she had 'swum out of our ken', but just a month later I Tatti and its inhabitants were stirred out of their lethargy by her unexpected arrival:

> Suddenly Gladys came ... & she has been filling our time & thoughts. She is radiant and sphinx-like. Strange likenesses to her mother flit across her face. Placci has come to adore. She has been marvellous.[22]

The Berensons took Gladys with them on a trip which included Pisa, Massa, Viterbo and Siena, where they stayed for a week. Mary wrote in her diary the first of several perceptive descriptions of Gladys, which gave the best possible picture of her at this time:

> The event of this month has been the reappearance of the radiant Gladys, so beautiful, so brilliant 'with her soft elixir ways', her hard clear youthful logic, her gaminerie, her lively imagination, her moods, her daring .... Gladys has been enchanting, but tiring. A wonderful creature, but too young to talk to as an equal, and so [sic] much of a born actress to take quite seriously. But so beautiful, so graceful, so changeful in a hundred moods, so brilliant that it is enough to turn anybody's head. Part of her mysteriousness comes from her being, as it were, sexless. She has never changed physically from a child to a woman, and her doctor said she probably never will. She calls herself a 'hermaphrodite', but she isn't that. Brought up by a mamma who thinks of nothing but Dress & Sex, her mind plays around all the problems of sex in a most alarming manner with an audacity and outspokenness that make your hair stand on end. She is positively impish. But she has never felt anything, so she dares.
>
> Her defects are bad form – for she is distinctly in bad form – and lying; but as Bernhard says, she is so wonderful she can afford the first, and she may outgrow the second.[23]

Four days later Mary returned to the theme:

> Gladys is of course interested in nothing except herself, or what touches her, and, being so brilliant a creature, she can-

not be 'put down' as so young a girl naturally would be. Therefore all our endless talk centres around the things that interest her. Still she has read & felt to a certain extent, & sometimes it is less boring.[24]

Mary worried that B.B. was inviting trouble by caring so much for Gladys. She also worried about the persistent rumours concerning 'the supposed relations' between Gladys and the Marlboroughs. After Siena, the three returned to I Tatti for another week before Gladys left for Blenheim in May. Before her departure she took Mary aside and told her that Consuelo was 'nearly broken-hearted because the Duke would make such wild love to her'. Mary became more anxious about the fate of the 'brilliant, beautiful, cruel, selfish, untrained' Gladys. Nor could she be sure whether or not to believe her: 'I never knew a person who told so many lies as that beautiful & radiant creature.'[25]

England was preparing for the Coronation of Edward VII on 26 June, and a wonderful season of entertainment was planned. Gladys began the season at Blenheim and sent news to Mary:

The sniffy Oxford Dons are very displeased at the prospect of having to receive the holders of the Rhodes Scholarships, & are grumbling that it is going to cause great expense to the University. Among the political men I have seen there seems to prevail little else than jealousy, & it is only among the upper & the upper middle classes that unstinted praise is given to the Great Man.[26]

Consuelo was not so broken-hearted as Gladys had suggested. She escorted Gladys all over London during that festive season. And Gladys floated from party to party like a Grecian goddess, dressed innocently and simply in white. She was never far from the apex of high society and everywhere she went the heads turned to gaze at her. On May 8 she sat in the stalls of Covent Garden with the Marlboroughs for the opening night of the opera season, attended by King Edward and Queen Alexandra. A fortnight later she was there again to hear Melba, Caruso, Scotti and others sing in a night of Italian opera. *The Lady* reported that 'two of the most beautiful girls in London, or indeed, anywhere' were to be seen side by side in Madame von

André's box: Muriel Wilson* and Gladys, 'the lovely American, with her fair, golden hair and exquisite pale damask complexion'.[27] Both the girls wore white and Gladys carried pink roses. On 10 June Madame von André took her to an Austro-Hungarian concert at the Royal Institute of Painters in Water Colours in Piccadilly, and then Gladys retreated to Blenheim for a week.

Two days later the Berensons came to England and drove to Oxford in dismal rain, accompanied by Roger Fry. They spent the day cataloguing the drawings in the Christ Church Library. They were to have seen Gladys, but the work in hand was so important that they wired her not to come. Gladys was livid, and not being one to be easily put down, she dashed off a furious note to B.B. Mrs Baldwin also spent June and July in London. She took a house, 3 Hyde Park Place, in the Bayswater Road, near Marble Arch. On 19 June she had a dinner party to which she invited Mary and B.B., Norman Forbes and Douglas Ainslie. According to Mary, Mrs Baldwin was 'radiantly beautiful in a head-dress of golden and purple' in contrast to Gladys who was 'pale and worn-out in a huddled up black dress, and could talk of nothing but the "Beauty Ball" she was getting up'. The decor was good, but the conversation 'pitiable'.[28]

Mrs Baldwin and Gladys were eagerly awaiting the Coronation on 26 June, but a mere two days before the great event the news spread that the King had fallen victim to perityphlitis, the Coronation was postponed, and the stunned nation waited anxiously for the result of the operation. It was successful, and Mrs Baldwin, in black velvet with tiny diamond tassels, took Gladys to the Crystal Palace Ball on 2 July, which became a celebration for the King's miraculous recovery. Twelve thousand square feet of parquet flooring was specially laid down for dancing, £15,000 worth of furniture and ornaments were lent for the night, and the glass palace became alive with palms, plants and flowers, with private boxes for the less adventurous, content to gaze on the scene from a safe vantage point. The band of the Life Guards played and members of the St James's Theatre Company danced a grand quadrille.

The Duke and Duchess of Westminster had invited guests to

* Youngest daughter of Arthur Wilson of Tranby Croft (where Lt-Col Sir William Gordon-Cumming, Bt, was caught cheating at cards in the presence of the Prince of Wales in 1890).

a ball at Grosvenor House on the same night, but they postponed it for a week until the King was absolutely out of danger.
The King and Queen would have attended as guests of honour,
but instead they were represented by the Duke and Duchess of
Connaught and their daughter, Princess Margaret. Lady Curzon
of Kedleston recalled that the ball was the most outstanding of
the season, and singled out the beauty of Consuelo as 'of a most
distinguished elegant kind'. Crown Princess Marie of Roumania,
whom Gladys thought very clever, was beautifully gowned in a
snow-white dress with a long train. This train, made of a cling-
ing material, wrapped itself round the legs of other dancers,
felling more than one, so the Princess had to retire to the royal
dais. There in safety she watched the dancers whirling round in
the specially erected supper hall amongst the silver plate, blue
hydrangeas and white lilies, observed by Gainsborough's Blue
Boy, which still adorned the wall. Rumour persists that Gladys
was reunited with the Crown Prince of Prussia at this ball, and
that the two were 'swept up with the corks at dawn, to the fury
of their host'.[29] However, on that day, the Crown Prince was in
Bonn, meeting with the carriage accident he might so nearly
have had in Oxfordshire. A horse fell, he was thrown out, but
he escaped serious harm. Thus the story of an indiscretion at
the Duchess of Westminster's ball can be relegated as apo-
cryphal.

The season continued with the Imperial Coronation Bazaar at
the Royal Botanical Gardens in Regent's Park on 11 July.
Gales tore through the awnings and thunderous rain drenched
the guests. A Canadian lady was killed by a piece of coping-
stone which fell on her head as she waited to see Queen
Alexandra arrive. Gladys was a stall-holder along with twenty
Duchesses, sixteen Marchionesses, and sixty-two Countesses. So
hectic was her life at this time that it was not unusual for her
to attend several events a night. She looked 'very lovely' at Lady
Howard de Walden's reception for colonials and Indians at
Seaford House, attended by Princess Helena Victoria surrounded by tiaras and Garter ribands. Then she went to Cla-
ridges for a *diner-dansant* given by Princess Hatzfeldt and Lady
Cunard, and sat at a table which included Lady Marjorie
Manners and Count Mensdorff.

It did not suit Mrs Baldwin to remain in London for the postponed Coronation, now fixed for 9 August, but Gladys was

determined to see it and so she stayed on. She found herself in something of a quandary, because all her friends began to leave London for a quick stay in the country before the ceremony. The Duke of Marlborough was at Blenheim, Consuelo and Verena Churchill were away, Lady Blandford was staying with her sister, Lady Norah Churchill was in Norway and the Leslies were at Portsmouth. Then to Gladys's fury an invitation from Mrs Cornwallis-West, the former Lady Randolph Churchill, was suddenly cancelled. She decided to stay on at 3 Hyde Park Place, because she did not want to have to go about asking to be taken in, so for four days she was entirely alone. She promised her mother: 'I am going to tell no one I am alone & shall receive nobody. Like that it will be all right.' It would have invited the most disparaging comment for a twenty-one-year-old girl to be discovered there unchaperoned. She was well aware of this, for she urged her mother not to tell 'Minnie A[nglesey] who might write it to some of her cat friends and make mischief'. Meanwhile, she lunched one day with Lady (Arthur) Paget and spent the day at Cliveden with the Crown Princess of Roumania, who was enjoying a stay of 'absolute happiness' with her new friends the Astors.

On Saturday 9 August King Edward VII was crowned. The ceremony was curtailed somewhat in order to preserve the King's strength. The Duke of Marlborough, who had recently been given the Order of the Garter, acted as Lord High Steward, while Consuelo carried the canopy during the anointing of Queen Alexandra. Gladys watched the procession from a vantage point in the Mall. The Queen smiled in her direction so gracefully that the picture remained with her vividly all her life. Gladys was impressed by her bearing and the way she could wear an enormous quantity of jewels and still look relaxed and natural.

After the Coronation Gladys went to Hillington Hall, King's Lynn, the home of Sir William and Lady Ffolkes and the neighbouring estate to Sandringham, to enjoy the peace and quiet of a Norfolk summer. But peace was shattered when *Le Matin* in Paris began to serialize the story of Gladys and the Crown Prince under the title 'Les Deux Aigles'.[30] Instantly Gladys became world news as the story was flashed from Paris to New York and from there to London. The *Daily Telegraph* described it as 'romantic' and related that it had caused much amusement in Berlin. It caused none to Mrs Baldwin, who wrote to *Le Matin* on 13 August:

> My daughter has no other protector but me. . . . I know better than anyone the true nature of the short relations that a meeting of forty-eight hours at Blenheim, the home of the Duke and Duchess of Marlborough, has caused between the Crown Prince of Germany and my daughter, both of whom are mere children.
>
> A lot of imagination is needed to transform them into an affair of state.

Gladys protested to the *Telegraph* that the statements were 'absolutely false' and demanded their emphatic contradiction. Yet *Le Matin*'s account though written in a romantic vein, tallies surprisingly well with the later version told by Consuelo in *The Glitter and the Gold*. Considering how few people there were at Blenheim that weekend it would be fascinating to know exactly how the story emerged. Following Mrs Baldwin's letter, the editors of *Le Matin* dropped the serial, explaining that 'the intervention of a mother is something we hold sacred'.[31]

The article had far-reaching results. Those people she had as yet failed to dazzle now became acutely aware of Gladys's existence, and she reached the dizziest heights of fame. She became so celebrated that a manufacturer even produced a cardboard doll with clothes that slotted on to it, named 'Miss Deacon'. Contemporary writers talk of her having 'burst into society'. Her friend Albert Flament wrote that she 'traversed Europe like a meteor in a flash of dazzling beauty and of conversation no less exceptional'.[32]

It would be nice to freeze the frame there, with the meteor burning brightly at the end of a London season, caught in the fullness of her beauty at the age of twenty-one. But one cannot freeze a meteor which flares up and then fades away, and this was to be Gladys's fate; not that she would not flare up again to dazzle further in the course of her extraordinary life. But never would it be so perfect in the future. Meanwhile, as Gladys left London for Paris, she was sure in the knowledge that she had taken the city by storm.

Chapter Seven

MONTESQUIOU'S WARNING

Versailles awaited Gladys on her return to France. She was no stranger there, being accustomed to making day-trips from the rue Jean-Goujon and to spending part of the season in a hotel such as the Hôtel des Réservoirs, close to the Château, destined to be the place where Marcel Proust first set eyes on her four years later. The city was full of Proustian figures in the rather depressing autumn of 1902. Montesquiou, who relished Versailles as the perfect setting for his entertainments, had rented a house. Here Sarah Bernhardt would declaim his poetry to a rigidly selected circle of friends. On 10 September Comte Bertrand de Fénélon, another of Proust's intimates, entertained guests at the Hôtel des Réservoirs. Gladys attended together with Montesquiou, Comte Georges de Lauris, and his lesbian friends Elsie de Wolfe and Bessie Marbury, who shared a house at Versailles and were particular purveyors of Parisian gossip to Berenson. Parties of this kind were very different from those of the London season but Gladys felt more at home in France, speaking French, than ever she did in London, though she found Fénélon himself 'serious . . . gloomy-spirited . . . a prophet of doom'.[1]

For some years there had been hints that Gladys was not strong enough to cope with her great success. She became frequently tired and depressed and at the beginning of October was sent to Biarritz for a rest. From there she returned to England to stay at Ugbrooke Park, the seat of Lord and Lady Clifford of Chudleigh. In the peace of Devon she read the works of Gibbon, which inspired her to write to B.B.: 'I am filled with giant ambition when I think of the vast stores of bravery, learning, [and] virtue which have been amassed by passing generations for us poor minions.' At the same time Gladys was happy to reassure the art critic that she was moving in more sober circles than hitherto: 'I am divinely happy here, no longer "wound" with those awful people of the racing set, whose tongues do "kiss one into madness". I now understand why Jupiter was a drunkard and Venus so fast and giddy. They lived on the fats of the land and had to pay for their godhood & comfortable living in hundreds.'[2]

Consuelo was also staying at Ugbrooke, but returned to Blenheim in the middle of November to prepare to join the party going to India for the Delhi Durbar. Gladys was reluctant to understand why the Marlboroughs should desert her for so many months and put her case to the Duke in forthright terms:

Sterne says that 3
travel   – Those who do so from
                Imbecility of mind
or from – Incapability of body
”   ”   – Inevitable necessity.

The 1st he says, comprise all those who travel by land or by water labouring with pride, curiosity, vanity or spleen. As for the 3rd class they are all the peregrine martyrs who live by the traffic & importation of sugar-plums, we'll say, & boots.
    Does this explain the Durbar? You, of course, belong to the first & second, most obviously. Don't you now?[3]

Before Consuelo's departure, she was able to assist Gladys with some introductions for another traveller, for Montesquiou was about to set off for a two-month visit to the United States to give lessons in beauty to the citizens of New York. Gladys thought they would spoil him so much that he would never return: 'You will be the king of taste', she wrote to him on 19 November, 'the most elegant arbiter of the new world.' Montesquiou's imminent departure was the talk of Paris. Gladys, back there for Christmas, hastened to pass the news of the Count's latest activities to B.B.:

He has been seized at this last hour with a terrible funk and yet dares not back out. He speaks quite openly of his 'trousseau' & asks people to visit it at Charret's in the Rue de la Paix. One moment he fancies he is Beau Brummel, the next he speaks of evangilizing the United States in the names of Desbordes – Valmore – Verlaine – de Noailles, etc.[4]

Yet another traveller was Mrs Baldwin who sailed to New York in January 1903, returning before Montesquiou's departure and in time for Gladys to instil a last minute panic into the wretched Count: 'It appears the sea is very rough these days. I've seen Mamma!'[5] However, Montesquiou's visit was a wild success. Though the Americans were amused by him and at times laughed at him, they liked him. Gladys reflected on the matter in 1977: 'Well, he was not evil', she explained, 'and he was elegant. One could dress like that today.'[6]

During Mrs Baldwin's visit to New York, she met the American writer, F. Marion Crawford. For some time he had been fascinated by Gladys, whom he had often seen in Paris and in Rome. He asked the Duchess of Sermoneta what she thought about Gladys, and gave her his view:

> ... though we talked much, and she talks well, I never got anywhere near to understanding her.... My friend and I agreed that she would make a marvellous Beatrice, but what character may really be under that strange archaic type of beauty goodness only knows. I like to think that the one may suit the other. She is like the Archaic Minerva in the Naples Museum.[7]

The Duchess of Sermoneta replied that she thought Gladys's beauty was 'weird'. Marion Crawford continued:

> Yes, she inherits what one might call 'natural publicity', she cannot help attracting attention, and people will always talk about her ... she interests me very much, her gifts of mind seem to be extraordinary, and I cannot help believing that she has a generous and enthusiastic nature.[8]

Meanwhile Gladys was spending quiet days living in the rue Jean-Goujon with her sisters. Her day seldom varied. She rode for three hours in the morning, enjoyed having a friend such as Leo Stein to lunch, read all afternoon, dined at 6.30 and retired to bed at 9. She wrote to Berenson: 'I melt into sleep with a voluptuousness so delicious that I am content never to go to a party again.'

Despite the relaxed picture she painted, Gladys was not content for long. The pace of her brain quickened and she bubbled over with questions for B.B.

> Does Mme de Montebello still dazzle you with a bird's eye view of continental politics?
>
> Does she tell you that war-fare is become a spiritual process because the combatants now see each other across Shrupp-swept plains, with the eyes of faith? Does she still magnetize very young men sitting in electrified circles about her throne? Does Carlino count himself among them? Has the Grazioli at last laid her bones to rest?
>
> Speak upon all these & other things O Belial & come with me to Spain whither I would go.
>
> P.S. How are Mr Botticelli's feet? Less swollen I hope. Give my love to all the invalided virgins even though there be 11,000 & quickly write another book to point out the beauty of their putty faces . . . .[9]

It was while she was ill and in a highly strung state that Gladys committed a serious folly. Mrs Baldwin was away and she was left to her own devices. For a long time Gladys had been intensely fascinated by her own face. Mabel Dodge Luhan wrote that 'she was content to lie for hours alone on her bed, happy in loving her own beauty, contemplating it'.[10] As she gazed, she worried about the slight hollow between the forehead and the nose, which, to her mind, denied her a true classical beauty. Her bizarre love of the classics, combined with a reckless vanity, set her to consider how she might achieve the perfection of the Hellenic profile she had so often admired in museums and galleries. Marthe Bibesco condemned what she did as 'her obedience to a barbarous conception of the rules of Greek beauty'.[11] Was she remembering also the words of that fortune-teller? He may well have contributed to Gladys's search for perfection.

Gladys's first step was to visit Rome where she explored the Museo delle Terme and measured the distance between the eyes and nose of a statue there. Returning to Paris she took advice from a professor at the Institut de Beauté, who gave her instructions. Then she had paraffin wax injected into the bridge of her nose to build it up and form a straight line from the forehead down to the tip. At first the endeavour had a measure of success, but in the long term it was a disaster.

This catastrophic interference with nature might never have

happened if Gladys had not been ill. Montesquiou was very depressed when he learnt about it, the more so because he saw great dangers in the temporary success she was having with the experiment. He wrote Gladys a long letter in which he quoted Madame de Sévigné: 'Look after your health, my girl. It will help you in all things.'[12] He warned that decisions taken in a state of nervous debility could have dark and ominous consequences that could last as long as life. Gladys would have done well to heed his words.

When Mrs Baldwin returned to Paris she was alarmed to find her daughter in such a bad state, and decided that she should be sent to a *maison de santé* for a complete rest. Gladys explained her plight to B.B. on 11 February:

> One line before I am imprisoned for 6 weeks or 2 months. After having been in bed for 5 weeks it has been decided that I am to go to a Sanitarium to be under treatment for some sort of nervous trouble! ! !
>
> I am to be there in company with *morphinomanes*, ether drinkers and goodness knows what not! I have grown much taller, thinner and all my hair has been cut off! Audrey says I look like a consumptive collégien ... take care of yourself or they will send you to some acquarium or other.

The beautiful Gladys of the previous season had declined rather quickly to a nervous wreck and was duly placed in an institution called Sollier's in Paris. Visited only by her mother, she remained there until April.

Fortunately Mary Berenson passed through Paris on her way to Haslemere in Surrey and took the chance to pay her a visit. So alarmed was she by Gladys's condition that she did not return to I Tatti until May, making B.B. very angry at such a prolonged absence.

On 3 April Mary lunched with Mrs Baldwin who gave a 'frightening account' of Gladys and showed her a 'frightfully depressed letter'. Mary called on Gladys the next day and found her 'well and jolly, and getting fat – awfully affectionate'. Gladys fell on Mary and could not stop hugging her, so delighted was she to see her. Mary gave this report to B.B.:

> Her attention is a little wandering and hard to fix, she jumps inconsequently from one subject to another, but I made her

1 Gladys photographed in Paris as a child.

2 RIGHT Gladys with her mother,
Florence Deacon.

3 Edward Parker Deacon with his daughters (*left to right*) Gladys, Audrey and
Edith, with Mrs A. Robertson, Mrs Sturtevant and Miss Dora Donavant at
Sturtevant Farm, Sunset Hill, Center Harbor, New Hampshire, USA, in
June 1895.

lu

Po Kui Piste a Pictré

du vieux Versailles: Lobre...

(les Perles Rouges. Sonnet IV.)

son affectionné

Robert de Montesquiou.

4 'The Poet' – a photograph of
Count Robert de Montesquiou
dedicated to Maurice Lobre,
the painter of Versailles.

5 Bernard and Mary Berenson at
Fernhurst, Sussex, *c.* 1898 (*Florence,
Berenson Archives, reproduced by
permisson of the President and Fellows of
Harvard College*).

6 Gladys in a tomboyish pose
with her mother and a guide in
the mountains.

7 A crayon portrait of Gladys by
Boldini, 1899.

8 'Your silly old Coon' – Consuelo Vanderbilt, first wife of the 9th Duke of Marlborough, with her sons, Blandford and Ivor.

9 LEFT Crown Prince William of Prussia – love burgeoned on the tennis court at Blenheim.

10 ABOVE Audrey Deacon, Gladys's favourite sister, an example of a Grecian profile.

11 BELOW Gladys in 1905.

12 RIGHT 'The Chinaman' – Hermann von Keyserling, the Baltic philosopher in later life.

13 Claude Monet, a great painter and a simple man, photographed by Gladys in his garden at Giverny.

14 Florence Baldwin painted by Boldini in 1906 (*in the private collection of Mr. B. Gerald Cantor, New York, Beverly Hills*).

15 RIGHT 'The great Alphonso'– Prince Doria Pamphili, Mrs Baldwin's friend.

16 The Villa Farnese from a print – Mrs Baldwin's summer house.

…he staircase of the Villa Farnese,
…w enough to climb on
…back.

…IGHT Gladys's portrait by
…ni, commissioned by the
…of Marlborough in 1916.

…ELOW Edith Gray, Gladys's
…, with her two elder daughters,
…ey and Milo.

20 Winston Churchill momentarily
disturbed by Gladys's camera in the
Long Library at Blenheim.

21 'The Etruscan Bust' – the first study of Gladys by Epstein in 1917.

22 The Duke of Marlborough and Gladys with her 'Anaconda', Walter Berry (*right*).

23 'The Irish Duke' – H.R.H. The Duke of Connaught photographed by Gladys at Nice.

24 A sketch of Gladys by Boldini in the possession of the author.

get out of bed and stand with her right hand upraised and scream : 'black and blue, cut me in two' that she would let me bring her back to I Tatti with me.[13]

Mary also found that her memory was impaired and that the lying was getting worse. She told Mary a half-dozen contradictory things during the visit. Mary again lunched with Mrs Baldwin – 'as hopelessly foolish & lying and indiscreet as ever' – and met Audrey, who, she thought, 'hadn't a quarter of Gladys's bewildering charm'.

In her haste to write to B.B. Mary forgot to give her impressions of Gladys's nose, which had been swollen but was now somewhat better. She had great difficulty in extracting a remotely plausible version of what had happened from Gladys herself :

She said that she must have knocked it, she couldn't remember where. One doctor after another asked her if she was sure she hadn't been monkeying with it and she always vowed she hadn't. It got worse & worse, swelled up & became an open sore. At last, when she came to this Maison de Santé, the doctor threw her into a hypnotic sleep, and, as she said 'got the truth out of me, so that he was able to cure me'. 'What was the truth, Gladys?' 'I don't know, I can't remember any more, but he got it out all right.'[14]

On Wednesday 8 April, a few days after this encounter, Gladys suddenly arrived at the rue Jean-Goujon to the astonishment of her mother. She was accompanied by an attendant from Sollier's and announced that she was on her way to the Louvre to buy Easter eggs. On Saturday she intended to leave for an hotel at Versailles. 'I suppose I must let her have her way', was Mrs Baldwin's rather feeble comment.

Though Gladys was in need of plenty of peace and quiet it soon became clear that she was unlikely to achieve it. Lord Francis Hope was still pressing his suit and had just broken his engagement for her sake. Then the Duke of Marlborough, recently returned from the Delhi Durbar, arrived in Paris for a few days. Mrs Baldwin was suspicious that Gladys was up to something with him and worried that she might elope with him just to spite Consuelo. 'What a hateful silly muddle it is', wrote Mary to B.B., 'and poor Gladys with her excited brain drifting about in it with no one to guide her. I haven't half told you how silly and hopeless the mother was. She is worse than useless to her children.'[15] Berenson was very muddled: 'Poor dear Gladys. I'd give anything to have her well and happy. I feel so much more fatherly than lover-like to her.'[16]

Mary Berenson continued to worry about Gladys, who was very elated at the arrival of Marlborough. In the middle of all these worries, Mrs Baldwin casually left the city for an automobile trip with Audrey, while Gladys went alone to the Hôtel Vatel at Versailles. Mary was determined to persuade her to come to I Tatti and plans were made for the visit, despite Gladys's complete inability to make contact. B.B. himself wrote to Gladys and at last she replied, saying that she was awaiting Mary's 'kind wing' to shelter her on the journey to Italy. Then at the last minute, another Duke arrived in Paris. Mrs Baldwin, back from her trip, conceived the idea that Gladys should marry him. Ever keen to upstage Consuelo, Gladys warmed to the notion and I Tatti was forgotten.

The new suitor was the fifty-nine-year-old Duke of Norfolk, a widower since 1877, who had lost his son and heir, the Earl of Arundel, the previous summer. At this point he was in search of a new wife. Gladys was one of the candidates, and so hypnotized was the Duke that he allowed himself to be subjected to a ridiculous charade at a dinner-party in Paris. Gladys addressed him as 'Marie', put an antimacassar on his head and made him pretend he was the Pope. Meanwhile she dressed another guest as the King and the two acted a long interview between the King and Pope. Then Gladys said to him: 'Marie has another game he loves to play – play your game Marie.' Promptly, the Duke of Norfolk, Earl Marshal of England and Premier Duke of Great Britain, left the room, removed his coat and returned on all fours with a large green cushion on his back and trotted around the room like a dog.[17]

But these antics did not herald a marriage, and the Duke remained single until February 1904, when he married the heiress to the Barony of Herries; a match which produced the sixteenth Duke of Norfolk (who died in 1975) and three daughters. In 1907 Gladys amused Berenson by telling him that the Duke's highest ambition was to be 'in society'.

Gladys spent the summer of 1903 in England. From Blenheim

she wrote to Montesquiou: 'Restored to health, thanks to my rest, I am enjoying myself smugly and stupidly.' She suggested that he should repeat his American success in England. She also contacted B.B. after a long silence:

> The clouds are springs pouring cascades over the poor swimming garden. Such weather fosters friendship. It makes one long for bright fires &, well, for B.B.'s life-enhancing thoughts.
>
> I feel so well and cheerful that I long to make you adopt my cure and go to Sollier's. He is a fraud of course, but then his method is so good that even incomplete application is telling.[18]

The smug and stupid pleasures in which Gladys indulged were shared this year by her favourite sister, Audrey, who became a debutante at the age of seventeen. Mrs Baldwin took a tiny house in London in order to repeat for Audrey Gladys's success of the previous summer. Gladys was keen to assist and 'do her duty to Audrey'. However her conception of this duty manifested itself in the out-dazzling of her younger sister, whose season was, in consequence, a failure.

Gladys trailed through London in the summer of 1903, alluringly dressed in a variety of costumes, which again tended to be vestal white. For the Countess of Warwick's dance at Brook House on 20 May she appeared in tier upon tier of white tulle, while Audrey did her best to compete in a 'white spotted net frock, trimmed with little pink rose-buds'. Gladys chose white tulle again for the opera at Covent Garden in the presence of the King and Queen at the end of the month, and was 'all in white' in Mrs Frank Mackay's box on 11 June to hear *La Bohème* sung by Melba and Scotti.

In what was, even so, a less successful season for Gladys, she did not pass unnoticed. She 'carried off the palm for girlish beauty' when she danced an American quadrille with Minnie Paget, Lady Cunard and others at the London Hospital Ball at the Albert Hall. The Americans wore white chiffon with the sash of the stars and stripes and high pointed crowns of gilt spangles, and performed very well. Certain of the dancers were somewhat under-rehearsed as a result of which a number of the quadrille came to grief. No one appeared to know what was expected of them. Gladys thoroughly enjoyed the evening, especially since the Duke of Marlborough failed to recognize her in her strange attire.

Gladys also secured an invitation to the magnificent gala given by the King and Queen for President Loubet of France, who made a state visit to Britain in July. The royal box was packed with Princesses including the young Princess Alice of Albany,* and was surrounded by dozens of artificial pink roses: it was felt that the perfume of natural roses combined with the summer heat might overcome the more susceptible members of the audience. Gladys also attended Lady Ilchester's garden party at Holland House and a cotillion given by Mrs Mackay at the end of July.

In August Daisy, Princess of Pless, and her husband, Prince Hans, invited Gladys to sail with them at Cowes. On 7 August they climbed into a shore-boat to make way to the *Meteor*, the Kaiser's yacht. Just as they pushed off, the Princess was handed a note from Admiral Eisendecker, informing them that the *Meteor* would not be sailing that day on the pretext that there was no breeze and they did not want her to lose the race, thus spoiling her admirable record. Rather disappointed, they returned to dry land for a second more leisurely breakfast. Then the real reason suddenly dawned on Prince Hans. They had Gladys in their party, and the incident of the Crown Prince still weighed heavily on the Kaiser's mind. Gladys herself was unperturbed:

> Cowes week was rather amusing. It was like a pandemonium without the cheery bustle and noise – All manner of people walked about dressed all alike in yachting clothes which likeness only seemed to accentuate the differences.[19]

In September Gladys retreated to Blenheim as usual. Her days followed a set pattern. She got up at ten, read, continued to read or talk throughout the day and retired to bed at midnight. One afternoon she went down to the boat-house by the lake and wrote to B.B. Mrs Baldwin had taken Audrey to Maloja, which had much amused her: 'For some weeks past Mamma complained that Dorothy (picture of health) was looking pale and needed Engadine air. In due time Mamma left with – Audrey!'

* Princess Alice, Countess of Athlone, last surviving grandchild of Queen Victoria, born 25 February 1883.

The Berensons went to the United States that winter, and so Gladys did not see them for a long time. She returned very regularly to England from France, and in November was spotted at a private view of the New Gallery, in the company of her actor friend, Norman Forbes, who himself owned a gallery in Bond Street.

Meanwhile, Mrs Baldwin tired of Paris. She gave up her house at rue Jean-Goujon at the end of the year and the Deacon entourage directed their steps to Italy.

Chapter Eight

ROMAN DAYS

Mrs Baldwin and her daughters moved into the Palazzo Borghese in Rome at the beginning of 1904. For nine years she rented an apartment in the Palazzo, a sumptuous building shaped like a harpsichord near Ponte Cavour, and here the family spent the winter. Mrs Baldwin declared she was going to conduct the apartment on an opulent scale, and was assisted in this aim by Prince Doria, who became her escort and companion until his death in 1914. He often travelled to St Moritz with the mother and daughters, and everybody joked about the 'whole family' being gathered together. Princess Doria still lived in Rome at that time and was an influential figure in Roman society. In January 1904 Carlo Placci spotted that Mrs Baldwin had been a guest at a party given by Lady Anglesey with 'the Dorias and other people whom it is chic to meet'.[1] At the same time Mrs Baldwin's avowed intent to be extravagant led to the first of many rumours that she was short of money.

Gladys loved riding and Rome gave her the opportunity to ride in the park by the Villa Borghese. Here she met Gabriele d'Annunzio who challenged her to jump a large gate on a borrowed horse; Gladys thought he secretly hoped she might fall off. This undersized, singular man had not yet become a romantic legend as novelist, poet, and founding father of Fascism. Eleanora Duse was prepared to give up her career for this latter-day Casanova. 'Chips' Channon recalled 'the story that d'Annunzio fainted when he saw [Gladys] such was her beauty,'[2] but attractive though this idea is, there are no witnesses for it and Channon cannot be trusted. It was also recalled by one of Gladys's sisters that she and d'Annunzio were 'engaged' at one time, though the term was used loosely. However,

Gladys was not one of the numerous beautiful ladies whose photograph lay beside d'Annunzio's bed; nor were they correspondents. Speaking of him in later life she dismissed him as 'someone the nobles did not accept'. And she was aware of his reputation for immorality. 'He slept with anyone!' She did not think him a great man. 'He had spark, but not fire',[3] she declared.

Scarcely had the family arrived in Italy when a tragedy befell them. In April 1904 Audrey fell ill and was put under the care of a matron known to the Dorias at the Casa di Cura in Florence, suffering from what transpired to be an incurable heart-disease. The doctor told Audrey that she had developed endocarditis as a result of influenza, and that she must rest as much as possible and avoid any exertion or excitement. It was not easy for her, as the matron described on 9 April:

> Audrey finds it dreadfully difficult to rest! She has a really brilliant mind and a very erratic one too, I find, on nearer acquaintance. It is difficult to follow her always, so quickly does she pass from jest to earnest.

The matron feared a mental illness, inherited from her father, but concluded:

> I would describe her as unusually balanced in mind – or rather in soul, for the soul, the real Audrey is extraordinarily clear and forceful but the mind is at times, strange, erratic, melancholy.

Audrey languished in Florence for several weeks as her condition slowly deteriorated. She was on a regime of digitalis, but it did no good. In May she became excited and delirious, and was frequently given morphine so that her heart could rest. Her mother was summoned and sat with her, and as Audrey's mind wandered further and further Mrs Baldwin kept telling her to 'leave your dreams alone, darling, they are not true'. On 21 May Gladys came to sit with her, and tried to will her to sleep.

> Audrey knew her, kissed her, & laid her head on her shoulder. Gladys held her, and Audrey liked the scent of her (she has always been very sensitive to scent as to sound) going off after a little into a quiet sleep.

The next day Audrey had a terrible convulsive fit. Caffeine was given her, and she made one more agitated struggle before slowly sinking into long hours of shallow breathing, realizing, it was thought, the presence of those around her, until at 2.30, as the matron wrote, 'she simply stopped breathing; the exact moment one hardly knew'.[4]

Tall, dark Audrey had been Gladys's favourite sister and the accomplice of her childhood. She was buried in Florence. Gladys began to worry that she had been in some way responsible for her death. The matron reassured her to the contrary:

> You must never feel that Audrey said anything unkind or un-true – if I have heard such things it has never been from her – that you did not understand how ill she felt, & tired her – yes – but never anything more. . . .[5]

Her sister's death upset Gladys deeply. In answer to a loving and sympathetic letter from Consuelo, she replied:

> My numb heart cries unceasingly. The pain in me has burned away all but what is the nucleus of immortality in us and I feel as much in death as I do in life, now that I see how close bound they are – the one the pathway to the other. . . . If this living be of importance, why should she have been with-drawn?[6]

The pain caused by Audrey's death remained with Gladys for a long time. Even a year later, when Yturri died, she wrote to Montesquiou:

> You have many friends and they will all share your sorrow; but none more than I, who have, since last year, lived on happy and sad memories, which open the heart to the sharing of grief.[7]

An unpleasant sequel to the death of Audrey was a cruel rumour that Gladys had murdered her sister. In the years in which Gladys had been traversing Europe, her behaviour had attracted considerable attention and her father's attempts to mete out justice were still fresh in the public mind. It is a sour reflection on the power of malicious gossip that the story was still being hinted at in New York, Boston and London as late as 1976. There is not a shred of evidence to support it. Rather was

Gladys made miserable by the death, and over the ensuing years her diary regularly recorded the sad anniversary. She became a more solitary figure in her family, because Dorothy was too young to be an intimate friend, and she often quarrelled with Edith, who was already spending more time with Marraine Baldwin in the United States than with her mother in Europe.

In Rome Gladys felt a yearning for Paris friends and so decided to make contact with Montesquiou again; she began a long and flattering letter to him:

> I am very frightened of you because like all the angels your power is fearsome and, above all, like petrol, an unknown quantity. I am afraid to draw your attention to me, but I want to tell you that I think of you and talk of you often and I wish you all the happiness that poets deserve.[8]

Gladys bemoaned the fact that he never came to Rome and begged him to record his voice on a wax spool so that she could play it on her gramophone. 'I will even take the liberty of making you repeat yourself, which alas never happens', she wrote. Shortly afterwards Gladys and the Count were united on a project to get an article of his published in an English review. Gladys offered to make a translation and eagerly awaited the arrival of the article. 'Can you not send it to me now?' she asked. 'I have been burning with a desire to read it since the first day you mentioned it.' Finally it arrived, delayed by the Italian post. Gladys read it 'with the attention and admiration only you can command'. She struggled with a translation but found it very difficult. 'How can one render all the finesse, the malice and the irony that only you know how to lavish upon it?' Marion Crawford agreed with her and so she suggested that Montesquiou find another translator. Meanwhile she would make an attempt and he could choose the one he liked best.

In June Gladys and her mother made a pilgrimage to Audrey's grave in Florence. After some days there on their own, they contacted Berenson. He invited them to dinner, an occasion which left him with a bad taste in the mouth, as he explained to Mary who was elsewhere:

> I have been fighting with it all day, & can not define it in the least. They were very nice yesterday evening, and what it

was that got on my nerves I can not tell. Perhaps it was my nerves climbing up their noses.[9]

Gladys was still in an emotional state and promptly invited herself to stay at I Tatti, while her mother returned to Rome. At the last minute she got cold feet and sent Berenson a note via his driver, Damiano:

B.B.! Oh B.B.!
I find Damiano waiting here, just as the train is going – with my trunks. Did that besotted Express man not reach you with my note?

B.B. I love you so much, please forgive me! I can imagine you sitting at I Tatti expecting & I shall be sitting in the train between two band boxes.

They are calling me! I must go! But I'll come back whenever you wish.

Your G.[10]

Berenson was thoroughly relieved that Gladys did not come. A week later she joined the Marlboroughs in Paris.

In Rome Gladys was not without suitors, and among them was the friend mentioned to Montesquiou, Roffredo Caetani, Principe di Bassiano, a particularly eligible bachelor of thirty-two, and one who, by more than one account, could have made her very happy. Edith's friend Julia Meyer,* daughter of the American Ambassador in Rome, thought Gladys made a serious mistake in not marrying him. Roffredo was the second son of the fifteenth Duke of Sermoneta, at one time Italian Minister of Foreign Affairs, and his English wife, Ada Bootle-Wilbraham. He came from the Black Nobility, descended from a brother of Pope Boniface VIII. The family lived in Palazzo Caetani, and had a highly cultured background. Roffredo himself was a gifted composer and was considered very attractive to women.

For the next four years the possibility of his marriage to Gladys was a regular topic of conversation in Italy. One night in Rome, Gladys finished Madame de Broglie's *Ilse*, found she could not sleep, and as a cat 'croaked' sleepily in the street outside, she took up her pen to write to Roffredo about aspirations she would never fulfil:

* Later Donna Brambilla (1886–1979).

It wd be nice to get up at dawning and run up and down mountains in buggies, to see trees lying in swathes on hillsides and hear the murmurs of waterfalls torn on hundred feet of jagged rock. Oh dear it makes me ill to think of all I have not seen, the volcanoes, the swamps of ooze, vegetation, the rumbling geysers, steaming cataracts, the still lakes, the storming lakes, the salt lakes, the silent hills & deep canions, broad rivers & tumbling streams full of shooting salmon, the deserts, the seas, the forests and I know not what else.

Fancy living such days as we do when 'tis possible to see such dawns, such noontides, such evenings & nights!

It's simply disgusting! Roffredo, think of all the queer people one misses knowing, the opportunities of interest, of amusement. I long to hear the stories of commercial travellers, of stage drivers, of 'braconniers', of miners and more especially of cattle drivers and inlayers of wood! What fun to really learn not from books which are finite dead things, but with nature's infinite capacity and receptivity.[11]

The romance was forever changing direction. In July 1904 B.B. chatted to Count Rembrelinski who told him that Gladys got on his nerves and had ruined her chances. Roffredo would certainly have married her, but instead she had set her cap at Prince Torlonia. Yet a month later, Rembrelinski reported that it was Mrs Baldwin who was ruining Gladys's chances in Rome but that Roffredo was keener than ever to marry her. That September, B.B. and Montesquiou were in St Moritz together. The two went over to Pontresina to visit Roffredo who was residing in 'a little chalet consisting of 3 rooms panelled like an English 3rd class railway carriage'. This time Roffredo told Berenson that he had never been in love, but was ready to sacrifice everything to the experience, which he feared would never come to him. He did not mention Gladys to B.B. but soon afterwards indicated to Carlo Placci 'nothing less than a desire to marry her'.[12]

Gladys herself fell ill in the summer of 1904, suffering like Audrey from a racing heart. Mary Berenson became seriously worried about her, and reflected too on the effects of Audrey's death:

How I wish Gladys would fall into the right hands, just at this crisis I do not know exactly whose hands those would be, but certainly not her friends in Rome. She ought to have the right things to read too – the revelation will fade unless it is strengthened from outside. But her letter makes me feel as if there was less chance of her becoming a Satey Fairchild than sometimes we feared – she is capable of sailing into seas that the other [Audrey] at her most radiant moment of flowering, never imagined the existence of.[13]

Prince Doria drove Mrs Baldwin, Gladys and the other sisters to Vallombrosa via Perugia, Assisi and Gubbio. They travelled in his motor-car on the orders of Gladys's doctor – 'less likely to agitate the bell clapper in my chest', she explained. She was meant to rest, but instead felt the need to explore each new town. 'Whenever we arrived anywhere, instead of resting I struggled numbly and clayishly up and down every street & lane, into every church & museum.' Gladys confessed in a letter to B.B. that since Audrey's death, the wonder had gone out of her soul. She continued:

Things had grown remote & changed in receding & I was grown in a manner impenetrable. Then I saw your Giottos. Suddenly, something in them, a sincerity of existence as of an overwhelming fact literally startled me into a responsible consciousness. Then in a rush came back the world and with it the love of things (because I felt sure of their existence again) and changed, for now I know of something higher and deeper and aweful which is the very core of them all.[14]

B.B. was happy to get this letter and replied:

I am so glad to ascertain your growth, and to be assured in my hope that you can & that you will become a real person, with deep humanity & keen mind. . . .[15]

Vallombrosa near Florence, praised by Milton in *Paradise Lost*, had a soothing effect on Gladys:

During the day it is geographical, at least what I can see from my window of it – but in the evening it is marvellous. When great rivers of mist come pouring into the valleys, swelling to the edge of peaks, overcoming the ruggedness, the rockiness of the mountains making them glamorous phantoms with yet a poignant reality in them. And clouds gathering at the same time, clustering mysteriously about the mountain tops (one of them a huge purple-black one like an island lingers in the sky each day, overlooking the show) assailing the sun jealously!

Oh, you cannot think how wonderful it is! I sit and wonder and wonder of it late into the night.[16]

From Rome, Roffredo sent regular letters and postcards to Gladys, giving her news and begging for her photograph. Meanwhile at Vallombrosa Gladys lived a quiet life, finding even the most trifling conversation with her sisters quite exhausting. Nearby there was another suitor, who recalled to her years later:

I do not forget Vallombrosa, the Tyrol, Versailles . . . ! all of which reminds me of a delightful and very often cruel child, wearing an old black boater any old way, over her golden hair, at whose feet – so badly shod, with black soles with holes in them – I so often longed to lay myself down . . . but only Frank* was extended the privilege.[17]

It was Octave, Duke of Camastra, a bachelor of forty, who had fallen in love with her. The Duke did not have an easy time as he pressed his young friend with invitations to take walks, make donkey rides deep into the forest and allow him to escort her to the picnic of the day. 'You will not be unaware', he wrote to her, 'that I take an exquisite pleasure, albeit thoroughly honourable and disinterested in finding myself in your company, looking at you and listening to you. It is like a *bath of light*, sovereign treatment for rheumatism and my soul is terribly rheumatic. . . .' One night in anticipation of a meeting the following day he resigned himself to '*une nuit blanche*' (a sleepless night) or, as he put it, '*blonde* for I shall be thinking of you'. There were frequent delays and postponements, for Gladys was no respecter of punctuality. If all the hours that men spent in waiting for her ran concurrently, months and months would be accumulated. Camastra was patient:

I bow down respectively before this heroic resolution which deprives me of the great pleasure of seeing you before midday. Rhenish legend relates that the hotel-keepers die in the whirls of the great river when *La Lorelei* combs her golden

* Gladys's dog.

hair on its banks. Being neither hotel-keeper nor the Rhine, and not being admitted to contemplate the charming spectacles of which you speak – oh! how much more fortunate is Octave! – I shall not die, but I suffer most cruelly for having to wait so long to see you. . . .[18]

Leaving Vallombrosa, they went to the Dolomites and to Innsbruck. Then Mrs Baldwin and Edith left for Marienbad, while the faithful Duke of Camastra drove Gladys and Dorothy to Achensee Tyrol. Camastra was at the wheel of his car for two weeks. In due course the news reached Berenson, who wondered how ever Gladys tolerated him: 'C is a beautiful creature but I could not stand a fortnight of him.' A little over a year later, the Duke married Rose Ney d'Elchingen in Paris. Both remained close friends of Gladys for years.

It was a period of deep reflection for Gladys. Again she passed on her thoughts to B.B.

> All things about me, which until now I have known and loved as existing materially in themselves, I now feel to be *spiritual wholly*. Have I lived part blinded in some enchanted forest? I now live out of the world seen, or rather living more in it see through the 'appearance' into a part of the reality.[19]

But as ever there were moments when Gladys's sense of humour was uppermost. Achensee had a beautiful lake with a green valley at the far end. Many Germans flocked through the mountain passes from Bavaria to spend their holidays there:

> Germans, nothing, absolutely but Germans seen, slow, heavy laden immensely fat folk who walk for pleasure or instruction or perhaps appetite. To me they seem stomachs. But such stomachs! Imagine the stomach so sovereign in the man that every part of him slaves and endures for it contentedly. At all hours they are ordering, admiring, comparing, discussing, sharing, devouring mountain and valley herds, whole fields and vegetable gardens, faces greasy with satisfiable desire and pleasure.[20]

Such descriptions amused B.B. enormously – B.B. who had once declared to the disgust of his wife that taste only began where appetite ended. Mabel Dodge confirmed that the Berensons loved Gladys for her intelligence as much as for her beauty. 'She had an appreciation and she felt it to be her duty to observe values wherever they existed',[21] wrote Mrs Dodge.

In the autumn of 1904 Gladys joined her mother at Versailles, where they stayed at the Hôtel des Réservoirs. Mrs Baldwin reminded the sculptor, Auguste Rodin, that he had promised to lunch with them on Sunday 30 October. Rodin confessed to Mrs Baldwin that he had never been to Italy. She was horrified and the following January she invited him to stay at the Palazzo Borghese in order to rectify this terrible omission. 'A great artist like you owes this courtesy to your predecessors', she wrote, promising from herself and her daughters an admiring but discreet friendship. Rodin was still unable to go, but Mrs Baldwin never ceased to press him with invitations.

In December 1904 Gladys and her mother spent some days in Florence at Signore Pacini's in Lungarno Acciacola on another sentimental visit to Audrey's grave. B.B. went down to see Gladys, who kept him waiting for a long time, which did not surprise him, but then emerged 'looking anaemic and badly dressed'. They took a stroll together. 'I felt as one does with a person one loves, does not trust and has not seen for some time', confided B.B. to Mary, 'shy, slightly embarrassed, also like a bottle too full, and with too narrow a neck.'[22]

B.B. had guests at I Tatti. R. C. Trevelyan, often known as 'Trevy', was an elder brother of G. M. Trevelyan the historian, and a lifelong friend of B.B.'s. David Garnett described him recently as 'a very good poet, now forgotten',[23] and Nicky Mariano, B.B.'s secretary, remembered him as 'tall, lean, uncouth, with dishevelled grey hair, a long inquisitive nose, corduroy trousers, heavy boots, very poor table manners'.[24] Berenson described his wife, Bessy, who was Dutch, as 'a fine, fairly open-minded appreciative intelligent person'.[25] The 'Trevys' were rather taken by the idea of making Gladys's acquaintance over dinner and so decided to prolong their stay. Mrs Baldwin, 'as innocent, simple, childlike and protection-inspiring as ever', gossiped about America and her friends. Gladys, on the other hand, bewitched the 'Trevys' and the other guests with her extraordinary conversation. But though the 'Trevys' found her irresistible, they disapproved of her, and it was not until some thirteen years later that Bob Trevelyan fell desperately under her spell.

While still in Florence, Gladys and Mrs Baldwin were often guests of Carlo Loeser, an American collector who held a rival court to I Tatti. They also visited the Actons at La Pietra. Ever socially ambitious, Mrs Baldwin invited the Japanese Minister, Mr Oyama, to dine with her. His reply was indicative of the way many people treated Gladys's mother: 'The Minister of Japan does not know Mrs Baldwin and does not wish to dine.' Mrs Baldwin was too experienced a social campaigner to take the rebuff to heart. From Florence Gladys again joined the Marlboroughs in Paris, before returning to Italy for the winter.

The early months of 1905 were spent in Rome. In January, Berenson, travelling, as so very often, alone, arrived to stay at the Grand Hotel de Russia. A chic friend of Gladys's, the Duchess of Grazioli, had lunch with him and reported that Gladys 'was making herself thoroughly disliked with her flightiness and insolence'. Her three main suitors – Roffredo Caetani, the Duke of Camastra and Prince Torlonia – had all broken off relations with her. Nevertheless B.B. was anxious to see his old friend and so he made his way to the Palazzo Borghese. To his disappointment the apartment was closed, and Gladys was staying alone at the Minavia. Berenson tried to contact her there, but she was undergoing one of her periodic bouts of seeing nobody. B.B. wrote that there was 'no sight nor odour of Gladys' but they were due to meet the following Friday at the apartment of Princess Jane di San Faustino in the Palazzo Barberini. Princess Jane was an enormous American, noted for her boundless hospitality, wit and sense of humour, of whom the Duchess of Sermoneta wrote 'she collects human beings as others collect postage stamps or moths'.

A few weeks later, the Berensons accepted an invitation from Gladys to stay at the Palazzo Borghese. They arrived on 21 March for a week. Mary thought Mrs Baldwin had 'a perfectly marvellous fine taste', but Carlo Placci warned them that they would be more or less 'taboo', on account of staying with Mrs Baldwin, whose 'goings on' with Prince Doria had set all Rome by the ears. Mrs Baldwin was visiting couturiers in Paris, so Gladys was alone with Dorothy. Gladys – 'that wonderful siren' – had been ill yet again but told Mary that she was enjoying herself. Illness had given her 'the leisure to become acquainted with herself and to notice and enjoy the difference of things'.

Previously when she had been in society, having a wild time, everything had appeared to be the same, 'all boring and all exciting à la fois'.

Gladys and Mary talked all evening, and Mary found her an 'enchanting but naughty, untruthful child. It is terrible the way one gets to feel with her after a very short time, the impossibility of believing a word she says, but the equal difficulty of disbelieving everything!' Gladys told Mary 'such wild and improbable tales of her illnesses and operations and so on that one cannot possibly tell how serious it is, or whether it is really serious at all. But all the same she is an Enchantress!!' The following evening B.B. had a long talk with her. Before they left Mary came to the conclusion that Gladys was 'still an awful liar, and she won't face her situation, or live on any plan'.[26]

Apart from ill-health, Gladys had to cope with the problem of her mother and Prince Doria. Their friendship was again bringing the Deacons into disrepute. Mrs Winthrop Chanler's daughter, Laura, a friend of Edith and Dorothy, recalled that her parents never allowed her to visit Mrs Baldwin's apartment. Though Edith and Dorothy were welcome to come to them, Mrs Chanler felt it was too shocking to allow her daughter to accept hospitality from someone as infamous as Mrs Baldwin. Edith once asked Laura why she never came to their home, but although Laura secretly knew the reason, she refused to reveal it. As Mabel Dodge wrote, Mrs Baldwin's conduct resulted in Gladys being considered 'a free lance'. 'She was beautiful, as Judith was beautiful, or like Salome and she loved only herself so she was not bothered about lovers.'[27] Nevertheless Gladys did not like the ostracism that descended on her family due to the Doria friendship and it stirred her ambition to regain her mother's lost status.

Gladys was in Roncegno, recuperating from her illness of the spring, when she heard from Nicolette Grazioli that Montesquiou's secretary, Yturri, had died at the Pavilion des Muses in Paris after twenty years with the Count. Yturri had been ravaged by diabetes. Gladys hastened to console her old friend: 'I loved this poor Yturri so much. He was so good, so understanding to those who loved him, so entirely devoted to you. . . .'[28] Mrs Baldwin heard the news at Maloja from Maurice Lobre, the painter of Versailles. She wrote to Montesquiou that she was sad that Yturri 'had left for the great voyage without a word of remembrance from me'. According to Mrs Baldwin, Gladys was 'not really very ill', but she stayed on at Roncegno, while her mother made the annual visit to St Moritz.

B.B. spent August in St Moritz as well, and it was not long before he met Mrs Baldwin at a lunch party given by the Duchess of Sermoneta. Mrs Baldwin informed him that Gladys had recently been 'all but engaged' to Lord Brooke, son of the Earl and Countess of Warwick. She then lowered her voice dramatically and enquired whether or not he thought Gladys was fit for matrimony. B.B. could not work out what answer was expected of him, so he parried the question. When his wife Mary heard this, she remarked that it was unlikely Gladys would ever marry, nor should she, 'at any rate without a full explanation such as would put most people off'.

As if by chance, Prince Doria then appeared in St Moritz. He insisted that B.B. should not contact Gladys, who, he said, had been causing terrible family rows. Later in the week, Doria drove B.B. to Sils, where they were joined by the Raoul-Duvals and Mrs Baldwin, 'looking more beautiful than ever, and very happy in the presence of Doria'. The Prince's devotion to her, thought Berenson, 'is so complete, so courteous, so service-ful and I feel pretty sure so innocent'. On the drive back to St Moritz, Doria went into raptures about her kindness, goodness and gentleness, and then cried out: 'Ah if only Gladys were not so cruel. I tell you, she is a real thorn in her side.' Berenson detected that Doria very nearly said 'our' side. Doria then assured him that the poor Lord Brooke was broken-hearted over Gladys and that she was very fond of him; but he added significantly that Gladys would marry nobody who would not give her the *pas* over Consuelo.

Gladys was getting slowly better in Roncegno, but earnestly wished to stay alone. Meanwhile, in St Moritz, news circulated concerning Mrs Baldwin's life in Rome. She made things impossible for Gladys by carrying on as though she was Doria's mistress. It was generally believed that she was not, but Roman society naturally turned in sympathy towards Princess Doria in the face of such calumnies. Prince Giovanni Borghese told B.B. that if only Mrs Baldwin had had the slightest tact, she would by now be received everywhere in Rome.

The close of 1905 brought Berenson a greeting from Gladys in Rome. 'I am exceedingly well in all ways', she wrote, 'and I enjoy the luminous immobility of my life.' Once again she decried the Christmas season: 'I hate Xmas – but perhaps you don't and so I must tell you, I suppose, that I wish you all plum-pudding cheer – & I do sincerely wish it you, only I find Xmas lunch more a day of sad recording of changes come than a day of satisfied banter.'[29]

Prince and Princess Doria celebrated the New Year with a reception at Palazzo Doria to which both Gladys and Mrs Baldwin were invited. Tina Whitaker observed both ladies, Mrs Baldwin with 'a hard, determined face, handsome still', being openly courted by the Prince, and Gladys 'handsome, but her eyes are too wide apart, and although she has a beautiful figure, there is want of grace in her movements'.[30]

Gladys remained in Rome until May. Then, one cold Monday morning when it was pouring with rain, Mary Berenson met her in Florence, 'looking divinely beautiful', and was rather disappointed that Gladys had not told them she was there. Gladys made a rendezvous with B.B. which she then failed to keep. On 23 May Mrs Baldwin called at I Tatti and proudly announced that Gladys was now engaged to Lord Brooke. This confused the Berensons, and the next day they went down to Florence to call on Gladys. She made 'a deplorable impression of vulgarity and restlessness and cruelty and flirtatiousness'; but a day later, Mary found herself writing sadly in her diary that Gladys had won back B.B.'s heart with 'her soft elixir ways'.

B.B. had many talks with Gladys during her stay, but there was no further mention of the unfortunate Lord Brooke. Roffredo Caetani was very much under discussion, and B.B. did not fail to impress upon Gladys what an ardent admirer she had in the young composer. Roffredo had evidently sought B.B.'s advice some two years earlier concerning certain reports about Gladys circulating in Rome. B.B. foolishly gave this as the example to prove the sincerity of Roffredo's feelings, but Gladys took it entirely the wrong way. She wrote to Roffredo, accusing him of gossiping to B.B. She went so far as to say that Berenson had complained that Roffredo had kept him up one whole night talking about her in a way he prayed never to hear again. On 16 June Roffredo accused B.B. of trying 'to do harm to the friendship I have for Miss Deacon' and demanded an explanation for what he called 'this ridiculous exaggeration'. B.B. explained that he had been trying to give Gladys the best advice possible, and apologized for the misunderstanding. At this Roffredo quoted Goethe: 'Lass das Vergangen vergangen sein',* and the matter rested. Somewhat later, from Roncegno, Gladys could not resist letting B.B. know her opinion of it all:

Much amused dearest B.B. at the exchange of letters between you and another great friend. Cupid's messengers must not be a year late. Now you know why I was so amused at your – forgive me if I say it – rather silly words. The intention was probably good but a little ill timed and ill clothed.[31]

Also in Florence in the early summer of 1906 were the writer Gertrude Stein and her friend Alice B. Toklas. Meeting Gladys after a winter in Montmartre, Gertrude dismissed her as 'too easily shocked to be interesting'.[32] Gladys remembered Gertrude in 1976: 'I hated Gertrude. I disliked her. She was hard and ugly, and a hard man or woman isn't worth bothering about. No, never! ... She was absolutely round ... hideous she was! She wore hideous clothes in a disgusting way ... but she was clever.'[33] Once at a dinner-party in Paris, Gladys declared suddenly: 'Stein and I are the only two people who have had enough courage to put the manners they were born and bred with completely aside and have therefore been able to live an unencumbered life.'[34]

On 10 August 1906, instead of going to St Moritz, Gladys and her mother went to Versailles to stay at the Hôtel des Réservoirs. The room below theirs was occupied by Marcel Proust, who had incarcerated himself there for five months. During the last three months of his stay he never left the hotel at all. 'I haven't left my bed, I haven't seen the palace, the Trianons, or anything', he wrote to Madame de Caillavet. 'When I open my eyes it's already the dead of night, and I often wonder whether the room I lie in, lit by electricity and hermetically sealed, isn't anywhere in the world rather than at Versailles. ...'[35]

However, during August, he was still seeing his friends. One of them was Hans Schlesinger, the brother-in-law of Hugo von Hofmannsthal, who was seldom far from Mrs Baldwin's entourage. It was not long before Proust became aware of the fascinating presence in the room above his. He informed Rey-

* Let byegones be byegones.

naldo Hahn of Gladys's arrival, but exhorted him on no account to discuss her with Schlesinger. He became exceedingly sensitive on the subject, and related the full circumstances of his knowledge of her to Madame Emile Straus.

One day he was lying on his bed when he saw Gladys through the window, heavily veiled, stepping into an automobile. He did not meet her, his excuse being that he was never well enough. One evening he left his room, climbed the stairs nervously and knocked on her door. Mrs Baldwin answered and told him that Gladys was in bed. Proust begged Madame Straus to inform Robert Dreyfus that that was the full extent of his association with the Deacon family. At the same time he took the trouble to write to Hahn, urging him to tell Montesquiou that he was not interested in meeting Gladys. 'I am beginning to prefer *objets*',[36] he wrote in reference to a poem in *Les Hortensias Bleus*, which the Count had sent him.

On the contrary, Proust yearned to make Gladys's acquaintance, but he had to wait until the following year before doing so. He never forgot his first attempt and when Mrs Baldwin died in 1918, he reminded Gladys of it:

> I remember your mother so well at Versailles, her beauty and her goodness. I had gone upstairs to make your acquaintance but you were in another room, you were ill. I felt that just a very thin wall prevented me from seeing you and kept us apart. Alas it was a real wall and a symbolic one which was to extend endlessly in the plan of time. Very often I have thought of this evening. . . .[37]

Chapter Nine

SEPARATION

For some years the Duke and Duchess of Marlborough had wanted a divorce, but to obtain one at that time the Duke would have had to prove unfaithfulness in Consuelo, and she physical cruelty and unfaithfulness, or desertion and non-support. In October 1906 they went their separate ways and in January 1907 a legal separation was granted. Apart from their long-standing incompatibility, both had found interests elsewhere. When, in August 1906, Gladys was declaring herself engaged to Lord Brooke, Mary Berenson noted that 'she still keeps Marlborough hanging on'. Nor was Mary surprised to hear that the Brooke engagement was off: 'She has inflicted herself rather seriously with the Duke of Marlborough I am afraid.'[1] On the other hand, Mary Crawshay, sister-in-law of Lady (Leonie) Leslie, and Berenson's informant on Marlborough matters, told him that it was Consuelo, not the Duke, who had strayed from the marital path. B.B. told his wife: 'Gladys has nothing to do with the impending separation of Marlborough and his wife!!! Who knows Gladys may be Duchess of M. yet – but on what?'[2]

This theory was proved true by the remarkable journalist W. T. Stead, founder and editor of *The Review of Reviews*, and a friend of Gladys's. In 1910 he lunched with the Duke of Marlborough's solicitor, Sir George Lewis, who confirmed what Gladys had told Stead – that she had nothing to do with it, nor was her name introduced in any way.[3]

Daisy, Princess of Pless, had noticed a tendency towards flightiness in Consuelo as early as 1902. When Consuelo went to Vienna, Daisy sent her friend, a certain Prince Z., to look after her. Arriving there herself a while later, Daisy found

Consuelo saying: 'I knew you would come and take him away from me.' To which Daisy replied, 'You can't take away in five days a loyal faithful friend to me for more than five years.'[4] Then on 21 March 1907 Tina Whitaker heard from Marchesa Lea Rudini that Consuelo had paid a visit to Paris with Lord Castlereagh (later the Marquess of Londonderry). The Duke wired that he did not want her back, but Consuelo chose to ignore this. Lady Castlereagh, the political hostess whose 'shrewd worldly wisdom', Consuelo wrote, 'proved a whole-some antidote to any sentimental tendencies on my part',[5] inter-vened to rescue a situation which was dangerous for both of them; and finally King Edward and Queen Alexandra themselves made it clear that any question of divorce between the Marl-boroughs would be met with distinct disapproval.

Another friend in common who strove hard to reconcile Marlborough with Consuelo was the Duke's cousin, Winston Churchill. He succeeded in remaining very friendly with both, but the separation did not dispose him favourably to Consuelo's successor. On 13 October 1906 Winston wrote to his mother from Blenheim informing her of the definite separation and asked her to call on Consuelo. 'We are all very miserable here. It is an awful business.'[6] Lord Hugh Cecil (later Lord Quicks-wood) also joined the fray and gave Winston an opinion of how society reacted to the news:

> I am satisfied after hearing much talk that Sunny is in danger of falling between two stools. What I said to you is evidently true: what he is doing pleases neither the Christians nor the fast set. The Christians feel that whatever his wife may have done, at any rate he is to blame as himself unfaithful: the fast set do not like a fuss made about such a matter and the implied rebuke at their own lives. His position, that his wife is unfit to live with him because she went wrong before he did and because the standard for women in these things is higher than for men, is not defensible either before the Church or the World. I am sure he will do himself harm.[7]

The Duke certainly harmed his position at court. On 1 June 1908, on the instructions of the King, Lord Knollys wrote to Winston Churchill asking him to notify the Duke and Duchess that they 'should not come to any dinner or evening party, or private entertainment at which either of their Majesties are expected to be present'.[8] The Duke was a Knight of the Garter and there were occasions when he attended the chapters of the Order at Windsor, but on these occasions his carriage was called before the other Knights Companions sat down to feast with their Sovereign.

The Duke also made himself unpopular in other quarters. On 27 November 1906 the President of the United States, Theodore Roosevelt, wrote to Whitelaw Reid:

> I thoroly dislike . . . these international marriages . . . But the lowest note of infamy is reached by such a creature as this Marlborough, who proposing to divorce the woman when *he* at least cannot afford to throw any stone at her, nevertheless proposes to keep and live on the money she brought him, come my dear Sir . . . surely you don't object to my consider-ing the Duke of Marlborough a cad![9]

In April 1907 the Duke took a motor trip in France with Jennie Churchill, Daisy, Princess of Pless, and others. The journey was fraught with problems from the start. First of all, the car ran out of 'essence or whatever the stuff is called . . . a most inappropriate name for a substance that smells so hor-ribly'. Then, after dinner, the Duke accidentally tipped the table over with a mighty crash, converting a corner of the dining-room into a pigsty. 'The Duke was miserable', wrote Daisy; 'by the way he looked at the debris one might have thought he was peering at his own life, which, at the moment is in much the same state.'[10]

If nobody in England was especially pleased to hear that the Marlboroughs had separated, Mrs Baldwin was delighted. She went about Paris boasting that Gladys could marry Marl-borough whenever she liked. Gladys herself brimmed with con-fidence. The Duquesa de Montellano related with horror that Gladys had snubbed Prince Gorchakov, 'the most renownedly courteous gentleman in Russia'. She accused him of not know-ing how to be polite to ladies.

Any possibility of Gladys marrying Marlborough was still a long way off, and in Paris, life continued as normal. Marcel Proust was still as eager to meet Gladys as he was reticent to talk about

Poor Doria I miss dreadfully – I used to think him sometimes a terrible bore yet he was very sweet and always helpful and sympathetic and now all is a wilderness and my voice is heard by no answering one.[4]

Less than a fortnight later, Bertrand de Fénélon was killed at Mametz. His death, which so distressed Proust, upset Mrs Baldwin too, when news of it emerged several months later. Her heart went out to his mother 'who does not know where his mortal remains lie'. Another casualty of the war was Charles Lister, three times wounded in Gallipoli in August 1915. In happier days he used to like riding over to Caprarola when he was at the Embassy in Rome. Another young friend, Louis Bessina, was killed on the very day his baby was born. 'His eyes haunt me', wrote Mrs Baldwin.

Gladys's unmarried sister, Edith, was busy nursing at the American Hospital in Paris. She became something of an expert on new treatments. Wounded limbs, instead of being bandaged, were dressed with antiseptic, left uncovered and placed under powerful electric rays which speeded the healing process. Edith had quite an adventurous war. On a visit to Girgenti in Sicily in April 1915 she was taken for a spy and had to ask the American Ambassador to prove her innocence. Presently she returned to the United States, where in 1916 she married a New York lawyer, Henry G. Gray, the son of Judge John Clinton Gray, Chief Judge of the New York Court of Appeals, the second most important court in the United States. She was the mother of three daughters, Audrey, Milo and Alison.

Italy joined the war in May 1915. 'Well', wrote Mrs Baldwin to Gladys, 'the great event has at last taken place. Italy has declared war and vindicated herself but to my astonishment the Austrian Ambassadors are still in Rome.' In the agony of it all, she wrote disconsolately, 'I wonder if we will ever meet again.'

In August 1915 Florence Baldwin lured B.B. to Caprarola. 'The House is a house of shade & silence & freshness. Bring yr books & yr papers and pens & come', she urged him. Mrs Baldwin welcomed him and Geoffrey Scott, dressed in creamy white, with a thick purple veil over her mahogany-coloured hair. She told B.B. that Gladys had been in Belgium and was busy taking the Belgian Army, Navy and Royal Family under her charge. She had spent a great deal of time with the intellectual set of the British Museum and South Kensington. Mrs Baldwin also said that Gladys had converted a loan of £400 into £16,000 on the Stock Exchange and that she 'would marry no one but M[arlborough] & perhaps not even him'. Berenson loved being at Caprarola: 'Meanwhile a round moon was shining around the round court and outside it was fairyland.' The food, though delicious, was sparse due to the limitations of Mrs Baldwin's purse. She was hoping to find someone extremely rich to hire the Casino in the garden, and contemplated taking up interior decorating.

Berenson studied Gladys's mother closely. In the dim light she was extraordinarily like her daughter with 'the same raucous voice rather *canaille*, the same vehemence of gesture and the same flash of the eye'. Yet Mrs Baldwin was growing old, albeit reluctantly. 'Her eyelids have dropped and her hands and throat are peppered over with brown spots',[5] he reported.

A month later Mary travelled to Caprarola, again with Geoffrey Scott. She took up the theme:

> But what an in-cred-i-ble central figure!!! With all she has gone through, her standards are those of a frivolous debutante. No maturity, no revaluation, no development morally....[6]

On the other hand Mary was forced to admit that Mrs Baldwin was one of the most useful women in that part of Italy. She had opened a workroom and was on the point of converting Caprarola into a hospital for the wounded. 'It is an inconceivable mixture. One admires her & one is horrified with her at the same moment.'[7] Mrs Baldwin told many tales about friends in common and many lies about money. She admitted to having spent £6,000 on the villa. Mary reckoned it was more like £20,000.

> There are huge traits in her that are simply appalling – so appalling that it is almost a miracle that one can like her. Only Dostoiewsky could do justice to her.... Solitude & old age if they weren't accompanied by decay might liberate a very remarkable character.[8]

All in all, Mary Berenson was anxious to get back to I Tatti. In December Mrs Baldwin paid the Berensons a visit. Geoffrey Scott and Mary took her to La Pietra, the villa of Arthur Acton (father of Sir Harold). They visited the grave in which Audrey had lain for eleven years and then returned to I Tatti. Mrs Baldwin exhausted the entire household with irrelevant and unceasing chat. She left on 13 December to their 'immense relief'.

Gladys spent most of 1915 in London, and that May became a naturalized British citizen. Her life revolved entirely around the Duke of Marlborough. His letters to her were short and to the point, making appointments to see her, promising her flowers (usually orchids), perhaps an acquamarine brooch or some game from Blenheim. They dined together when he was in London and sometimes the Duke would send his chauffeur, Troubridge, to pick Gladys up at Burlington Gardens, a meeting point convenient to Savile Row, and bring her to the station to meet him. He worried about the loneliness of her life and was consistently overjoyed to see her. Not that everything ran smoothly. After one particular letter from Gladys, he replied: 'Beloved, your spiteful letter I expected. I felt that the OB was beginning to get her hackles up, and that I was to get a scratch or two. . . .'[9]

They had their own nicknames for each other and for the characters who peopled their correspondence. 'MG . . . YS' was often his greeting: 'My Gladys . . . Your Sunny.' She would reply 'MS . . . YG'. Then 'OB' stood for 'Old Bird', and sometimes the Duke addressed her as 'Bird Darling'. Mr Asquith was known as 'Squiff', King George v as 'King Log', and Lord Lansdowne as 'Little L'.

Until September 1915 the Duke was the guardian of his sons. Then they went to Consuelo. He frequently visited them at Eton and Gladys would come down, have lunch at an hotel in Windsor, and they would meet surreptitiously 'in the usual place' in the Long Walk. Gladys was the only light that shone in Marlborough's life and he often wrote rather shyly and formally thanking her for her kindness and goodness to him. She provided a striking contrast to Consuelo, who caused him many worries:

Now I do not often complain – but few men have been plagued with such a woman as C – truly her life is spent in doing harm to the family whose name she bears.[10]

When Gladys was in France, an intrigue developed concerning the appointment of a new Lord-Lieutenant for Oxfordshire. Lord Jersey had died and Marlborough believed he was the rightful successor. He heard that Consuelo was backing Lord Lansdowne, and that there was also a move to appoint the new Lord Jersey. The Duke stormed round to Berkeley Square to beard Lansdowne at his London house. 'Never has he had such a plain spoken statement as I made to him!' he reported. Marlborough marshalled allies in the form of F. E. Smith, Winston Churchill, Sir Edward Carson, Bonar Law and Max Aitken, to combat Lord Valentia, Consuelo and their team. The decision rested with Asquith and the Duke noted 'every kind of pressure is being brought to bear on him from the C gang'. He fought for all he was worth and finally he won a battle which was highly significant to his whole position in later years. From France Gladys wrote that one good thing emerged from it: he would now know on whom he could rely in the future.

In the New Year of 1916 Gladys paid a visit to Paris. It was a chance to see Rodin again. Reminding him that she was 'amongst the most fervent of his disciples', Gladys proposed a cup of tea with him before he caught his train to Meudon. But her latest new excitement was that her old friend Boldini was commissioned by the Duke of Marlborough to paint her portrait. The Duke was delighted that Gladys had agreed to sit, knowing that she hated the process, but hoped that Boldini would not make her look like a tart – 'he can't help it the brute' – or fill the background with cushions.

Very soon, however, the Duke became angry because the sittings continued endlessly and Gladys refused to come home. On 6 February he wrote to her:

> Oh that picture. Of course it will never be completed; that pig B likes your company and will in a day or two rub out the head for the third time.

He became increasingly angry that Gladys would not come back to England; she was relying on three excuses – her mother, the portrait and influenza.

The portrait shows Gladys seated facing left on one of Boldini's traditional Empire sofas, an ostrich-plume fan in her hand. The pose selected was striking to the point of exaggeration, and not unlike the poses favoured by Rodin. The Duke cursed 'that Italian (who must have painted 6 pictures by now)', but when it was completed, he liked it and persuaded Gladys to let him have it for Blenheim. Mrs Baldwin was less impressed:

> It doesn't do you justice, there's that tooth effect I don't like, which in *you* is certainly not apparent. I, too, think the dress un peu décolleté.[11]

Mrs Baldwin and Gladys were staying together at the Quai Voltaire. Mary Berenson who, despite frequent complaints, remained a loyal friend to Mrs Baldwin, was also in Paris, staying with Edith Wharton. She called at the Quai Voltaire and found Gladys's mother in bed with influenza. Gladys began by playing her well-tried game of hide and seek, and refused to come in until Mary was on the point of leaving. Then she rushed on her and smothered her with kisses, declaring as she did it how improper an act it was to kiss another woman in that way.

Mary observed Gladys in her short striped skirt and flat hat, which seemed to cut off the top of her head. She had not seen her for some years and was distressed at the deterioration of her face since those first wax injections thirteen years earlier:

> Isn't it awful? Her face has grown very full and heavy-jawed, and all her colours jar – hair too yellow, lips too red, eyes too blue. . . . She looked *deplorable* not a lady. It made me v. sad.[12]

Sir Francis Bertie (now Lord Bertie of Thame) also saw her for the first time since the outbreak of war and observed: 'She still has fine eyes and good features.' Mrs Baldwin worried about the face, and recommended electric massage. Princess Marthe Bibesco recorded her opinion of Gladys's appearance at about this time. The Roumanian Princess and Gladys shared a distant dislike for one another for reasons not unconnected with the fact that they were both considered extremely beautiful and were lionized in intellectual circles. Marthe Bibesco never saw Gladys at the zenith of her beauty, before the wax had taken its toll. The Princess much regretted this 'real crime against beauty' which had converted Gladys's features into 'a Gorgon's face'. The Princess noted that the wax had not only damaged her face but run under the skin and down into the neck, leaving terrible blotches which obliged Gladys, at least during her encounter with the Princess, to disguise the deformity with a cloud of tulle. Another guest muttered, 'I thought she was a marvel, but she's nothing but a curiosity.'

Marthe Bibesco attributed the disaster to a 'savage admiration of the old world by a daughter of the new'. Contemporary photographs show a thickening at the bridge of the nose and a swelling around the mouth, combined with a general deterioration in the complexion. Further comparisons can be made by studying the two heads by Epstein, one sculpted in 1917, the other in 1923. By the later date, Gladys's lower jaw had begun to protrude somewhat. The wax had loosened the epidermis so that the lower part of the face slipped, the skin from the jaw forming, as it were, a second and false chin. At some point the wax was taken out, leaving four tiny scars along the jaw. There is a legend that Gladys received a certain visitor while sitting by the fireside. According to the rather dramatic account, she refused to look him full in the face, and appeared to be gently massaging the wax, melted by the heat, back up into the bridge of her nose.

Legion are the stories that circulate about Gladys's face. The majority suggest that she was most self-conscious about it, and several go so far as to suggest that it caused her withdrawal from the world into the life of a recluse. All the stories hitherto related assume however that Gladys injected the wax into her nose in the 1920s, whereas the deed was done as early as 1903. After a mild success, the operation failed. But she was far too intelligent to allow this to destroy her life. She continued to mix in society, to pose for artists, to marry the man she had sought for twenty-five years and to lead an active public life as the chatelaine of Blenheim. Any further damage to her features came as the natural deterioration of oncoming old age.

Marthe Bibesco left further recollections of her evening with Gladys; it was on this occasion that Gladys discovered a friend in the Abbé Mugnier. He caught her attention by interrupting a long and argumentative discussion about the classics and the romantics by announcing: 'Romantic! Classic! What is all that? Take me for example! Every day I wake up in the morning classical and I go to bed at night romantic!' The room dissolved into laughter.

Gladys launched into a diatribe against French poetry, comparing it most unfavourably with English poetry. Marthe Bibesco remained silent for a long time, and then cried out:

'How lucky that we have both!' Gladys and the Princess then joined conversational battle. Gladys provocatively declared that there had been no poets in France since Villon (who lived in the fifteenth century). Marthe then conducted Gladys on a voyage through the world of poets, finally arriving at Alfred de Musset. 'Musset?' said Gladys scornfully, 'but he's a poet for my *femme de chambre*.' Princess Bibesco reckoned that she won the day by replying: 'How lucky for a poet to be liked at the same time by your *femme de chambre* who is no doubt French and by me who am not!'[13]

Marthe Bibesco disliked Gladys enough to write of her in a malicious tone and even to describe her as 'Medusa'. But Gladys's power to fascinate others was certainly not lost. In 1916 Jean Giraudoux was still able to describe her as the most beautiful woman in the world and to observe with amazement the effect she had on passers-by as they walked together to lunch. Gladys was an hour and a half late for her appointment with him, but he felt that for someone of her beauty, an hour and a half was 'the minimum' time to wait. She ran towards him 'with the speed of light' and the Parisians, already emerging from the restaurants, gazed in wonderment. This is how Giraudoux painted the scene:

> They all looked at Gladys, she reminded them of someone they had once seen, but they could not recall exactly where. It is not true, she reminded them of someone they had not seen and who is the most beautiful woman in the world. A hoop passes before her, she runs and catches it in flight. She becomes the most beautiful girl in the world. All that is free is married to Gladys. I see her marriage with the Sunday sun, with the pigeons, with the little boy of the hoop who is an exacting husband and doesn't want to leave her. I take her away. Gladys must be married to the Arc de Triomphe which one can see sparkling above the arch of the merry-go-round.

Giraudoux saw in Gladys's beauty something unique. She had no lazy zones and even the tiniest movement of a finger came at the command of the shoulder. When she listened, she listened with her ears, her hair, her eyes, her voice, and even her big toes, thought Giraudoux. Gladys sat opposite him with her head resting on her crossed hands. 'I am being listened to by the most beautiful grown-up child in the world', he wrote. Every part of Gladys was breathlessly lapping up the writer's words.[14]

Gladys was in London during April and May and saw the Duke regularly, though she suffered one of her intermittent bouts of ill-health. She never much liked London and by the end of May became restless and unhappy. This led to a quarrel with Marlborough. He tried to explain to her that his life over the past ten years had been one of worry and anxiety, relieved only by occasional days snatched in her company. In the month of May 1916 alone he was wrestling with five major crises. George Cornwallis-West had let him in for £4,000, the Government had announced that they were intending to sequestrate part of his fortune, his land manager had departed leaving the entire burden of administration on his shoulders; this would mean a decrease in the already slender returns on the land, and, as usual, his family, public bodies, and dependants were all clamouring for money. Furthermore he worried that he might have to close Blenheim (to the delight of the Americans), and he resented the fact that his attempts to provide Gladys with money from time to time were met with contempt.

> I realize quite that you cannot appreciate my position. You have few responsibilities and my own are tremendous – the effect of responsibilities on my character is a source of annoyance to you, because possessing none yourself you *cannot* understand how anyone else can have thought for the morrow.[15]

Marlborough was very worried that Gladys might have taken it into her head to return to Paris permanently, for in spite of his complaints he missed her. Instead she went to Brighton for June and July where he was able to visit her.

Meanwhile, from Paris, Boldini was pressing his 'incomprehensible friend' to return there. He longed to show her his new portrait of the American, Mrs Leeds, already wearing a princess's coronet for she was about to marry Prince Christopher of Greece.* Boldini was most insistent that Gladys should come, and chided her for being a bad correspondent. He explained the reason: 'It's love'. He extracted a promise that his 'Parona'

---

* Nancy, widow of William Bateman Leeds. Born 1873. She did not marry Prince Christopher until 1920, and died in 1923.

would come on 25 June. He assured her he would be good: 'I promise you that I will keep my hands in my pockets.'

Gladys crossed the Channel in July without making any explanations. 'I ask no questions about yourself', wrote her mother, 'since you evidently desire me to remain in ignorance of all that concerns you.' Marlborough hoped Gladys would have some fun and be in the company of amusing friends. Her main interests were attending the Academy luncheons and dabbling with her investments. Marlborough hoped Boldini might quickly paint another portrait of her before she was exhausted by too many Paris *fêtes*, but by the end of July she was refusing to see him any more, and thereafter he addressed her as 'Parona (ex)'.

Soon after her departure, the Duke of Marlborough fell from his horse at Blenheim and suffered a compound fracture in his foot. For weeks he was immobile, but he worried seriously that he might be permanently lame, and worried all the more since Gladys had expressed her hatred of lameness when discussing Lord Francis Hope. Very nervously he wrote on 9 August: 'I expect to have a limp for all time. It is as well to tell you this for if you hate that – you will have an excuse for leaving me.'

The summer passed and the war continued to rage. Mrs Baldwin's poverty grew worse and she wondered if Lady Clifford of Chudleigh might find her a place as a companion or take her in herself. All she wanted was board and lodging. She also tried to persuade Gladys to part with $8,000 of capital in the United States Trust Company of New York, but Gladys was unmoved. Mrs Baldwin continued to live at Caprarola and her debts steadily mounted.

Gladys stayed in Paris during the autumn and captured the imagination of the Abbé Mugnier. The Abbé told Berenson that he had witnessed an occasion on which Gladys had been 'as brilliant as he could conceive'. (On the other hand the philosopher Henri Bergson, to whom Keyserling had once recommended her, was unimpressed.) In October Marlborough came over to see her, and hoped that he might find a cure for his lameness. Back in London he awaited Gladys's proposed arrival with impatience. In one of his many bouts of melancholia he wrote:

The world for me is growing grey – and since without you it

would be hardly worth the effort to go on living – you must bear with me when I attach importance to your arrival. The time for us to be together may indeed be short – for who can foresee the requirements of the year 1917?[16]

Chapter Thirteen

ARMISTICE
1917-1918

During Christmas 1916 Marlborough seriously reviewed his situation, and resolved that the time had come to break his last bond with Consuelo. Gladys had patiently waited for many years; and he realized that if he did not take a definite step she would make up her mind to settle down without him, and this was the last thing he wanted. He was relying heavily on the possibility of a new divorce law, which had been under discussion since 1909, and which would make desertion for more than three years one of the grounds of divorce. But the war delayed the Bill and nothing constructive happened until as late as 1923 when Lord Buckmaster's Matrimonial Causes Act was passed. And so the Duke and Gladys remained in their present unsatisfactory state.

1917 witnessed the passing of many old friends and the making of new. At the end of January Mrs Baldwin gleefully announced: 'Rodin has married his old wife!' The sculptor made an honest woman of Rose Beuret on 29 January at Meudon after a shared life of fifty-three years. Two weeks later she died of bronchial pneumonia in their cold, half-empty house, leaving the confused old man alone in a world of miserable dreams. Gladys responded quickly by offering her condolences on Rodin's great loss:

Madame Rodin's very sweet charm and her exquisite simplicity struck me greatly, and I realise what the loss of a lifelong companion must be to you, Dear Master.
The last time I saw her, you remember, was here with Miss Grigsby....[1]

Gladys hoped that Rodin's strength would return with the

spring and that when she came back to Paris she would find him in his garden restored to perfect health. But Rodin was not to linger long himself; on 17 November, a few days after his seventy-seventh birthday, he died, and was buried with Rose in the shadow of 'Le Penseur' at Meudon.

In contrast to the august, white-bearded figures of Rodin, Monet, Degas and Anatole France (and to the elder statesmen she knew such as Clemenceau and Aristide Briand) it was a refreshing delight for Gladys to meet in London the young and talented sculptor, Jacob Epstein. On making his acquaintance she threw up her hands and exclaimed: 'Un génie qui est jeune!' Epstein joined the ranks of Gladys's circle when he was thirty-six, through a new friend of Mrs Baldwin called Mrs Fletcher-Robinson. She had an unfurnished apartment in Cheyne Walk which she was prepared to let Gladys have for £100. Mrs Baldwin reported that 'she said a Mr Epstein was in it and that if you wanted it please hurry'. Gladys did not take up the offer, but she made friends with the tenant.

Epstein had already tasted success with works such as the Strand statues, the tomb of Oscar Wilde at Père Lachaise cemetery, and with portraits of Admiral Lord Fisher, Augustus John and the Countess of Drogheda. In April 1917 Gladys paid Epstein £150 as a contribution towards a marble clock she commissioned but which was never made. In the same year she sat for the first of two portraits. Epstein sculpted the straight nose, the lips already more naturally open than closed, the lower part of the eye more exposed than is natural and the chin grown heavy.

Through it shines the striking quality of her beauty. Epstein saw it as something eternal, and the finished bust was different from anything else he ever did; nor did it belong to any period. While Epstein pronounced it 'somewhat stylized', his second wife called it 'The Etruscan Bust'; Richard Buckle has written that her 'striking looks' were 'rendered with a grand archaic simplicity which recalls nothing so much as the Delphic charioteer'.[2]

Gladys herself loved the bust, and Epstein was duly appreciative of her judgment. She was, he wrote, 'a woman of great discrimination in Art ... and thoroughly understood what an artist was aiming at'.[3] However, when the bust was exhibited it caused 'great uneasiness' amongst the English ladies who patronize artists. When a photograph of it appeared in the *Chicago Evening Post*, a friend of Gladys's wrote furiously: 'An artist (?) ought to be severely punished for work like this.' Epstein wrote angrily of critics such as these:

> [They] expect a work to be entirely lacking in character and would rather have a portrait lacking all distinction than one which possessed psychological or plastic qualities, and a combination of these qualities is abhorrent to those ill-educated snobs who run about London airing their money-bag opinions, and who dominate with their loud-voiced arrogance the exhibiting world.[4]

Having discovered Epstein's immense talent, Gladys worried that he might be enlisted into the army and sent to an early death. She prevailed upon Marlborough to approach Sir Edward Carson to ensure that this did not happen. Eventually the Duke dined with Max Aitken (by then Lord Beaverbrook) who promised to do his best. On 4 March 1918, the Duke reported the outcome:

> Well I have fixed up Epstein for you. He is to join the Canadian Forces as an artist to mould figures and make sketches in the manner he thinks best. He will therefore not get killed and one day no doubt in recognition of your efforts he will present you with something from his chisel. Beaverbrook has been most painstaking in the matter. Never again say I do not get things done for you according to your liking.

Ill-health dogged Gladys during much of 1917. In March the Duke was appalled to hear that she was in London with not even a nurse to look after her. As sympathy did not come easily to him he relied on a letter to express his anxiety. Gladys was livid: 'Why did you write me this? So as to draw my attention that you wd not even telephone to me? Ah, my friend, how strange, how little human you are!'[5]

Gladys retreated to Brighton for the summer and stayed there until September in the Bedford Hotel, and later in the Norfolk: Marlborough wondered if her move was a belated tribute to 'the lately defunct nobleman', Gladys's former friend, the fifteenth Duke of Norfolk, who died on 11 February 1917.

In May, Austin Harrison invited the Duke to write an article about horse-racing in the *English Review* following a speech he had made on the subject. Marlborough wrote at once to Gladys suggesting she should do it and that like a number of previous contributions it should go out under his name. The Duke enormously valued any public esteem he managed to earn, no doubt because of the bad press to which he had so often been subjected. It is interesting to find him relying so much on Gladys in these matters.

Meanwhile the Duke worried about Gladys's safety in Brighton, and both were convinced that the war had at least two more years to run. On 16 June he wrote to her:

> I note you think the war will last as long as we continue to kill the wrong men in battle. It will cease the day we could be certain of killing all the right ones.

In September Mrs Baldwin came to England, and she and Gladys returned to Paris together. She avoided mentioning the Duke until they arrived in Paris; then she did so in terms of abuse, which surprised the Duke when he heard about it, since he was aware how much Mrs Baldwin expected of him. He was glad when she returned to Caprarola leaving Gladys at the Quai Voltaire. There she remained for the rest of the year, living in her little apartment at 23, two doors away from her mother's. For Christmas the Duke sent her a pearl necklace, but Gladys did not like it. To tease her, he wondered if he should not give it to Lady Diana Manners* instead. (She had been to stay with the Duke in 1917. Her mother, the Duchess of Rutland, armed Lady Diana with a revolver and instructed her to announce that her maid slept in her room.)

As the war progressed, Marlborough became increasingly depressed. He contemplated closing Blenheim and wondered if he could find a seminary in Spain where the monks would be kind to him, and where there would be sunshine and silence. He was annoyed when Lord Beaverbrook suggested that he should give Blenheim to the nation, and worried about Lord Blandford who was about to go to war. He found himself living in dark days.

Furthermore, he quarrelled bitterly with Winston Churchill over the 12½ per cent increase in wages for skilled workers. One day he met Clementine Churchill by chance and she invited

---

* Later Lady Diana Cooper.

him to lunch, saying 'It is such a long time since Winston and I have seen you.' The Duke wrote to decline, confiding in Gladys:

> I do not mean to go into their house again – till order reigns in this country – and they have learnt their proper place. That 12½% I can never forgive. It means 150 millions a year more in wages. I wonder what the French would have done to their Minister of Munitions.[6]

In March 1918 he made another attempt to get divorced. Again he hoped the Divorce Commission would make a move, but nothing happened. His solicitor told him that none the less he could be a free man in about six months. Marlborough wrote to Gladys asking her views in the matter. Gladys replied with an 'anti Divorce Reform letter', and so yet again the matter dragged on.

On 23 March 1918 the first of the German shells hit Paris from points seventy miles from the city. The shells were fired from huge naval guns of the kind that were nicknamed Big Bertha, after Bertha Krupp of the German industrialist family. The shelling persevered for some months and the Quai Voltaire became a danger zone. 'For nearly a fortnight one had to offer large tips to taxis to come to this quarter', reported Gladys.

Gladys had a narrow escape when a shell landed thirty yards in front of her, as she was ambling back from the house of Comtesse Edith de Beaumont one Sunday. Suddenly her skirt was blown almost over her head, while she was thrown on to the sidewalk, and a piece of iron waste pipe, dislodged by the explosion, fell on to her shoulder. She was saved a bad breakage by a fur shawl collar she was wearing, but suffered a badly bruised arm and pain in her side and back. Gladys related what happened:

> Four people were blown to atoms. For ten days I was constantly seasick from the memory of the sight I saw when I was helped to my feet by those who came up.[7]

Marlborough was very alarmed to hear of her misadventure and in vain urged her to leave Paris. His anxiety increased when she told him of a visit she had made to see the damage done by the German guns. Gladys was delighted to hear that Haig had departed and felt more confident in Marshal Foch than she had done in Pétain.

Mrs Baldwin had become the driving force behind the Farnese Relief Fund and enlisted Gladys's help to write an article for them with her 'clever pen'. In January 1918 Mrs Baldwin went to the United States to do canteen work and to raise funds. On her way through Paris she carefully avoided Berenson, 'fearing', he supposed, 'that she might have to say something about the small sum we lent her'. Gladys was full of advice for the journey over. In the event of trouble, her mother must drink brandy, keep her life-belt on and if possible keep a firm grip on that brandy bottle. All in all she thought her mother would be safe: 'You'll have too many spies on board. They make travelling safe!' Mrs Baldwin stayed with Bessie Marbury in New York until the end of May.

The artist Edgar Degas died in Paris at the age of eighty-three on 27 September 1917. Gladys had known and admired him, and when the first sale of Degas's work took place in his studio on 6 May 1918, she went along as a bidder with Walter Berry and Madame Hennessy. She purchased two signed pastels of dancers, both executed in the late 1890s.

She found the atmosphere at the sale 'fearfully exciting'. A particular source of amusement was Mrs Robert Woods Bliss of Dumbarton Oaks, who steadily climbed 'the ladder of prices' in her attempt to secure one of Degas's pictures. Gladys informed Mrs Baldwin:

Hers is a very good one though & as her purse is castor oil, I sd think it must be fat enough to draw upon. She has a pretty, extraordinarily mean little face, & her expression became so rapacious during the bidding that it stirred even Mr. B. into laughter.[8]

The Duke had been worried when he heard that Gladys was going to the sale, convinced she would pay too much. She succeeded in allaying his doubts, and eventually he was persuaded that her sound knowledge of art had ensured that her pictures were good examples of Degas's work.

Her companion at the Degas sale, Walter Berry, struck up a great friendship with Gladys, who discovered in him a thoroughly honest and highly cultured man. She said of him: 'He was an inspiration to people's lives.'[9] Like her, he was an

American born in Paris. At this time he was hovering around the age of sixty. A brilliant lawyer with a fine literary mind, his tall, thin form of six foot three inches cut an imposing and elegant figure in the streets of Paris. He was of aristocratic appearance, with a long straight nose and piercing blue eyes. In Paris he held the important position of chairman of the American Chamber of Commerce. As such he was a useful ally to Americans there, since he could arrange special banking facilities during wartime.

He was one of the best known Americans in Paris and a vociferous campaigner to bring America into the war. Proust dedicated his *Pastiches et Mélanges* to Berry, explaining it was 'because he won the war'. Proust attributed the German defeat to the arrival of the Americans and the arrival of the Americans to the efforts of Walter Berry. Berry soon became a member of Proust's new circle of friends and regularly partook of oysters and champagne with him at the Ritz. Paul Morand described him as 'like an American in a Henry James novel', but he is perhaps best recalled as what Mrs Winthrop Chanler described as the 'dominant seventh chord' in the life of Edith Wharton. There had been a time in their early lives when marriage had been talked of. Though nothing came of it, they remained very close friends until Berry's death in 1927.

Berry also had a reputation as 'the most noted lady's man in America', the lifelong bachelor whose eye could be diverted from the most serious study by the passing by of a pretty face. He was always interested in some lady or another, invariably a rather rich and beautiful one with a tendency towards frivolity. His love of intelligence in women inspired someone to ask, in a New York club, how he was able 'to seduce the minds of our women'. To this, Frank Crowninshield, the editor of *Vanity Fair*, replied: 'If only he left them in an interesting condition.'

Walter Berry's friendship with Gladys developed from a rather formal 'Dear Miss Deacon ... yours sincerely, Walter Berry', to his addressing her as 'Gardenia' or 'Gladysissima' and signing himself with a solitary 'A'. The 'A' was short for 'Anaconda', the snake that crushes its prey. He used it when speaking of himself – 'The Anaconda has only rudimentary paws and consequently isn't much at writing ...' – and their mutual language he called 'Anacondiac'.

Their friendship revolved around lunches, teas, theatres and stocks and shares. The invitations with which he regaled her were always entertaining and from time to time written in verse. Firmin Gémier, the actor, sent him two tickets for *Antony and Cleopatra*. Berry wrote to Gladys:

Shakespeare in French is always a peculiar joy!
    Don't you want to go?
    Do.
    They are terribly serious about it and close the doors during the acts – and it begins at 1.15. Would you mind – if you can go, and I do so hope you can – having a *casse-croute* with me somewhere *en route*?

Then on another occasion he wrote:

Ohio Gas 37 +
Sticks tight, and bull at heart
Gladys-Marie
consults her *carte-du-jour* inscribed thus:
'Lunch in some *bouge* today with Walter B'
Who will come at 12.30.

Sometimes he called her Marina – 'that is because you are the Sea'. He addressed her as such when he proposed a lunch at his home with Jean Cocteau and Madame Murat:

We'll gorge –
Don't think I'll ever ration, like Lord Rhondda;
I'm your most unrestricted Anaconda.

While on the subject of Lord Rhondda, who had the unenviable task of being Food Controller from June 1917 to July 1918, the Duke of Marlborough passed on a contemporary limerick for Gladys's amusement:

There was a young lady of fashion
Whom her husband loved with great passion
When the clock struck eleven
She cried out 'Thank Heaven!'
'There's one thing Lord Rhondda can't ration.'

Mrs Baldwin remained in America, writing occasionally, but Gladys, like many others, was sick of the war:

You don't tell me abt Americans as you find them. You know

that war-news are very stale to us who've lived on them for
so many years now, & one tries not to speak of 'la guerre' in
any of its forms over here. It's bad enough being under it. Tell
me abt the people you see. Are they amusing? Are any
beautiful to look at? Do they say witty things? Are the girls
conventional or the reverse? Is the food *amusant*? Remember, I only know them through novels.[10]

According to Elsie de Wolfe, Mrs Baldwin returned to Europe
'prosperous & jolly'. She spent a few days with Gladys, before
returning to Caprarola. The contrast between Italy and America
disheartened her enormously, as she explained to Mary Berenson on 29 June:

I came back with great plans, but how difficult it is to move
anyone or anything in this country. One beats one's wings
against the iron hand of ancient laziness & lethargy & there's
hardly an appreciable result, try as we may. I am trying to
organise a class for knitting socks for the front with knitting
machines that I have brought back & also 40,000 flyswatters
for the Italian hospitals. . . .[11]

She complained that she had received 'a stiff cold note' from
Dorothy and nothing from Gladys. 'I am disgusted with both.
They really carry indifference to its ultimate limit.' Mrs Baldwin concluded that she was 'disenchanted & weary'. She felt she
had given too much of her soul to the war effort and she was
consequently exhausted and depressed. Her last words to Mary
were: 'I feel it cruelly there's not a human being in this land
that I can call **friend.**'

Gladys was staying with the Ménians in the Loire when, three
weeks later, doctor Lombardi telegraphed the Quai Voltaire to
say that her mother was gravely ill. Chester Aldrich, director of
the American Academy in Rome, telegraphed the next day,
again in vain, beseeching her to come. It was too late, for Mrs
Baldwin died peacefully at Caprarola on 15 July, aged a mere
fifty-nine.

One of the worst aspects of death in Italy in those days was
the pillaging that followed in its wake. Many odd stories grew
up about Mrs Baldwin's death, stories of how the staff fled, and
how the pillagers did their worst. None are true. Fortunately
Prince Maffeo Sciarra moved into Caprarola and remained at

the palace until Gladys arrived there. Thus nothing was lost. There was, however, a disturbing account of Mrs Baldwin lying in state at the palace: as one mourner approached the bier, a cloud of flies dispersed from the corpse.

Mrs Baldwin left debts and chaos for Gladys and her sisters to clear up. For years creditors had been doing their utmost to keep up with her extravagance and for years Mrs Baldwin and her daughters had been staving them off. Edith Gray, who admired and adored her mother, related tales of how the endless flow of insistent creditors would arrive at the villa, and how Mrs Baldwin would turn lovely eyes on each one and say: 'Mon cher monsieur, la plus belle femme du monde ne peut pas donner ce qu'elle n'a pas, et moi, je n'ai pas un centime!' The creditor invariably retreated in disarray. In May 1918, very shortly before Mrs Baldwin's death, Gladys told her the story about the rent at the Quai Voltaire:

> The Ruissiers are making fresh trouble abt your unpaid rent – we exhaust stores of weeping eloquence on them, here at the 23. We speak of inability to get news because U.S.A. fills all her ships with food & soldiers, that private correspondence is usually suspended for great official reasons etc etc. They don't seem convinced, we cry in dusters. I speak of myself as of a possible orphan etc.[12]

As soon as possible Gladys came to Rome and stayed at the Grand Hotel. Her mother was laid to rest in the English Cemetery and an auction was held at Caprarola to pay her debts.

Yet again there were contrasts. A year after Mrs Baldwin's death, her war efforts were recognized by the posthumous award of the Italian Red Cross. And one of those who wrote to Gladys saw her death very differently from those interested in debts and pillaging. It was Marcel Proust:

> The war has not accustomed me to death. The death of young people does not appear to me to lessen the sadness of the death of those who were not so young where it sweeps away less hopes but destroys more memories. I remember your mother so well at Versailles, her beauty, her kindness. . . . I hope that the phase will not last too long for you until this terrible illness which is grief and the suffering of the loss is

soothed so that you can appreciate the divine sorrow of remembering.[13]

The Duke of Marlborough tried to be nice about the woman he had so often insulted:

My heart bleeds for you in your sorrow. I was very fond of your mother. We never had a quarrel and I liked her for some of her wonderful qualities.[14]

Gladys's mother died a few months before the Armistice. As the Armistice approached so the social world revived. The Ritz in London was filled with every type of society and the un-crushable social war horses put on their harnesses again. Lloyd George went to Versailles and was heard to announce that he had won the war, while the world situation was reappraised. Marlborough was aghast to consider the Empires that had fallen, the Slavs, the Teutons, the Mohammedans. Now power would rest with the Rockefellers and the Carnegies. Shortly before the Armistice, Marlborough had to cope with the inevitable problems of being a Marquess's father. Blandford became enamoured with a musical comedy actress and had to be dissuaded from his matrimonial plans. The Duke reckoned it was his common American blood prompting him to such a course.

When peace came, London filled with drunken crowds and ten thousand bottles of champagne were consumed at the Automobile Club. Gladys became thoroughly depressed. She seemed at this moment to see everything black, her spirit was crushed and she felt she had failed in her life. Well used to such depressions, Marlborough tried to cheer her up, believing she would do well to spend forty-eight hours laughing with a buffoon. She concluded that the remedy was to leave Paris for the South of France.

Chapter Fourteen

LAST DAYS OF LA DOUCE BOHEME

Bernard Berenson lived on until October 1959, but he and Gladys met for the last time some forty years earlier. Mesmerized for years by her extraordinary personality, he found that the attraction at last wore off. He ended by being bitter towards her, as he explained once to Umberto Morra:

> I decided to stop seeing Gladys Deacon when I convinced myself that in human relationships she offered nothing but an offensive arbitrariness, pursuing people in a flattering and ensnaring fashion, only so as to be able to break off with them noisily when the fancy struck her.[1]

Their last meeting was a strange one. Berenson was walking near the Petit Palais in Paris when an old horse-drawn coupé drew up. A curious figure, dressed in widow's weeds, stepped out and though he thought she was 'the Gladys type', he did not immediately realize it was she. Gladys approached him furiously, almost poked her finger into his eye and demanded: 'Horrible B.B., you mean you don't recognize me?' She was accompanied by Boldini, whom Berenson described as 'an even more deplorable figure all bundled up in shawls'. Over the ensuing years, Berenson heard news of Gladys from her sister Dorothy. From afar he remained interested in her life, and she in turn read some of his books, and wanted to know the fate of his excellent library at I Tatti.

In January 1919 Gladys travelled to Nice to look for a cottage. In the spring she moved into Tells Cottage, in the Chemin de Fabron, a secluded and pretty neighbourhood just behind the main town. The Chemin de Fabron was not far from Beaulieu, where a distinguished old gentleman of military bearing spent the winter months. Of him Anita Leslie wrote: 'On one or two occasions a slight fear arose that certain ambitious ladies had designs on the handsome old widower.' Her grand-mother Leonie Leslie would then be despatched to his villa to protect him. As they said in the Leslie family: 'We send you out like the Fire Brigade.'[2]

The gentleman in question was His Royal Highness the Duke of Connaught, the last surviving son of Queen Victoria. Born at Buckingham Palace in 1850, he had been a godson of the great Duke of Wellington and his christening was the subject of Winterhalter's famous picture 'The First of May'. He lived on to be the godfather of the present Queen.

Throughout his sixty-nine years he had lived at the very centre of the nation's life. He was a Field-Marshal in the British Army, had been Governor-General of the Dominion of Canada from 1911 to 1916, was a Knight of the Garter and held the Grand Cross of all the British Orders of Knighthood. He was the respected Colonel of numerous regiments and president of a wide range of charities and organizations. His Prussian-born Duchess had died to his everlasting sorrow on 14 March 1917, and just prior to his arrival in the South of France, his im-mensely popular daughter, Princess 'Pat', had married Captain the Honourable Alexander Ramsay, of the Royal Navy. So March that year heralded a lonely phase in the life of the man whom Marlborough and Gladys called 'The Irish Duke'.

Gladys wrote to the Duke of Connaught inviting him to renew an acquaintance of many years ago by coming to see her at her cottage. He replied that he would be delighted to come, but hoped that she would not go to the trouble of inviting anybody else. Meanwhile he looked forward very much to meeting her again. A rendezvous was fixed for Wednesday 19 March at 3.30. The Duke enjoyed the visit and sent Gladys some pictures of his daughter's wedding. 'I only hope that you won't be bored with so many pictures of the damn thing', he wrote.[3] He suggested a further meeting and hoped that Gladys would not be too bored if once again they were alone. The Duke was staying at La Réserve at Beaulieu until 11 April. One day he drove to Cannes, 'very resortish & uncared for', he told her, '& very unlike what I remembered it in the time of my brother, of the Bob Vyners, of the Gr. Duke Michael & Ctss. Torby and others'.[4]

Several times the old Field-Marshal called on Gladys, and they discussed books and articles and their shared feelings about the losses of his wife and her mother. Gladys clearly made much of the demise of Mrs Baldwin, for on 2 April the Duke wrote: 'I grieve to know how lonely and unhappy your mother's death has left you. Having so recently lost my wife I know what a blank the loss of a beloved one leaves in one's life.' He hoped to be allowed to comfort Gladys and trusted that his next visit would not 'grate against your lacerated feelings'.[5]

Time was running out, and what little remained was already quite filled. Gladys was expecting guests, which would have prevented the Duke from calling, but due to an accident to the guest room, she put them off. Then on 3 April the Duke was to pay an official visit to a hospital. But before returning to Paris the Duke discovered that his car had to go to Nice for petrol. This provided him with the excuse for a farewell call. Following this visit 'Dear Miss Deacon' became 'Dear Gladys', and the Duke requested a photograph: 'I am very anxious to have it. If you again forget to send it to me I will very reluctantly have to come to the conclusion that you don't consider me worthy of possessing one!!'[6]

In his sadness at saying goodbye he was comforted by the company of her wrist-watch, which he had promised to get repaired for her at Cartier in Paris. He assured Gladys that he was her 'respectful & devoted friend'. Just before setting off in the direction of Paris, he expressed his feelings:

> Although you may not realise it, you have added a new joy and interest to my now rather lonely life – you know how I feel towards you; I have confided in you & trust you completely and I am sure that you will never disappoint me.[7]

The Duke was then driven to Marseilles and caught his train despite the fact that his car had knocked a man down on the way. From Marseilles he took the train to Paris, where he was elated to hear that Gladys was due to arrive in connexion with Mrs Baldwin's affairs. Her train was due in at 8.45 a.m. on 15 April and his was due out at 11 a.m. on the same day. That morning he left the Ritz and made his way to the Quai Voltaire in the hope of a quick glimpse of her.

Arriving at the building he saw his letter of the previous day still in the concierge's rack. So Gladys had not yet returned, and the Duke was obliged to hurry to meet his daughter, Lady Patricia Ramsay, at the Gare du Nord in a state of desolation and disappointment. He was thoroughly depressed on the journey home and tortured by the knowledge that Gladys must have been within half a mile of him for some two hours.

The Duke of Connaught went home to Clarence House in London, and then down to Bagshot Park, his country house near Ascot. Gladys was never far from his thoughts. Indeed during Sunday matins his attention wandered during the prayers and sermon and he began to wonder what she was doing. He was anxious not to lose touch with his new friend and forever concerned that he might bore her. While she lived in the centre of life in Paris, his own existence in the country was very quiet. On Easter Day he wrote to her: 'You are so much more intelligent and cleverer than I am that I often feel that what I write is dull and perhaps too much about myself.'[8] As April turned into May, the Duke busied himself with a round of royal engagements.

Gladys remained in Paris in the 'rathole' as she disparagingly called the servants' quarters of the Quai Voltaire. Though residing in uncomfortable conditions Gladys found Paris life very interesting. The Peace Conference was in full swing, and the city was awash with diplomats and politicians. It was not long before Gladys surmised that President Wilson's concept of the League of Nations was impossible. On 30 April Jean de Gaigneron invited her to dine at the Ritz in the company of Marcel Proust, Harold Nicolson, Marie Murat and Carlo Placci. Gladys sat between Proust and Nicolson and Nicolson observed the contrast between Gladys, 'very Attic', and Proust, 'very Hebrew'. Nicolson suggested that a passion for detail was 'a sign of the literary temperament'. Proust was hurt by this and cried out 'Non pas'. He then blew what Nicolson described as 'a sort of adulatory kiss' across the table in the direction of Gladys. The conversation turned towards homosexuality – whether it was a matter of glands, nerves or of habit. Proust was of the opinion that it was 'a matter of delicacy'.[9]

A regular stream of letters arrived from Clarence House. One contained two photographs of the Duke. He asked Gladys to choose a favourite and was delighted when she kept both. In May he returned to Paris on royal duties, and for some days enjoyed teas with her at the Loidan and Colombiers. On his return from one such outing he found the British Ambassador already waiting for him at the Ritz. The Ambassador would no doubt have been surprised to learn the reason that had delayed His Royal Highness. As ever the Duke was grateful to Gladys for her kindness and assured her: 'our friendship is so close and so delightful to me'. On 14 May the Duke left for London and two days later Gladys went back to her cottage at Nice.

They did not meet again until the end of 1919, but the Duke of Connaught continued to be a source of interesting news in high places. He informed Gladys that the Empress Marie of Russia still believed that her son and his family had not been murdered at Ekaterinburg. He let her know that Sir John French, whom he called 'a vain little man & not quite a gentleman', hated H. H. Asquith. In June he received a visit from his other daughter, the Crown Princess of Sweden, and her five children who all had 'ugly noses like their father'. He confided to her the strictly private information that Lady Patricia was expecting a baby in December. Members of the Royal Family take such matters seriously and the Duke impressed on Gladys the necessity of saying nothing about it.

One controversy which played on the Duke's mind was the fear that the Kaiser might be brought to trial in London. The Kaiser was the Duke's nephew, and he thought the best solution was to 'let the wretched man disappear into oblivion'. In his view the idea of a trial was a vote-catching effort by the Labour Party:

> The King is very worried about it; the Kaiser is such a near relation of his, he is also Queen Victoria's eldest gr:son & he has been entertained here in London as a most honoured guest by 3 successive sovereigns. I don't believe the Dutch will give him up. I very much hope they won't.[10]

At Tells Cottage Gladys waged war on the weeds that had sprung up during her absence in Paris. When the Duke of Connaught fell ill, she recommended Horlicks before bed to prevent insomnia. Later in the year she worried about Dorothy, who was proposing to divorce Prince Radziwill and marry again; and for a time, she told the Duke, she suffered an attack of sunstroke. The Duke complained that her letters did not come as frequently as he would have liked but when they did he found her 'always interesting perhaps a little satirical'.[11]

During her mild and innocent friendship with the Duke, another relationship was reaching something of a crisis. In the autumn of 1917 she had met Bob Trevelyan again in Paris, where he was in charge of the Quakers' Library. Renewing a friendship that had been forged at I Tatti in December 1904, Trevelyan suddenly discovered himself violently in love with Gladys. There is a legend that Gladys would lie on a bed behind a screen, while he read his poems aloud to her. In the first months of 1918 he sent Gladys editions of his poetry with the frequency that other men send flowers. His love for her grew and he suffered very much. As his son wrote, 'He was very much changed by meeting Gladys.'[12]

In 1919 the matter had got so out of hand that Trevelyan's friends began to intervene. One of them was Francis Birrell, a fringe member of the Bloomsbury group, who was proud to be artistic and bohemian; he was the son of Augustine Birrell, the distinguished Liberal statesman. Gladys thought Frankie Birrell brilliant, whereas his father thought him stupid. 'There was this rift between them', she recalled. 'He was not a genius, but his father was harsh on him.'[13] David Garnett recalled in 1975 that Gladys entrusted to Frankie the delicate task of calming Trevelyan down. 'Frankie was given to exaggeration', he wrote, 'but he made it sound hectic.'[14]

On 22 September Birrell gave Gladys a progress report. As with so many of her friends, there was a secret code. He called her 'Frances II' and he signed himself 'Claude'. He began by apologizing for muddling in her affairs and complaining of the inconvenience he had endured on account of them. Bob Trevelyan had 'more or less regained his equilibrium' in the three months that had passed since he left England in June. Then events took a turn for the worse. Birrell continued: '[I] discovered him shattered by a p.c. he had just received from you à propos of his visit to the Riviera, & have since been endeavouring to shepherd him off to Madrid, though I am not sure with what success.' Trevelyan was so stricken with love that he was unable to work or settle to anything. He was 'rapidly becoming intolerable to himself & everybody else'. Birrell suggested that

Gladys should 'summon up the brutality to say that you cannot bear seeing him regularly or something to that effect'.[15]

Gladys replied to Birrell and he in turn promised to send on to Trevelyan 'one or two abstracts from your letter'. He agreed with her that the situation was a serious one. 'Bob sometimes appears hardly sane – & is on the high road to worry himself into a mad house.'[16]

Nor did the matter rest there. Another 'Bloomsberry', Roger Fry, the art critic, intervened in January 1920 to give his assessment. Bob Trevelyan was in 'a very agitated situation'. He wanted to establish a relationship of pure friendship with Gladys, but doubted he would be able to keep it on that level. Roger Fry thought it unlikely that Bob would 'obsess' Gladys again. He was remaining silent only in order to speed his recovery. Fry's mind dwelt on that strange thing which is love:

> It's a funny disease, isn't it, and very painful and worst of all tends to make one ridiculous though I must say that Bob has never appeared to me to better advantage than when re-counting his woes – he's very simple and very honest and hasn't the ordinary share of *amour propre*.[17]

By June 1920, Trevelyan was more settled. Edmond Jaloux, the writer and literary editor of *Grasset*, reported to Gladys: 'Did you know that I saw Trevelyan, a Trevelyan clipped, at ease, elegant, unrecognizable? He has a very melancholic expression when one talks of you in front of him!'[18]

Few letters written by Marlborough to Gladys in 1919 now survive, but their relationship was still very much on, though the distance between them was greater. She informed him of the progress of her friendship with the Duke of Connaught and Trevelyan, while he continued in his efforts to extricate himself from marriage with Consuelo. Thus Gladys's life was a curious mixture; there was her trusting friendship with the Royal Duke, and life with more bohemian friends. Boldini was thoroughly baffled by her absence from Paris. 'What are you doing at Nice? You'll freeze', he wrote. Boldini's letters to lady friends were always brief presumably because he had so many to write.

Sometimes the different worlds threatened to meet. In December 1919 she wrote to the Duke of Connaught about the impending arrival of some 'artist friends'. He was confused:

What do you understand by 'artist friends', singers, actors or what. If they are good & are also nice I don't think we look down upon them in England – I can't imagine who your 'English intellectuals' are who you refer to. I know some who are nice & others who are not – of course you are a regular Bohemian & may like some people who others don't like.[19]

The Duke arrived at the Hotel California in Cannes at the end of December, following the birth of a grandson. Buoyed up by the hope of seeing Gladys, he was disappointed that she would not come over from Nice. And he was cross that she signed herself 'Yours respectfully'.

Surely 'Gladys' is enough. There is no other Gladys to my mind; you really must not do that again; I know you did it out of respect, but really it is unnecessary, our feelings of respect are I hope quite mutual & my feelings towards you are also of great affection; if you will not think it rude or impertinent to say so.[20]

While the Duke continued to press Gladys for solitary encounters, she issued more unusual invitations. He found himself in an unlikely world: 'I should be very glad to have tea with you at the New Club, where the nigger jazz performers are ...'[21] he replied to one such summons. At the end of December he called at Tells Cottage, but he was not admitted. Gladys pleaded a bad attack of influenza. Instead he wrote to her and passed on some local gossip: 'Your friend the Duchess of Marlborough!! is building a villa near here.'[22]

While he was at the Hotel Bristol in Beaulieu, the Duke of Connaught and Gladys continued to see each other. Friends such as Mrs George Keppel and Ethel Boileau were in the neighbourhood, and Gladys would come over for lunch and tennis or occasionally meet the Duke in Monte Carlo for tea at the Café de Paris. Then on 9 April he left the South of France.

There were some who believed that Gladys seriously considered the possibility of becoming the Duchess of Connaught. Certainly this would have upstaged Consuelo, for she would then have taken precedence as the tenth lady in the United Kingdom; but it was quite out of the question. Nor does the Duke give the slightest indication in his cautious letters that he was even thinking along these lines. She valued his friendship, because if she was to marry the Duke of Marlborough she would need friends at court to ensure her acceptance. This matter became a growing preoccupation for both Marlborough and Gladys. Nevertheless the Duke of Connaught was surrounded by jealous lady friends who felt the time had come to divert him from Gladys before their friendship ripened further.

On 1 January 1920 a libel was printed about Gladys in the *Daily Graphic* in an article about the matrimonial problems of Dorothy and Aba Radziwill. The article resurrected the old story about Gladys and the Crown Prince of Prussia, and went so far as to state that Gladys had been 'the centre of a great outcry in Germany' and had been banished from that country. Represented by the Duke of Marlborough's solicitors, Messrs Lewis & Lewis, who briefed Sir Ellis Hume-Williams and St John Field as counsel, Gladys was awarded £500 damages with costs before the Lord Chief Justice. The publicity engendered by the case may well have provided the ammunition needed by the Duke's lady friends. Certainly, either Lady Leslie or the Countess of Essex told the Duke a number of stories aimed to make him feel that Gladys was making a fool of him.

The Duke fell into the trap and questioned Gladys about what he had heard. She replied in 'cruel and seething words' which expressed nothing less than a violent hatred of him. On 17 April he wrote from the Ritz in Paris, begging forgiveness and accepting all the blame. 'I feel that you are right', he continued, 'in abusing me in the unmeasured terms you did, but I have felt none the less – your terrible letter is I fear intended to show me that you cease your friendship which I have valued so much. It is hard at my age to part with friends like you that I have liked & had up to that cruel letter trusted so completely.' Utterly miserable and downcast, the Duke begged her forgiveness but recognized that she was determined to part from him. He signed himself 'a grateful friend who prays for your health & happiness throughout life'.[23]

The Duke of Connaught's troubles were not over; on the day of his seventieth birthday his elder daughter, Daisy, the Crown Princess of Sweden, died suddenly from erysipelas and blood-poisoning at the age of thirty-eight. The tragedy brought an immediate response from Gladys:

Sir

In the midst of my bitterness yet do I remember the agony of

losing one near and dear to one – the sense of sudden empti-
ness, of collapse, of loneliness. This therefore, is to tell you
that I hope God's help be with you through these grievous
hours.[24]

It was impossible for the Duke of Connaught and Gladys to
avoid one another forever, especially after her marriage to the
Duke of Marlborough. Yet Gladys never forgave him. Normally
invitations sent to Blenheim were marked 'A' if accepted and
'R' if refused, but an invitation to meet H.R.H. The Duke of
Connaught was very firmly 'declined'. The friendship that the
Duke had called 'so true and so pure' was over.

The days of Gladys's bohemian existence were also coming to
an end. After years of hesitation, Consuelo at last agreed to a
divorce, because she now wished to marry a French aviator,
Colonel Jacques Balsan. Nothing positive had yet come from the
Divorce Commission, so the Marlboroughs had to go through
the ridiculous ritual of being seen to cohabit once more. The
matter was conducted on the lines approved by their respective
solicitors. The various deeds of separation were revoked and the
Marlboroughs returned to live under the same roof for just over
a fortnight. The scene was Crowhurst, Consuelo's small Tudor
manor house in the North Wolds. The Duke's sister, Lady Lilian
Grenfell, also came to stay to help them through this tiresome
but necessary period. Marlborough left Crowhurst on 15
December 1919 leaving a letter to the effect that they had
grown too far apart to resume their union, and Consuelo replied
in kind. Further letters were exchanged and then on 28
February 1920, Marlborough spent the requisite nocturnal
hours 10.30 to 8.30 with an unnamed woman in room 193 at
Claridges. He booked in under the name of Spencer.

Other family events occurred. Marlborough's elder son, Lord
Blandford, having outgrown his fondness for stage-door petti-
coats, was married on 17 February to the Honourable Mary
Cadogan, daughter of Viscount Chelsea. Gladys was not
amongst the guests. Then Consuelo's father, William Kissam
Vanderbilt, died on 22 July. After a visit to the United States,
Consuelo put Sunderland House and Crowhurst on the market
and moved to Paris. On 10 November a petition for divorce was
entered.

The termination of his long endurance filled Marlborough with tremendous excitement. He was determined to be seen at as many London parties as possible, moving in society unabashed despite the divorce proceedings going on around him. He was, indeed, very anxious that both he and Gladys should do the right thing. He urged her to keep in touch with her rich cousin Eugene Higgins, because everyone in England from the Royal Family downwards was impressed by money. Meanwhile he dined with the Pembrokes and the Cornelius Vanderbilts but felt that he should not go to the Merry del Vals. His main fear was how 'King Log' and the court would react. 'That fortress one day will have to be raised [*sic*]', he noted.

Fortunately the unveiling of the tomb of the Unknown Warrior superseded the divorce as the main topic of conversation. Meanwhile Gladys softened the French gossips and consulted Léon Renault, her family lawyer, who was most approving. On the day the divorce petition was entered Marlborough wrote:

> Thank Heavens it is all over – The last blow that woman could strike over a period of some 20 years has now fallen – Dear me what a wrecking existence she wd have imposed on anyone with whom she was associated.[25]

Gladys remained at Nice. Edmond Jaloux tried to persuade her to translate Henry James into French for *Grasset*. After a visit to her, he was most flattering about her looks and her intelligence:

> I know few besides you with whom it is so pleasant and refreshing to pour out one's heart, confident of that quick and deep understanding which intelligence gives. Yours is extraordinary! It is vast and quite naturally acquired. There is in you of the archangel (whom you resemble physically very much) and of the erudite. And to discuss with a seraphim as if with a very knowing spirit is a form of joy one rarely encounters, believe me![26]

But Gladys did no translations, for now that goal first contemplated at the age of fourteen and relentlessly pursued to the denial of other possibilities of happiness, came inexorably into view.

The Duke of Marlborough's decree became absolute on 13 May 1921 and he was free to marry her. Gladys, now aged

forty, had waited so long to be Duchess of Marlborough that the
sudden inevitability of the situation terrified her. When the
Duke put his proposal, she did not accept at once. He was
astonished and asked her: 'Haven't you had time to make up
your mind?'[27]

Finally Gladys surrendered her Bohemian freedom and her
beloved France for a palace and a title and man of whom she
wrote a year after their engagement:

> I feel again the thrill of terror which ran through me when
> I read it in the D. Mail. I loved him but was fearful of the
> marriage.[28]

Chapter Fifteen

PARIS WEDDING

With considerable foreboding, Gladys prepared for her forthcoming wedding. She dreaded the thought of having to behave like a Duchess with the clear restrictions on her freedom and solitude. On 21 April 1921 Gladys closed her Nice bank account and settled her affairs. Before leaving the South of France she implored Epstein to come and talk about art. So the sculptor travelled to Nice and stayed there for a week. Then Gladys braced herself to face the world and the clamorous publicity her wedding was bound to attract. Meanwhile, Marlborough hoped she would be happy 'with all the rough edges of life now knocked off' for her. He decided to wait until he arrived in Paris before buying her an engagement ring.

On 1 June Gladys took up residence at 16 rue Auguste Vacquerie, the home of Lord Wimborne. The same day the engagement was briefly announced in *The Times*. From that day until the day of the wedding Gladys was headline news. She was described as a well-known beauty and an intimate friend of Consuelo Vanderbilt. The Deacon family dramas were resurrected, and lists of Gladys's former suitors were published. Reports stated that at one time or another she had been engaged to Lord Brooke, Antoine de Charette and a Lieutenant Oliphant of the Royal Navy. Her father was wrongly described as a Boston millionaire and it was said that Whistler had painted her just before he died, for which there is no firm evidence. Inevitably the fable that she had been Consuelo's bridesmaid was circulated once more. A *Daily Telegraph* reporter attempted to interview the Duke at his Great College Street home in London, but the Duke had nothing to say.

Privately the Duke of Marlborough was delighted with the

way the engagement was received. The posters in the street announced 'Romance of a Duke', and Lord and Lady Curzon agreed that it was indeed a romance. Blandford and Ivor were charming to their father, Lady Sarah Wilson commented that Gladys was 'very beautiful', and his brother-in-law, Bob Gresley, that she was 'most agreeable to him'. The Duke's mother, Lady Blandford, remained silent for the time being.

The Duke derived much enjoyment from wondering how the 'Irish Duke' was taking the news. 'I hear that old Connaught announced at his table the other day that OB would never think of marrying OM – I hope he has had a colic today.'[1] In Paris Marthe Bibesco was horrified at 'the conquest of an historic castle by one American over another, the latter very lovable and much loved'.[2] On the other hand, the Byzantine historian Gustave Schlumberger was delighted that Gladys, whom he considered 'a marvel of beauty and of intelligence, one of the best known women in Europe . . . with many trump cards in her hand and certainly one of the most elegant charmers I have ever met', had given 'the most dazzling contradiction to the prophets of doom' who thought she had wasted her life, by becoming Duchess of Marlborough.[3]

The wedding was arranged in two parts, a civil ceremony at the British Consulate on 24 June and a religious ceremony at the home of her eccentric millionaire cousin, Eugene Higgins, the following day.

There was a flurry of pre-nuptial entertaining; notably the dinner on 16 June given by Madame Hennessy, known in Proustian circles as 'La jeune Faisanderie'. The Princesse de Polignac was there and Marcel Proust emerged from darkness to attend the dinner, wearing the famous sealskin dressing-gown to his ankles. The Duke of Marlborough met him for the first time, and despite the fact that Gladys was amongst his ardent readers, had no idea who he was. But they got on so well together that the Duke tried to persuade Proust to fulfil a long-held dream to visit England. 'You can go to bed immediately at the Gare du Nord', proposed the Duke. 'You can have a bed on the boat, and you can stay in bed while you are at Blenheim.' Proust was touched by 'so much consideration from a man that I was seeing for the first time'.[4] They discussed illness, and the Duke expounded the theory that the moment one believed oneself well one was well. He urged Proust to repeat to himself that he felt marvellous. Proust tried it, but as he wrote to Princess Soutzo, 'that made me go from bad to worse'.[5] He duly spent the next four months in bed.

It is sad that Proust was not able to accept the Duke's invitation to Blenheim. Miron Grindea, editor of *Adam*, imagined the scene:

> How one would have liked to watch Proust, walking through the splendour of Blenheim Palace, gazing upon the banks of sunlit lawns at Oxford, or just entertaining his English hostesses, thrilled by the enchanting beat of English peacefulness.[6]

After Proust's death in November 1922, André Maurois conducted him on a mythological visit to England in his book *The Chelsea Way*.[7] As Harold Nicolson was quick to point out, however, Proust was unlikely to have gone to Chelsea; he would surely have gone to Sudley Royal, Chatsworth and Blenheim.[8] In *The Chelsea Way* there is a character called Gladys Weston. Though largely based on Mabel Dodge Luhan, she is also invested with some of the eccentricities of the new Duchess of Marlborough.

On 22 June the *Daily Chronicle* announced that complications had arisen over the wedding plans. While the Duke would have settled happily for a civil marriage, Gladys was insisting on a religious one too. For this they were having problems finding a clergyman willing to officiate. The pastor of the American Church in Paris, Dr Goodrich, refused to bless the union, explaining: 'I have conscientious objections to remarrying anyone who has been divorced.' Then an English clergyman declined because the civil marriage at the Consulate, though perfectly legal, was in no sense a French civil marriage, and no French religious service could take place without a French civil one.

Doubts hung over the couple until the eve of the wedding; the headlines got bigger and the press reports longer. On 23 June, Gladys received a *Daily Express* correspondent and told him: 'All I know is that I am going to be married to the Duke of Marlborough on Saturday morning at twelve. I do not even know who is going to marry us.' She also told the reporter: 'You do not know what sort of time I have had the last two weeks. You do not know what it is to be married.' He protested that he did know, indeed that he was married himself, but she brushed his remarks aside and told him that even the destination of the honeymoon was a secret from her. The Duke feared otherwise that the news would leak out.

Lavish presents poured into the rue Auguste Vacquerie, amongst them a piece of Persian embroidery which had been in one of the palaces of the Sultans of Turkey for hundreds of years, a present from the wife of Azzet Pasha, daughter of Sultan Abdul Hamid. Gladys had asked for feathered fans. Eighteen arrived in a variety of different colours. The press were invited to inspect her trousseau of summer dresses from Callot Soeurs, which were hailed as 'fit for a fairy Queen'. Journalists and public relations officers feverishly pursued Gladys right up to the day of the ceremony, each one vying for the exclusive story.

The civil ceremony took place at the British Consulate at eleven o'clock. The Duke of Marlborough arrived from the Travellers' Club in the Champs Elysées in a Rolls-Royce, wearing a grey suit with cut-away tails, but double-breasted and like a frock-coat from the waist upwards. (The suit was thought to herald a new fashion in morning dress.) The Duke swung a cane and smoked a cigarette. He asked waiting press-men what the excitement was and they replied that they were waiting for the Duke's wedding. 'Well I'm Marlborough', he said and handed round cigarettes from a gold case. As he was photographed, he said: 'I have nothing to say – you chaps know more about my wedding than I do. Remember, the invitations are out for the religious wedding tomorrow noon. Be there and you'll see us married.'[9]

Gladys arrived in a navy-blue chemise dress of jersey *du soie*, thickly embroidered down the front, and a large blue hat. The colour blue was chosen as an omen of good luck. Gladys was accompanied by the beautiful Comtesse du Boisrouvray. The Duke kissed his betrothed's hand to the clicking of a battery of cameras. Gladys caught sight of a cine-camera, went up to it and touched it. She asked in French: 'Oh, is that a cinema? I didn't know. I shall come out frightful.'[10]

The bridal pair went inside the Consulate to unite their lives in law in the presence of the Consul-General. Eugene Higgins, Walter Berry, J. T. B. Sewell and Gladys's old family lawyer Léon Renault were the witnesses. What thoughts could have passed through Renault's head? A former Minister of the Interior, he had known Gladys since she was a baby. On the very day of her birth in 1881, he was on his feet reporting to the Committee on the Divorce Bill, that Bill which Dumas *fils* believed put an end to *crimes passionnelles*. He had numbered amongst his clients the Abeille family, and he had delicately dealt with Mrs Baldwin's creditors. Now before he sank into a very deep retirement, he was playing an important support role in a major society event, and he dearly loved talking about society in his sonorous old voice.

Gladys knocked five years off her age on the marriage certificate. After the ceremony she and the Comtesse de Boisrouvray smoked gold-tipped cigarettes and chatted to the Consul-General. Then the Duke took his new Duchess to lunch with the Wimbornes and to Auteuil for an afternoon of racing.

The religious ceremony took place at the height of a fierce heat-wave and drought that had descended on Paris. A wave of bad temper was in the air, but as one overseas correspondent pointed out: 'Post-war Paris would indeed hardly be Paris without a few Saturday or Sunday volleys of revolver shots in the streets or parks.'[11] A number of startling incidents took place that weekend, but nothing matched the spectacle in the drawing-room of 7 Place d'Iéna.

At the last minute, the Reverend T. H. Wright, 'a tall, lanky Scot, in rusty clerical garb', who was the rector of the Scottish Presbyterian Church in Paris, agreed to conduct the service. He stood at the end of a long drawing-room under a bower of green branches and white flowers with a horseshoe of white gardenias above his head. Eugene Higgins, who owned the house, was a bachelor with a bizarre collection of oil paintings of nudes. Every year he scoured the salons for the biggest and best he could find. Not long before she died, Gladys's mother had paid a visit to this room and was surprised to be confronted by four huge pictures of naked women, 'enough to put you off sex for life'. Thus, as he pronounced the sentences in a slow, monotonous voice, the poor rector was obliged to keep his head buried in his books to avoid a diverting confrontation.

Because of the stifling weather the drawing-room became insufferably hot and a number of the guests took refuge in a garden. A diverse company was gathered, including Princess George of Greece, Edith Wharton, the Princesse de Polignac,

Elsie de Wolfe, Mrs Robert Woods Bliss, Mr & Mrs Sheldon Whitehouse, Philippe Berthelot, Marshal Foch, Anatole France and Comtesse Anna de Noailles. Gladys's sister Dorothy attended, but Edith refused and no members of the Churchill family were present. Walter Berry acted as groomsman and Gladys was attended by the Comtesse de Boisrouvray's twelve-year-old daughter, Christine.

Gladys wore a picture dress of gold and silver brocade tissue in a classical style with a veil worn off the face, lent to her by the Duchess of Camastra, wife of her erstwhile suitor. The veil had been a gift from Napoleon to his wife. Gladys made an early stand for the feminist cause by insisting that the word 'obey' be omitted from the responses. The buffet was held in the garden and Eugene Higgins became increasingly agitated as he watched high heels sinking into his lawns, and canes, umbrellas and parasols being speared in the grass to free eager hands for the ice-cool champagne. One rather special guest was Irma, Gladys's old nurse, now aged seventy-nine. She arranged the veil before the ceremony and declined wedding cake in favour of a piece of bread.

'We are both awfully poor', replied the Duke to questions about the wedding present he had given Gladys. 'Oh, don't mention anything about that in the newspapers. One should not mention those things now, especially in the English press, with the miners starving. What will the miners think, reading about wedding presents, jewellery costing £50,000? It makes them dissatisfied, it creates trouble. You can say I gave the bride a motor-car as a wedding present.'[12]

A long photographic session ensued on the tennis court. One brave cameraman asked the couple to 'adopt an affectionate pose'. With some difficulty, Marlborough was prevailed upon to hold Gladys's hand. After standing motionless for a long exposure, she exclaimed: 'It's like a cow watching a train go past.'[13]

At four o'clock the Duke and Duchess left for their secret honeymoon, which was generally assumed to be in the South of France. Gladys wore a going-away costume of pearl grey *crêpe de chine*, with a long skirt, a black hat with long trailing feathers and a cape of flowing black crêpe. As they drove away in their motor-car, Gladys bade farewell to her freedom.

PART THREE

Blenheim:
The Pursuit of Profit
and Possessions

Chapter Sixteen

BLENHEIM

The Duke of Marlborough and Gladys returned from their honeymoon on 28 July 1921. As their car swept up the long drive to Blenheim and approached what Lord Randolph Churchill called 'the finest view in England', Gladys must have felt again the strange apprehension in the contrast between this and earlier visits. Never on previous visits had she signed the Visitors Book. Now the beginning of a new brief era in the palace's long history was marked by the two rather formal names side by side, 'Marlborough' and 'G. Marlborough'.

One of Gladys's first acts was to take a copy of *Burke's Peerage* from the shelf and work out exactly where she fitted in the pattern of Marlborough descent. Though Sunny was the ninth Duke, she was the twelfth person to bear the name of Duchess of Marlborough. As Duchess she was also mistress of Blenheim; she once declared to Epstein, 'I married a house not a man.'[1]

Blenheim Palace had survived many vicissitudes since its construction between the years 1705 and 1722. The celebrated gift of Queen Anne to the victor of the Battle of Blenheim, its architects were Sir John Vanbrugh and Nicholas Hawksmoor, with suitable embellishments coming later from Grinling Gibbons and Sir William Chambers. The task of creating the gardens and the lake was entrusted to Capability Brown. The lake sprang into existence when Brown threw a dam across one of the outlets. The first Duke was astonished when he saw the result, and Brown is said to have replied: 'Yes, my Lord Duke, I think I have made the River Thames blush today.'[2]

David Green, the authority on Blenheim, has called it 'the supreme example of the style of architecture known as English

Baroque'. And the Duke himself wrote in 1914:

> Blenheim is the most splendid relic of the age of Anne, and there is no building in Europe, except Versailles, which so perfectly preserves its original atmosphere.[3]

The seventh and eighth Dukes dispersed many of Blenheim's treasures, but Sunny was able to rectify much of the damage with the aid of the Vanderbilt money. Capability Brown had surrounded the palace with grass, but Sunny brought in Achille Duchêne, an architect and landscape designer, from France to repave the grand northern entrance court. Work began in 1900. On the east side of the palace where the private apartments are, a sunken garden, known as the Italian garden, was created and completed in June 1922.

During Gladys's period as Duchess, the western slope, which she called 'the crooked lawn', was being tackled. Work began in 1925 and she took a keen interest in its progress. As Sunny saw it, the architect's problem was 'to make a liaison between the façade of Vanbrugh and the water-line of the lake made by Brown'. He continued:

> To reconcile these conflicting ideas is difficult. The difficulty is not diminished when you remember that the façade of the house is limited and the line of the lake is limitless. As an example, if you turn your back to the lake and look at the façade, your parterre, basin etc. is in scale to the façade, but if you look at the same parterre from the rotunda to the lake it is out of scale with the panorama.[4]

The interior of the palace was grand and imposing and the state apartments were much the same then as they are today, hung with portraits and the famous Blenheim tapestries. Only in those days the rooms made no concession for the modern flood of tourists. It is well known that the dining-room at Blenheim was a ludicrous distance from the kitchen. Food had to travel sixty yards along a stone-flagged passage, up a lift and then fifteen yards by hand before reaching the ducal table – plenty of opportunity for hot fare to become cold. Another archaic feature was the absence of a telephone. Only after a protracted struggle was one installed in 1925. It was put in the gunroom with an extension to the office, and it was rumoured, falsely, that the Duke never made use of it.

Blenheim life was conducted on an imposing scale. There were forty servants inside the palace and as many without, though these numbers multiplied dramatically when guests came bringing their own entourages. The footmen were all said to be at least six feet tall and were attired in maroon coats decorated with a considerable amount of silver braid. Their hair was powdered daily with a mixture of violet powder and flour. A hunting establishment at Bladon, staffed by ten men, looked after the twenty thoroughbred hunters and the twenty carriage horses. There was a fire brigade of which the Duke was extremely proud. A fire was announced while a game of cricket was in progress. The players adjourned for an hour, put out the fire and resumed play. Twenty gamekeepers took care of the shooting and Lord Carnarvon recalled how sternly they were treated. The head keeper was ill one day and sent the Duke a message to say that he had entrusted the business of the day to his deputy: 'My compliments to my head keeper', replied the Duke. 'Will you please inform him that the lower orders are never ill.'

Lord Birkenhead recorded that 6,943 rabbits were killed in one day at Blenheim, the greatest number in the annals of shooting. He also remembered an afternoon when politics was being discussed, and, more specifically, the rise of the people. Suddenly the Duke pointed out of the window and screeched: 'Look, the people!' The other guests assumed that nothing less than revolution could have occurred, but when they looked from the window, the sight that greeted them was a hunched old man making his solitary way across the lawn.

In the best landowners' tradition, the Duke held a meeting in his farm office every Friday. Each bailiff was heard in turn, and reported how the cattle, cows, sheep, pigs and poultry were faring. The meetings began at 10 a.m. and could last until 3 p.m., while the prospect of lunches getting cold was ignored. If the Duke received unsatisfactory replies, he was not unaccustomed to burst into a rage.

Some years later, Gladys invited Lily de Clermont-Tonnerre to Blenheim. Lily wrote much about her visit, giving a French view of the place. She noted that Blenheim was heated by £2,500 worth of coal each year. The staff worked quietly and invisibly and Lily found that the 'majestic silence' of the place got on her nerves:

English servants and Chinese servants preserve the same silence, which is almost nerve-racking. I heard the fire crackling in my room without having seen it lighted, the curtains were drawn and breakfast was brought up without my being wakened, and at ten o'clock *The Times* was insinuated under my eyes. When I went down to the ground-floor, a groom of the chambers would murmur: 'Her Grace is in the Sir Peter Lely Saloon' or in the 'Long Library'.

By eight o'clock in the morning the lawn was rolled, the dead leaves removed and the flower stands filled with fresh flowers.[5]

This was the atmosphere which greeted the new Duchess. It was a cold world, peopled by Spencer-Churchills. Gladys had been acquainted with the Duke's sons, Lord Blandford and Lord Ivor Churchill, since they were boys. She and Blandford only tolerated each other at the best of times, but Ivor was a friend because they shared an interest in art. The Duke also found Blandford and his wife difficult, as Gladys noted:

Poor Sunny used his most deferential attitude to Bl & Mary. Poor thing, he is like a *pique-assiette* with them and so happy if the slightest attention is given him by them.[6]

Lady Randolph Churchill had died and been buried while Sunny and Gladys were on their honeymoon, but her sons, Winston and Jack, were frequently at the palace. Her elevation to Duchess did not endear her to Winston. If she tried to enlist his assistance on some project, his reaction was: 'You go ahead and organize it. I'll help.' Thereafter, she recalled, 'he'd leave you in the boiling-pot'.[7] Of Winston's wife Clementine, Gladys said: 'You couldn't discuss a thing with her. She had no opinions, only convictions.'[8] His brother, Jack, she felt, was always much in awe of Winston. On the other hand, she liked Lady Gwendoline, known as 'Goonie', who found she had to live with the Churchills and had accepted her lot with good heart.

Gladys became a firm friend of Sunny's intuitive mother, Albertha, Lady Blandford, who believed that Gladys understood her son's complicated character. And never far from the scene was another powerful Churchill in the shape of Sunny's aunt, Lady Sarah Wilson. In her day Lady Sarah had taken part in the Relief of Mafeking and had been captured by the Boers. Proud and authoritative and very much a Churchill, it was said of her: 'She could never resist a pungent comment or a withering gibe.'

Soon after her arrival at Blenheim, Gladys accompanied the Duke to a nearby fair. It was the first of many efforts made by Sunny to integrate his new wife into local society. In 1925, Lady Lee of Fareham wrote that 'they both try to do their duty by the county, although somewhat untactfully. She, however, has not yet been generally accepted or even much called upon.'[9]

It was very difficult. Oxfordshire society was stiff with county conservatism. They saw no reason why they should take this rather eccentric new Duchess to their hearts. There were confused views about her bohemian life in Paris and they were not unaware that she had been involved with the Duke one way or another for a considerable time. Nor did the villagers welcome Gladys with open arms. They had been very fond of Consuelo and felt the Duke had been unkind to her.

Some took it to the extreme of rudeness. One neighbour, Colonel John Eastwood, who lived at Woodstock, was invited to lunch at Blenheim, but declined with the excuse that he would be in London that day. Unfortunately the Duke rode by after lunch and spotted him in his garden. A terrible row ensued. For some years Sunny strove hard to have Gladys presented at court. He approached his cousin the Duchess of Devonshire, Mistress of the Robes to Queen Mary, but she was disdainful and said to him: 'Oh! No, Sunny. I really couldn't go that far.' Eventually he prevailed upon Lady Birkenhead to make the presentation. Lady Birkenhead was somewhat surprised to see the Marlborough state coach and six horses draw up outside her London home on the evening of 13 June 1923. After dinner, they made their way to Buckingham Palace where Lady Birkenhead made the presentation. Gladys wore a gown made from cloth of silver with a sixteenth-century train of venetian lace. After her curtsey to 'King Log' and Queen Mary she sat in the front row with the other Duchesses making disparaging remarks about the clothes and lack of coordination of the young debutantes who followed her. A few weeks later, on 21 July, she noted in her diary:

Garden Party at Buc Pal to which H.M. doesn't invite me

because terrified of articles published re divorced men's wives going to court! ! !

So the razing of the court fortress was not an unqualified success.

One person in Oxfordshire who did accept Gladys was Lady Ottoline Morrell, half-sister of the Duke of Portland. The legendary Lady Ottoline was one of the most intelligent women of her day; married to the brewer, and Liberal M.P., Philip Morrell, she was the friend of Augustus John, Bertrand Russell, D. H. Lawrence, Henry Lamb, Aldous Huxley and others. At Garsington Manor and in Bloomsbury she kept alive what Julian Huxley called 'a real salon – one of an intimate and infinitely attractive character'.

Lady Ottoline told her daughter that Gladys was 'the only intelligent woman in Oxfordshire'. The Duke of Marlborough thought Lady Ottoline magnificent, and she was a favourite with Gladys, who jokingly referred to her as 'Mrs Brewer Morrell'. She admired Lady Ottoline's individuality and re-called: 'She wore large floppy hats when everyone else wore neat little ones.'[10] She remembered that Lady Ottoline used to drop things here and there as she walked about. Her friends were kind and picked them up for her; 'You could follow her path by the things she dropped', she said. They shared an interest in cats, and Gladys gave a Siamese cat to Lady Ottoline's daughter. Appropriately Julian Morrell named it Malbrouk. In June 1922, Gladys asked Ottoline a favour:

> Do you think I cd later on send you one of my cats to make Malbrouk's nearer acquaintance? The pasha of my Siamese harem has fled to the open country these 2 months & is evidently lost forever.[11]

Unfortunately, Malbrouk proved 'too near a relation' and Gladys had to look elsewhere.

It was to Ottoline that Gladys confided the difficulties she had when trying to give a party. On 10 June 1922, there was a large party at Blenheim at which the Lansdownes, the Birkenheads, the Beaverbrooks, the Winston Churchills, Lady Irene Curzon, Lady Eleanor Smith and others were present. Another guest was the Christian Scientist Victor Cazalet, a frequent visitor to the palace, a young man with a promising political career ahead which ended prematurely in Sikorski's aeroplane during World War II. He suggested various Oxford undergraduates that Gladys might like to invite, amongst them Lord Morven Cavendish-Bentinck, Lady Ottoline's nephew, and Lord David Cecil. Both delayed replying for two weeks so that their refusals reached Gladys just two days before the dinner. Gladys wrote in despair to Lady Ottoline:

> Entertaining is at all times fraught with discomfort, but not to be left time to find another man without evident rudeness to him by an eleventh hour invitation is really rather trying, don't you think so?[12]

The Duke was equally indignant that Lord David Cecil had replied to Gladys in the third person and given no more substantial excuse than that he was engaged elsewhere. Despite a bad start, the evening ended in success. The band was excellent and Gladys danced until two in the morning.

Also staying at the palace that weekend was a friend from Gladys's Paris days, and he certainly did not enjoy himself. This was the artist Jean Marchand, whom Frankie Birrell described as 'a charming character'. Gladys had known him for years and owned two of his pictures, one of which was dedicated to her. She had often spoken of Blenheim and insisted that he should come and see it. Marchand was a vague and humble man; in the Great War he had served as a guard on the railways. He was very shy at the thought of his journey to Oxfordshire. Nevertheless he survived a chaotic journey to England and took the train for Woodstock. When he arrived at the station, the footman recognized him by his beard and asked him for his luggage. The artist handed him a small paper parcel and off they went.

When Marchand set eyes on Blenheim it was, in the words of his fellow artist Paul Maze, 'as if he had been dropped on the moon'.[13] The huge doors and the Great Hall bewildered and frightened him. His little parcel was taken to his room. In the evening Marchand prepared to come down to dinner at eight, but suddenly he lost his nerve. He ran for the lavatory and hid there. Gongs sounded but drew no response for him. Finally, at ten o'clock Gladys had his dinner sent up to him. The next morning she said to him: 'Où étiez-vous?' 'J'étais perdu,' he replied. Then she looked after him and showed him parts of the palace, at which he gazed in awe and fascination. But he was

not sad to escape from Blenheim. Gladys knew that Lady Ottoline wanted to meet him and took steps to arrange it. 'He looks
very frail, poor man', she warned, 'but gentle & delightful as
ever.'[14]

A continuing preoccupation during Gladys's first year at Blenheim was the condition of Bob Trevelyan. He was still wavering
and suffering from an inability to write. Gladys tried to help
him and even took him to the doctor. As Virginia Woolf reported to Vanessa Bell:

> Poor Bob Trevelyan – poor Bob Trevelyan – Well if one
> meets Bessy at the 1917 Club on a cold afternoon with her
> handbag and her great boots and her nice red Dutch nose, and
> her liberal sympathies – one does fall in love with the
> Duchess of Marlborough. I did at once.[15]

By January 1922 the situation had improved and Virginia
was able to inform E. M. Forster that Trevelyan was 'delicious . . . hungry greedy – growling – and divine'. She explained: 'His love for the Duchess (this is Gordon Square gossip)
has subdued and softened him, and he's having his arteries vivi-
fied in order to write more poetry, and out he pulls, as usual,
manuscripts – in fact he was bustling off to see a new
publisher.'[16]

Thereafter Bob Trevelyan, left with what Virginia Woolf
called 'the legacy of Gladys Deacon', adopted a more general
interest in the female sex. Nicky Mariano, Berenson's amanu-
ensis, wrote: 'From then on he became a sort of *Cherubino*
always infatuated in a schoolboyish manner with some young
woman, usually repulsed because of his uncouth manners and
ever yearning for an ideal fulfilment.'[17] For example, a female
visitor to I Tatti once met him after a swim. She announced that
she had come across 'un espèce de sauvage tout nu qui se
promène de long en large comme si c'était la chose la plus
naturelle du monde'.[18]

Before Christmas 1921 Gladys entered with zest into the running of the Blenheim estates. She took her place with potato-
pickers and laboured with them for an hour. In December
Sunny, who had been somewhat unwell, became a grandfather
for the first time when Lady Blandford gave birth to a daughter.
Less than a month later he was informed that he was also about

to become a father again. Gladys was miserable at the thought, and wrote in her diary for Monday 6 January:

> Ill all day & every day & so depressed! This poor thing so unwanted & has a pretty bad outlook to face. Why does it want to come!

A few days later, she wrote again:

> I am so sorry I am going to have a baby. I have nothing to give it. Its father wont want to leave it anything. What is it coming for!

By Friday Gladys was utterly depressed, frightened at feeling so ill and imagining she was about to die. Ominously she wrote: 'All sorts of accidents'. The next day her condition deteriorated: 'So ill it seemed death was coming. If only it wd. Feel so afraid & so alone.'

On Sunday Gladys had a miscarriage and was greatly relieved. When her strength returned to her, she noted:

> Glad it's over – I don't want a child. I don't want to stay here, so what wd I have done with it. Very lonely but the nurse is company.

It was some months before Gladys's health and spirits returned to her, but with the coming of summer, she began to enjoy all the good things that Blenheim could offer. She took drives in the park with Sunny and saw the may trees and chestnuts in full bloom. Together they lunched with Professor Lindemann* at Christ Church in Oxford and saw one of the Eights Week bump races. Gladys noted: 'Whole scene looked like a sporting picture.' At the end of May they spent some days in London and attended a dance which the Duke clearly much enjoyed. 'Sunny much to the fore and dancing strong.' At Whitsun they drove to Charlton for lunch with the Birkenheads, where there was a cricket match: Oxford versus 'Lord Chancellor and friends'. On Whit Monday Gladys distributed the prizes after a fête at Blenheim. During these months Gladys seemed content; she and Sunny were on good terms and enjoying things together.

On 12 June 1922, in the late afternoon, Gladys and Sunny went out on the lake for the first time. Gladys was enchanted: 'The pond lilies are closed & their leaves curled at the edges.

---

* Professor F. A. Lindemann (1886–1957), created Lord Cherwell 1941.

Beautiful extatic flowers! The accacias gleam all white among the green leaves.'

Restored to health, Gladys was able to resume her riding. While the Duke drove out in a buggy she would gallop down the monument avenue or attempt the jumps in the school. Sometimes they rode together, and on one memorable occasion Sunny noticed that the nether regions of his estate were serving a village couple well as a love-nest. From the security of his saddle, he sent them packing with some well-chosen words.

One of their favourite neighbours, Professor Lindemann, has written an account of one of Gladys's parties at Blenheim that June: 'The Blenheim dinner and dance was most amusing. They had got H. G. Wells of all people, and the Duchess made him dance, a most comic business.'[19] H. G. Wells was an interesting guest to find at Blenheim, and certainly Gladys's inspiration. The professor was surprised too to discover there 'numerous weird people like Jimmy Rothschild'. At another party, the 'Prof' played a joke on his fellow guests, which he much enjoyed relating. He put a roll of Debussy back to front on to the pianola and persuaded them it was one of the composer's more disturbed works.[20]

On 25 June Sunny and Gladys celebrated a year of marriage with a visit to Sunday matins and, on the way to Black Bourton, they had a picnic, the standard of which put Sunny into a grumpy mood. That night Gladys noted: 'Sunny reads Napoleon before dinner, after dinner & in bed.' The next day things cheered up and they attended the Christ Church Ball. Gladys loved the blue and white striped tent and the clusters of white and pink lights. The whole scene was 'quite Venetian'.

After a sentimental visit to the cowyards to photograph 'the poor Friesans' before they went to market, Gladys accompanied Sunny to London for the July season of receptions, concerts, weddings and dances. Again they were happy and one night they kept each other up until 2.45 a.m. laughing at their own jokes. They were present at the two big society weddings which took place on consecutive days in the middle of the month. Gladys wore a dress of tobacco brown jersey cloth and a black picture hat for Lord Porchester's wedding to Catherine Wendell. The guests included Lord Louis Mountbatten and Miss Edwina Ashley, who were themselves married the following day at St

Margaret's Westminster. Gladys and Sunny gave the Mount-battens a manicure set to add to their presents, which Gladys thought compared badly to the Porchesters'. 'Huge crowds in the church', she noted, '& Royal crowds outside. Took ¾ of an hour from St Margaret's to Brook House. Never saw as many police.'

At the end of the month Gladys prepared for a holiday with Sunny in her beloved France. She informed Lady Ottoline that she was both nervous and enthusiastic:

> It's been a great strain being always among foreigners & always speaking English & I am looking forward to going home – rapturously.... I do hope that the 'intransigeant' attitude of France won't make unpleasantness & that having married an Englishman I won't have to feel like an exile there too![21]

Gladys and Sunny made a smooth voyage across the Channel on 8 August, and met Lady Irene Curzon on the boat. Arriving in Paris, Gladys called on Irma, whom she found 'looking very well, but only able to move miserably'. They dined with Walter Berry at the Café de Paris and he joined them and the Abbé Mugnier the next day for lunch at the Plaza. At Fontainebleau Gladys was interested to see the rooms Napoleon had occupied as Consul. From there, they proceeded to Mont-Dore to begin a cure.

Days passed quietly amid cures, vapour douches, picnics and car rides, with only a little anxiety that Sunny was to be ill again, when he began to get twinges of sciatica. One night they went to the cinema, where Gladys observed 'lots of extra-ordinarily common, middle class people dancing'. At the end of the month Gladys spent three days in bed and then they trav-elled to Geneva and Montreux. On 2 September Gladys noted:

> We were to leave by 10 o'cl. Oberland but the weather tonight is rainy & cold and so we decide – or rather Sunny decides, for he does the deciding that we are to leave at 3 instead.

At Clarens, Gladys went exploring to try to find traces of Jean-Jacques Rousseau, who spent his youth in the vicinity, but with no success. She was disappointed to find it 'the ugliest place I've seen in Switzerland and like the new suburbs of Nice'. But she enjoyed Interlaken and was much absorbed in watching the waterfalls that fell a thousand feet from the steep mountains into the valley below:

> There like a vision of hell a huge swift shaft of water comes through the wall of rock, falls into a basin, from it into a narrow corridor at an indescribable speed and down another fall into a second basin where the water is churned into mighty eddies, then down into a long precipitous slide into yet another huge pocket and out of sight.

Gladys was forever in awe of the wonderful feats of nature which confronted her; for instance, at the Jungfrau: 'Our first view of the terrors of an ice mountain, a precipitous descent down a sheer cliff & a glacier yawning at our feet, immense, deadly, overhung by huge cones of ice.'

Whereas Gladys entered with zest into the spirit of the holiday, Sunny was more reserved. He was put out by a particularly hearty Swiss chauffeur who insisted on shaking hands with him at Grindelwald, and he declared that nothing would induce him to go near a glacier. Gladys succeeded in luring him into a grotto, where she left him, while she crossed the glacier, roped to a guide. She wrote in her diary:

> We do it in half the ordinary time so as not to keep my old tyrant waiting too long & I get boiling hot. It's a fine sight & exhilarating feeling to go up 500 feet in abt 18 minutes, walking into the steps cut into the ice along the edge of yawning crevasses.

From Interlaken they went to Bern where they had uncomfortable rooms, indifferent food and very bad wine. 'We go out for a walk in the drizzle and hate everything we see. Even the bears in the pit look philosophically disgusted.'

Gladys was delighted to be able to spend a few days in Paris on the way home. She had her side locks electrically curled, they lunched at the Ritz, inspected the Broglie Rembrandt at Duveen's gallery and had dinner with Walter Berry. Then suddenly Gladys caught 'the grippe' and so stayed on while Sunny went home.

When she was a little better, Gladys had the chance to see old friends and re-live for a while the life that made her happy. Lily de Clermont-Tonnerre told her that the manners of the masses were deteriorating and that there was a 'general disorganization towards a lower standard of civilization'.

Her writer friends told her they were depressed and complained that their colleagues' writing was '*de parti-pris*, thin and boring'. Edmond Jaloux said he was now editing a new Dada review since that at least amused him, and Paul Valéry announced that he was coming to Oxford presently to receive an honour. As for the painters, they had been at a loss to ascertain 'lequel est le vrai but' ever since Cézanne died in October 1906.[22]

On 25 September Gladys returned to London by the midday train. 'I felt no more emotion at leaving my dear France', she wrote, 'than if I'd been a trunk.' But at Charing Cross a deep depression fell over her. The footman came to meet her but did not have the carriage. Then she found that she was not expected at 15 Great College Street as her wire had not arrived. She was forced to dine off cold meat and salad since the housekeeper informed her the shops were closed. Her mind went back to a couple she had spotted at the station with whom she could compare her lot: 'Saw a woman at the station met by a man – she danced with joy & he seemed entranced.'

Gladys remained in a state of 'ennui noir' for days.

Chapter Seventeen

THE USUAL LIFE

The depression which overcame Gladys on her return to London was long-lasting. The contrast between life in Paris which she adored, despite her complaints about the noise, dirt and, surprisingly, the cooking, and her present existence hit her acutely. Suffering from a bad cold, she stayed in London, dreading the return to Blenheim. 'The mere thought of those huge rooms makes my acheing legs ache more',[1] she wrote to Lady Ottoline Morrell. By 27 September, she was so depressed that she almost gave up: 'I wonder how long it is before I go.' The following Saturday, however, Sunny collected her and took her to Blenheim by the 4.45 train.

Gladys was briefly cheered by the sight of a white frost, only to sink deeper into gloom. Her diary entries grew shorter until finally all she could write was 'Ah me!' Blenheim in the autumn was awash with shooting folk, or, as she put it, 'murderous with heavy people & talk of guns, game etc.'. Again the contrast between life in France and this intellectual wilderness was brought vividly home to her. The little statue given her by Rodin sat on a low table in the first state room, but the palace guests passed it by, neither knowing what it was, nor caring.

Fortunately, Gladys made what she called 'a grand and useful discovery'. By pruning the roses she was able to keep out of the way of everyone. One Saturday she succeeded in being alone from lunchtime until 6.30. When eventually every rose was pruned, she began to search for another line of escape, but it was a while before the solution came to her.

The wretchedness of Gladys's life was further aggravated by a tedious religious controversy. On 21 October the 'Bish row' began. This was one of those unnecessary issues which seized the imagination of the press and caused unpleasantness all round. As Lord-Lieutenant of Oxfordshire the Duke was an ex-officio member of the Oxford Diocesan Conference, according to its own constitution. The Bishop of Oxford, whom Gladys already disliked and referred to as the 'disgusting old Bish', took it into his head to publicly request the Duke not to attend any of the Conference's meetings on the grounds that he had not 'full status as a communicant', having been divorced and now re-married. By his act, the bishop suggested that the Duke's marriage to Gladys was not recognized by the Church.

As it happened, the Duke was regularly accepted as a communicant in parishes in Oxfordshire and London and since he had expressed no wish to attend the Conference in the first place, the bishop's attack was in somewhat questionable taste. The press accused him of making 'a public pariah' of the Duke, and Albertha, Lady Blandford, an Ulster Hamilton and a staunch Protestant, wrote to Gladys: 'I think the Bishop of Oxford behaved very wrongly, it was not religion, or religious what he did.'

Gladys was livid at the 'monstrous & uncalled for attack by the one now called here "Burgundy Burge" '. She wrote to Lady Ottoline that the issue would have been more appropriate B.C., and reeked of 1858. Once again the attack had been inspired by the Duke's enemies led this time by Lord Saye and Sele, an Oxford county councillor, nicknamed by Gladys 'Lord Stay and Steal'. She declared herself 'wounded, incensed, indignant beyond words'.[2]

Gladys was not content to remain silent and enlisted the help of her novelist friend, Mrs Boileau, to append her signature to a letter to the bishop. This would have added weight since Ethel Boileau was the daughter and grand-daughter of men of the cloth and had only been married once. The letter – which survives in draft – shows Gladys's clear reasoning and is surprisingly relevant even fifty-five years later:

My Ld Bish
Fraction re the Duke of Marlborough impels me as a member of the Church of England which up to now has prided herself on the freedom from bigotry, to ask you if you are aware of the serious and growing dissatisfaction among practising and

thinking members of the church with the Bishop's attitude towards divorce.

We can find no justification for the rigid attitude taken up by the heads of the church and in a free & democratic country, my Lord, those who rule exist by suffrance of the people. There is no right divine either in Church or state & the voice of God & of his Christ speaks as directly & clearly to the hearts of the humblest members of this Church as to his Bishops and priests.

I sometimes wonder & with despair if the priests of the Anglican Church know anything of the needs of the human heart – of its bitter loneliness – its painful struggle after right doing & its dumb despairs nearer to man in the tremendous mystery of the Sacrament. We ask that they sd help us to live more bravely, courageously and fully, & they hold out empty forms from which all life has long departed – a rigid ecclesiasticism which is far from the tender & merciful spirit of Christ our Master. My Lord, that Master turned once to his disciples and told them that 'The Sabbath was made for man & not man for the Sabbath.' I am impelled to ask you 'is the Church of England made for man – or is man made for the Church of England?'

For we are rapidly coming to the parting of the ways. Unless the Church of England sees fit to recognise the power of the English Courts to grant divorces to those living lives of misery & loneliness – or herself institutes eclisiastical [*sic*] Courts to grant annulments of marriages such as is the practice in the Roman Communion, then by her deliberate action she will drive from her an increasingly large body of men & women who will go reluctantly and with sorrow – but who do not intend to submit to tyranny & the dictates of a particular order.

Yours is the Supreme Office of bringing God nearer to men in the tremendous mystery of the Sacrament. You may elect to withhold it on a point of ecclisiastical law from those who feel the need of it – the responsibility is yours.

Christ laid down no laws as to who sd receive it – He only said 'Do this in remembrance of me.' . . .[3]

The outburst died down as suddenly as it had flared up, but it became a further incentive for the melancholy Duke to seek admission to the Roman Catholic church.

The last months of 1922 passed with a round of weekend visits and Blenheim house-parties. Sunny and Gladys went to Yorkshire, passing the 'Rotherham man-eating factories' in the train. They stayed at Wentworth Woodhouse with the Fitz-williams and occupied rooms lately used by the King and Queen. Sunny insisted that the sheets should be changed as the mattresses were damp, and for much of the visit Gladys felt 'too seedy to get up'. On 23 November she took her seat on the Duchesses' bench at the State Opening of Parliament, but her enjoyment of ducal status was somewhat marred by the scornful attitude of the other Duchesses.

At Christmas Gladys trod the neighbourhood visiting the poor and the sick with little enthusiasm. Sunny got a sore throat and a temper to match, and on Christmas Day, Gladys woke at six in the morning and wept. Sunny gave her a foot muff and Lady Sarah Wilson a workbag. They were the only gifts she got. On 27 December she sat alone in the palace as rain torrented down outside. She considered the two-year-old marriage to which she had so long aspired:

> Most interesting to me is Sunny's rudeness to me. Not very marked in public yet – but that will come. I am glad because I am sick of life here. Convention & commonplace & selfishness alone voice themselves over us. Quelle vie! But we will separate perhaps before long & I will then go away for good & ever.

1923 dawned quietly and Gladys walked in the garden, discovering primroses and supervising the rose-planting. She remained at Blenheim feeling listless and bored. In February she accompanied Sunny to London for the second Opening of Parliament in four months. 'It's becoming a bad habit', she noted. They did not go to the traditional Londonderry eve of session party out of deference to Lord Birkenhead. They took their places in the South Lantern of Westminster Abbey for the wedding of the Duke of York to Lady Elizabeth Bowes-Lyon in April 1923 at which Gladys was nearly frozen. They gave the bridegroom a decorated silver inkstand. A month later they were included in the house-party at Wentworth, when the

Prince of Wales came to stay. Royal occasions inevitably caused problems. When Queen Victoria's granddaughter, the Infanta Beatrix, and her aviator husband Don Alfonso de Borbon came to Blenheim, they insisted on departing at six in the morning. Gladys and Sunny had to be up and dressed to bid them farewell.

After a visit to Holland in June, which Gladys found 'as dirty as any other country', she settled once more at Blenheim. There was a memorable house-party that July, during the midst of a heat-wave, when the temperature sometimes reached ninety degrees in the shade. Gladys gathered the Birkenheads, the Winston Churchills, the Merry del Vals, Prince Paul of Yugoslavia, 'Shelagh', Duchess of Westminster and others and invited a new literary friend, Lytton Strachey. She enjoyed talking to him or rather listening to him. 'He was a pontiff, so you listened and kept quiet',[4] she explained. After his visit Strachey wrote to Mary Hutchinson that nobody except Gladys had been particularly interesting. It was really the palace which captured his imagination:

> I wish it were mine. It is enormous, but one would not feel it too big. The grounds are beautiful too, and there is a bridge over a lake which positively gives one an erection. Most of the guests played tennis all day and bridge all night, so that (apart from eating and drinking) they might as well have been at Putney.[5]

When Gladys sent Strachey a photograph she took of the house-party, he was amused: 'The ladies' skirts look oddly long and the tip of Winston's nose comes out beautifully.'[6]

As a further antidote to her loneliness Gladys invited her old friend Epstein to come and stay to sculpt a head of the Duke. They had kept in touch over the years and sometimes Gladys had visited his studio in London. Epstein was one of her most important links with the art world at this time, and through him she also became acquainted with Matthew Smith. She bought a picture of red and white flowers in a vase from Smith for £50 in October 1927.*

Epstein arrived at the palace on 27 July, and Gladys took him round to decide where the Duke's bust should be placed. Finally

---

* Sold at Christie's on 17 November 1978 for £3,800.

they settled on a niche in the entrance hall. At dinner that evening there was a heated discussion as to what dress the Duke should wear. Gladys noted: 'Epstein & I are of firm opinion it must be strictly modern – *de l'époque*. Sunny leans towards the picturesque because he hates the hard line of collar.'

This was not the only difference between the sculptor and his sitter. Epstein tended to dress in the bohemian clothes of his calling and the rumour soon spread that the Duke had ordered the staff to have all of them laundered. His casual appearance led to his being apprehended several times by the gamekeepers, and he greatly enjoyed informing them that he was a guest at the palace, which, as he wrote, 'always produced a comic fore-head salute of flunkeys and apologies'.[7] It was however made quite clear by the Duke that Epstein was a guest of the Duchess and not of his own.

Differences arose at every turn. Gladys liked to have an organist come to play an hour of Bach in the morning to inspire Epstein in his work. This irritated Marlborough, who preferred jazz and announced that his idea of a great man was Luigi, who ran a fashionable night-club. One day the Duke showed Epstein the chapel at Blenheim and the sculptor cast his eye over a building where there was little or no evidence of Christianity. He said as much to the Duke, who retorted: 'The Marlboroughs are worshipped here.'

During the next ten days Sunny sat regularly, often for as long as five hours in a day. By the end of the month Gladys noted: 'The Bust takes on a great fineness of modelling & surface since yesterday.' Sunny was exhausted by the long sit-tings, and this contributed to his general irritability. As the bust neared completion, Gladys agreed with Sunny that he looked a decade older than his fifty-two years.

The issue of the base of the bust now arose, Marlborough wanting to look like a Roman with bare shoulders, while Gladys and Epstein insisted on a costume. A row ensued and Epstein gave up after 'an acrimonious debate which ended in ill-temper on both sides'. The bust therefore remained a head and neck until 1926, when Gladys asked him to finish it. Before the row, Epstein attempted a second study of Gladys. This is a particu-larly remarkable head, because she allowed herself to be depicted with the ravages of the paraffin wax in full evidence. It confirms her love for what is real in art over a desire to be portrayed in a more conventional way; and it was a head she much liked.

When work on Marlborough's bust began again, things went more smoothly. The Duke agreed to pose in his Garter robes and at Gladys's suggestion, the hands were added. On 18 January 1926 Sunny wrote:

He is getting on famously and he will do a fine work. The man has immense talent and is in a good temper and very pleased with the result of his efforts.[8]

Marlborough wrote again as the sculptor's work approached completion:

We have discarded the chain [collar of the Order of the Garter] as it will be in the way – and spoil the lines of the cloak – which are good. The hands are coming out well – and are very Epsteiny – but at his best – E has taken great pains and I see a great improvement in his sense of beauty. I am tired from the ordeal and I shall be thankful when I am free – He keeps the cloak but does not work on the Garter badge. He wanted my uniform coat – but I told him that my servant wd give notice if I did not bring it back.[9]

When completed, the bust was placed in the entrance hall at Blenheim where it remains to this day. Ever since, it has been the subject of mild controversy. Marlborough used to say to young Churchill cousins: 'People will think I won the Battle of Blenheim!' A society friend, who particularly disliked Gladys, said of it: 'It showed very much the public image.' She thought it a horrible way to be remembered. 'He was pompous, but I know masses of Dukes and unless they are particularly intelligent, they are very pompous.' Sir Shane Leslie thought it brought out Marlborough's religious spirit 'as it were a Quixote designed by Greco', while Maurice Ashley recalled that by the 1930s the Duke 'disliked it intensely'. While Blenheim profited from a bust of the Duke and later of Ivor Churchill, Epstein emerged disillusioned from his attempt to adorn the great palace. He found himself 'out of spirits, and out of pocket'.

On 16 October 1923 Gladys had the second of three miscarriages and set off to the Prince's Hotel in Brighton to recuperate. She always believed this miscarriage was the result of a squabble with Sunny in the early months of pregnancy, during which she fell against a stool. She was also horrified that he allowed workmen to carry on their noisy labour as she tried to recuperate. Then in January 1924, after a visit to Mentmore, Gladys had an operation for appendicitis. Gradually she regained her strength, began sitting up in an armchair and then venturing out for a ten-minute walk. In February she went down to Brighton again to stay for three weeks at the Metropole Hotel – 'a very frowzly hotel famous in divorce courts as the place where defaulting husbands put up for a night with "a lady other than their wife". Certainly one must be pushed by very interested or passionate impulses to put up with such grubby surroundings!'[10]

Gladys was alone most of the time, though Sunny joined her occasionally. Early in her stay she received a letter from him, primarily dealing with his time of arrival, but including:

> I am much disturbed at your letter. You are evidently far from well.... Pray take care of yourself. I devoutly hope that the change will do you good at Brighton. B & I are both here – both well.

The letter annoyed her and she added at the foot of it: 'This is the kind of letter M. writes to help an invalid in hours of illness and loneliness.'

Brighton was not empty of friends. Gladys found Lady Alexandra Curzon there, and the Marquess and Marchioness of Milford Haven and Lord Alistair Ker. They went on to the pier and returned to laugh at the dancers at the Metropole. Lady Sackville invited her to several good lunches and she gave a lunch in return at the Metropole, after which she noted with disgust her annoyance at her fellow hotel guests: 'Great clouds of middle-class people all full of money, appetites & vulgarity.' All in all she was unhappy and found even keeping her diaries disappointing: 'They do not ever tell one the weather, but there are too many things I don't want to say and the rest I forget.'

Restored to health, Gladys returned to society, to lunch parties, to the Churchills and to Blenheim. There was some excitement in March when Winston Churchill, who had lost his seat in Parliament in the General Election of October 1922, stood in a by-election for the Abbey division of Westminster. On the day, Gladys went out to see the fun 'but saw nothing but a string of cars filled with men with hooters'. Winston, standing as an Independent and anti-Socialist, was defeated by a mere forty-three votes. Sunny advised him to stay detached from the Tories until he could command terms and 'get hold of the title deeds'. The following Sunday he joined Sunny and Gladys for a wet day in Brighton and left by the same train as Blandford. Gladys was amused to observe as he left, 'WSC "maided" at the station by a familiar person called Locker-Lampson,* lately in the service of Ly Birkenhead', as she put it.

Gladys was much occupied with this sort of gossip. She found Lord Haldane rejuvenated by ten years of being Lord Chancellor, Lord Buckmaster on the other hand 'very strained & ill at ease', and related a tale about the Earls and Countesses of Derby and Pembroke. 'I hear that the Derbys wdnt have Reggie Pembroke at Knowsley . . . so his wife is there & he is staying at Eaton for the Lincolnshire.' In solitude in 1946, she added '& on dit qu'elle et ld D . . .'.

In April 1924, Gladys found the first of two sound solutions to the boredom of Blenheim by beginning work on the rock garden. This garden had been laid down by the fifth Duke as 'a bold and rugged background' to his other horticultural plans. The garden was situated at the foot of the lake near Capability Brown's Grand Cascade, about as far away from the palace and its inhabitants as possible. Over many months, Gladys supervised the moving of rocks, the placing of steps, the clearing of undergrowth and the planting of saxifrages. At its best the rock garden was a mass of yellow flowers. Sometimes Gladys took friends to see it, driving them from the palace in her little estate car. Not everyone enjoyed the experience as the garden was so plentifully populated with snakes that it was sometimes possible to see several slithering about at one glance. Her usual accomplice in the work was a local craftsman, Bert Timms, who lived at Hanborough and was later immortalized as a canephorus on the West Water Terrace. They sat together at a Druid's table and ate a picnic lunch. Gladys used to chain-smoke, but rewarded Bert with chocolates for not following her example.

Gladys enjoyed the rock garden enormously, but had to give up her work there as she was not strong enough to continue

* Commander O. S. Locker-Lampson (1880–1954), Conservative M.P.

after her third miscarriage in 1925. Now nature has reconverted the solitary haven to its former overgrown state.

1924 continued with uninspiring social events, though Gladys enjoyed the visit of Douglas Fairbanks and Mary Pickford on 20 April. Another visit to Paris was planned for June and she looked forward to it eagerly, as did her old 'Anaconda', Walter Berry:

> Gladysissima!
> Hosanna!
> Are you really going to be here! What a wonderful pheno-menon telepathy is. Only the other day I came across a letter of yours. I tore it up, saying mournfully: She'll never come any more!![11]

Walter Berry fully understood the tedium of Gladys's existence at Blenheim. For some time he had been trying to entice her back to Paris: 'Aren't you EVER coming back? How can you spend *all* your days in Hyperboria? What are your brain-cells working on?' He hoped to '*dé-blenheimiser*' Gladys. When the plans for the visit were finalized, Berry assured her: 'of course you'll be in at everything – and we'll gala day and night'.

Sunny and Gladys arrived in Paris on 12 June as planned. Gladys was thrilled – 'in such a state of joy as never was'. She promptly lost Sunny at the Gare du Nord and disappeared into the Metro 'to instantly feel & hear France, Paris itself'. Berry's prophecy came true. For the rest of the month it was one long party – 'All my friends come beaming with joy pr me souhaiter la bienvenue.' Joy and gaiety were the order of the day with parties for polo matches organized by the Princesse de Polignac, lunches with the Duchesse de Broglie and Thérèse Murat, dinners, dances, balls, opera, ballet and the Grand Prix. Sunny returned to London on 30 June and that night Gladys dined with her 'Anaconda'. The next day she, too, left for London. 'Retour vers la morne Angleterre', she wrote. 'Déjà à Folkestone je suis frappée par la brutalité; le manque de politesse de tout.' Once again a state of depression engulfed her. 'Pendant le dîner ce soir, tout à coup je comprends que je suis rentrée en Angleterre, que Paris est loin, que je suis ici perdue de nouveau.' She sank once again into nothingness and did not revive until a snatched visit to Versailles and Paris in September.

Sarah Wilson and her son Randolph, and Colonel and Mrs

Keppel came for Christmas. Gladys received a grey rug and a book from Sunny and the other guests produced a blank book, a blotter and a small diary between them.

On the last day of the year, Gladys felt so ill that she did not get up. She had become pregnant for the third time but with no more success than on the previous occasions. A nurse was summoned and Gladys lived through several days of pain and illness. On 3 January 1925, she noted that the nurse thought 'no immediate devil expected', but the following day she became frightened and the doctor was sent for. Her final miscarriage occurred at three o'clock on the morning of 5 January, a month before her forty-fourth birthday.

Three hours later she awoke with a dreadful pain in both eyes, which had been burnt by the chloroform. The left eye was quite seriously damaged and still paining her as late as 1930. More seriously, however, the doctor told her that another miscarriage might cost her her life.

The early months of 1925 were given to recuperation and listless entertaining as Gladys was hostess to Lady Cunard, Lord Berners, Harold Nicolson and the Birkenheads. In February she and Sunny made an attempt to hear Paderewski in Brighton but muddled the time of the performance and missed him; and in March there was a lunch party for John Masefield and his wife and Sir Frederick and Lady Keeble.

As neighbours from Boar's Hill, the Keebles were frequent visitors, usually coming to parties, but sometimes when Blenheim was undergoing an open day, they would be summoned for lunch in an underground room where Sunny and Gladys had gone into retreat. The tourists were usually sufficiently adventurous to discover them. Lady Keeble was the dramatic actress Lillah McCarthy, famed for roles in Shakespeare, Galsworthy, Shaw and Masefield plays. She wrote that Gladys, 'wittiest and most brilliant of women, would make us all feel witty and brilliant'.[12] At this lunch a 'great fight' took place over Masefield's forthcoming play *Trial of Jesus*, ending with him telling Lady Keeble 'The Gospels cannot be translated.' On 9 May Gladys went to see the play and noted 'very adverse criticism on all sides'.

The summer passed with Gladys suffering from measles, a visit from the King and Queen of Portugal and a trip to France. Once again Gladys found herself surrounded by old friends –

Jacques-Emile Blanche, Albert Flament, Princess Soutzo, Elsie
de Wolfe and Walter Berry. In August Lord and Lady Lee of
Fareham came to lunch at Blenheim, and Lady Lee left a description of the visit, which she found 'a strange and somewhat
depressing experience'.

Lord Lee could not decide what interested him most, Gladys
or the house, while Lady Lee gave her opinion of Gladys:

> She is very intelligent and striking in appearance, with vivid
> colouring and enormous blue eyes, but she is not really
> beautiful, as she has a heavy chin which looks almost scarred
> and a coarse crooked mouth. She has also attempted to
> acquire a classic Grecian profile, by, it is said, having paraffin
> wax injected under the skin of her nose, but this appears to
> have got somewhat out of place.[13]

All in all, Gladys made quite an impression on the Lees. She told
them she was never tired, had no nerves, was not a snob and
had 'no sense of possession'. They had heard a rumour that
Gladys had once declared that she wanted to be a *grande
cocotte*, but even if this was true, it was nothing more than a
precocious remark made by a high-spirited child. Lady Lee concluded that Gladys was not immoral 'but merely unmoral'. She
came away thinking 'she is very executive and competent and
more than a match for the Duke whom A [Lord Lee] has always
thought a very poor creature ...'.

Chapter Eighteen

TO BE A CATHOLIC

Though he started his life as 'a total pagan', the Duke of Marlborough had been anxious for a long time to become a Roman Catholic. 'The need of contact with the sublime and the supernatural of which he was profoundly conscious', wrote Winston Churchill, 'led him to the Church of Rome. He asked for sanctuary within that august and seemingly indestructible communion, against which his ancestor had warred with formidable strength.'[1] His religious temperament was observed by another cousin, Shane Leslie: 'Beneath his liking for gaiety and pageantry he might almost have been called a mystic.'[2] The man who instructed him in the Catholic faith, Father C. C. Martindale, spoke of his 'almost disconcertingly vivid perception of the existence and privacy of the Spiritual',[3] and recounted that after an accident he had had in New Zealand in 1929, the Duke wrote to him, saying that he knew something had occurred and had prayed for him.

Father Martindale was a fashionable Jesuit priest, later on the staff of the Church of the Immaculate Conception at Farm Street. A balding figure with round glasses and a cleft chin, he suffered a great deal from bad health. He possessed the 'pale, drawn scholar's face, the high forehead, the slow, decided and rather affected speech, the muffler untidily thrown round the Roman collar, the unexpected smile, that would light up his features'. He was an outstanding preacher and writer and was responsible for many of the celebrated conversions of the 1920s.

The Duke was introduced to Father Martindale in Oxford through his friend Evan Morgan and announced his wish to be admitted to the Catholic faith. 'I need not fear to say that, in his circumstances, I was exceptionally careful about that admission',[4] said the priest after the Duke's death. He agreed to instruct him but could not receive him into the Church on account of his first marriage. Though Father Martindale accepted that Consuelo had been coerced into the marriage, he did not believe the Vanderbilts would ever give the necessary evidence for an annulment. Instruction continued for three years, but nothing more was possible.

Meanwhile the Duke attended mass at St Aloysius Roman Catholic Church as a non-communicant, and he became a generous supporter of Catholic causes. Normally Father Martindale saw him at Campion Hill, but later he visited Blenheim. There was a notable dinner during the stay of King Manoel and Queen Auguste Viktoria of Portugal in May 1925. Father Martindale had a tête-à-tête with the King, whom he thought 'a very pious creature and horribly lonely'.[5] Later in the evening the Duke came to sit beside Father Martindale, and showed him his jewelled crucifix.

It is interesting that even after several visits to Blenheim in 1925 and 1926 the priest was not sure whether or not Gladys had been baptized a Catholic. Nor was Sunny sure. Father Martindale knew that Gladys had been brought up in Rome and elsewhere in Europe, and would therefore have lived 'in conditions which enabled her to know all about Catholics', but try as he did, he failed to get a positive statement from her. 'I did not like to ask her point blank if she had ever been a Catholic and she eluded all the chances I offered for her to tell me',[6] he wrote later. She once drove him from Blenheim to Heythrop. Suddenly she turned and said 'I don't believe you are English.' He asked why not and she replied, 'Well, because you are so flexible.'[7] He felt only that they had not yet confronted a principle which demanded a show of rigidity from him. He recalled furthermore that Gladys was capable of saying pretty well anything she liked. Altogether Martindale found her rather confusing.

There is some lack of agreement as to whether it was Sunny or Consuelo (by then Madame Balsan) who instituted proceedings to have their divorced marriage annulled. In *The Glitter and the Gold*, Consuelo wrote that Sunny made the first move, wishing to regularize his marriage to Gladys in the Catholic Church. At the time, however, the Duke's solicitors announced that he wished it to be 'authoritatively stated that application for this annulment was made by Mme Balsan and not by him'.[8]

In 1925 Consuelo made the necessary application to the Sacra Romana Rota, the Supreme Court of Justice of the Holy See in Rome. It was hoped by everyone involved that the annulment could be granted without publicity. At first they were fortunate, and the Marlboroughs' marriage was annulled on 29 July 1926. News of the proceedings leaked, however, and on 11 November were splashed over the front page of the *New York Times*, causing an outcry which lasted for the next four weeks.

Controversy raged over whether or not a marriage of twenty-five years which had produced two children could be annulled on the question of coercion. The issue was an especially sensitive one, coming at a time when fears were prevalent that marriage was to be abolished altogether in Russia; moreover the first ever case in London of a woman being cited as co-respondent by her husband had recently been heard. One Brooklyn clergyman took the line that everyone should pray for 'the confused young people of today who have all the matrimonial inclinations mortals ever had and find themselves discussing promiscuously and in ordinary conversation trial marriage and every phase of the sex problem as unblushingly as we used to discuss the weather'.[9]

Gladys herself was happily a step away from the main issue. Father Mahoney, of New York, pronounced that as she had never previously been married, her marriage was valid in the eyes of the Catholic Church. Thus her name was only mentioned *en passant* when Bishop Manning rose to his feet in the Cathedral of St John the Divine in New York at a Thanksgiving Day Service to make his sensational attack. His words rang from the pulpit:

> Marriage is a civil contract, as well as a religious one, and the claim of any foreign court, ecclesiastical or civil, to pass upon the validity of marriages solemnized in this land between persons not of its own communion is an unpardonable intrusion and an impertinence.[10]

A variety of views were vociferously expressed. The Rector of St Margaret's Westminster, the Rev. W. H. Carnegie, stated: 'If such an action stands no one's marriage would be safe.'[11] In the *Observer*, J. L. Garvin went to excessive lengths to try and prove that the annulment made Lord Blandford and Lord Ivor Churchill illegitimate. Father Martindale was obliged to protect them by citing Canon Law. There were suggestions that Vanderbilt money in large sums had been handed to the Rota. This theory was discredited by the recent case of Boni de Castellane and the heiress Anna Gould, who had failed to have their loveless marriage annulled. In New York, Monsignor Belford was quick to point out: 'The annulment proceedings brought the Rota $200, and where in America could you get a divorce for $200?'[12] War was waged in the pages of the *New York Times* between Charles C. Marshall and Bishop Dunn. Their arguments became increasingly complicated, until they were left debating the question of whether or not cohabitation and the bearing of children constituted a marriage. 'Were this true', wrote the bishop, 'then there are many people now married who do not know it.'[13]

Some were more relaxed. The *Catholic Herald* stated: 'Rome has undone nothing. She only ascertained and declared there was nothing to undo.'[14] And Consuelo's mother got as near the truth as anyone when she commented: 'This is merely one of those adjustments that come into the lives of people.'[15]

In England Father Martindale wrote a letter which effectively put an end to the hysteria and the flood of correspondence. He pointed out that the Duke of Marlborough did not apply for the decree, that all the Duke had paid for was his fare to London to give corroborative evidence, that all the evidence given came from Protestants under oath, and that therefore if the press wanted to accuse the Vanderbilts and their friends of perjury they were free to do so.

In the end honour was satisfied and all parties were happy. Consuelo could become a Catholic, marry as a Catholic and be welcomed into the bosom of the Balsan family. Gladys was reassured that no Catholic could criticize her marriage, and Sunny was at last free to be received into the Roman Catholic Church. This was done at a private ceremony in the Archbishop's house at Westminster on 1 February 1927 in the presence of Gladys, 'Goonie' Churchill, the Countess of Lindsey and Abingdon, and Lord Lovat. Cardinal Bourne blessed Gladys's wedding-ring and she and Sunny confirmed before him their consent to marriage.

Then the Cardinal returned the ring. In gratitude for his help, the Duke then gave Father Martindale the first present he agreed to accept – the crucifix he showed him at Blenheim the night the King of Portugal dined.

Chapter Nineteen

AFFECTIONATELY YOURS G.M.

In October 1927 Gladys again visited Paris; the Abbé Mugnier wrote to Berenson: 'I am going to see her very shortly. From time to time she says she misses *la douce bohème* of the Quai Voltaire.'[1]

Her visit coincided with the last days of her 'Anaconda'. Walter Berry had been quite ill and his health was further impaired by a flurry of banquets and celebrations in September for the American Legation. On 2 October he suffered a stroke which he tried to keep secret. A week of paralysis followed and early on the morning of the twelfth, 'the first American citizen in Paris' quietly died. His funeral five days later was of almost unprecedented magnificence, the coffin being borne through the streets of Paris on a specially constructed hearse drawn by four black horses. Marlborough had always thought Walter Berry a bit of an old woman, and when his will was read, an unpleasant side of his character emerged; for he left the trinkets given him by one lady friend to a different lady friend, a potentially hurtful joke which he no doubt thought highly amusing.

Marlborough's conversion to Catholicism did not alas make relations between him and Gladys any better. Her fear of pregnancy was aggravated by the restrictions imposed on him by his new religion, and she found more and more that his temper, previously directed at outsiders, was now directed at her. She began to seek help and advice. In November she wrote to Abbé Mugnier, who replied that the Duke was just undergoing a physical crisis following his conversion and assured Gladys that he had seen many similar cases. Her Paris friends had thought her happy at Blenheim, and would, he wrote, now have another reason for regretting her departure from the Quai Voltaire. 'It is all very Shakespearian, but I prefer Shakespeare in books, Shakespeare printed, not lived.' At the worst, he reminded her, she could always return to Paris where everyone would ensure that she forgot 'the unjust treatment of which you are a victim'.[2]

On 28 February 1928, Gladys had her finest hour as Duchess of Marlborough when she gave a Leap Year Eve Ball at their new London home, 7 Carlton House Terrace. The party was kept quiet from the press and news of it only escaped later. Gladys welcomed guests 'looking very sprightly as a green pierrette with a Dresden china shepherdess hat on'. Among guests dressed as Ruritanians, cricketers and pirates, and in costumes they had worn for portraits, were Winston Churchill in a toga, Lord Birkenhead in cardinal's robes, which he kept specially for such occasions, and Duff Cooper as a French apache. The guest of honour was the Prince of Wales in a domino and mask, who transformed himself during the evening into a clown with two heads. Some of the guests came on from the French Ambassador's dinner and danced until dawn. As *The Lady* put it: 'The only solemn people present were the servants.'[3]

Gladys knew the Prince of Wales only slightly, but Sunny used to have him over to Blenheim for shoots when he was at Magdalen College, Oxford, before the First World War. For Christmas 1925 Sunny was inspired to send him a present of some gloves. The Prince was foxed and had to consult Winston Churchill over lunch to decipher the signature. Gladys's triumph in persuading the heir to the throne to come to the dance delighted Sunny, who fully appreciated the honour of having a royal guest after so many years of ostracism from court. Some years later Gladys revealed that after the party Sunny 'turned into a combination of Romeo & Chevalier Bayard for quite 3 days. I was allowed to express several opinions a day & no taunt abt my dislike of persons like Mr & Mrs Redmond Mc-Grath was forthcoming.'[4]

1928 reunited Gladys with two old friends. Hermann Keyserling met her in the spring after a silence of twenty years. He was now a successful philosopher and lecturer and had founded the School of Wisdom at Darmstadt under the aegis of the Grand Duke of Hesse. He sent Gladys a copy of his new book, *Europe*, 'in remembrance of the olden days'. Knowing she enjoyed intelligent company, he recommended his brilliant friend, Don Salvador de Madariaga, who had taken up an appointment as Professor of Spanish at Oxford, but Gladys's spirits were too low to follow up the introduction.

Delighted as he was to meet his former love again, Keyserling found that, like Berenson, the scales had dropped from his eyes. He was now convinced that Gladys had never read any of the books he suggested and certainly not two Emil Ludwigs she had specifically asked him to get for her. He did not realize how crushed Gladys's spirits were when, in 1929, he urged her to visit South America, 'a great continent as rich in Soul & Life as North America in material goods'. That Christmas he wrote to her, 'although I know how little sentimental you are', and repeated the request he first made in 1908:

> Would you not send me a photo or a photo after a picture of you which would help to fix old memories? I think you know that I am the most faithful of all friends. I am practically beyond space & time. And yet I love landmarks.[5]

But Gladys sent no photos and the two fell silent for another seventeen years.

The other old friend who saw Gladys again was Lily de Clermont-Tonnerre, who visited Blenheim in 1928. Her picture of Gladys is a glossy one:

> Silver-gilt vases modelled by Germain adorned the lunch-table one morning. The red roses, overflowing them, made a frame round the Duchess of Marlborough, so that she looked like a heroine of Shakespeare's: Rosalind in the Rose Bower. And the Duchess with her customary animation and wit entertained the Duke sitting opposite her with her paradoxes and anecdotes.

Nevertheless Lily was not unaware of a conflict between Blenheim and Gladys. Sometimes the palace won, and Gladys became a solemn, dignified Duchess:

> At other times, light as an elf, she frisks across the flowerbeds, laughs, sheds sunlight on everything and passes with her dog through the court of honour . . . and the Palace is annihilated before so much grace and beauty.[6]

The later years of the Twenties were brightened by a new literary friendship for Gladys. She used to attend the parties given by Lady Colefax who, though neither rich, beautiful nor aristocratic, was a wildly successful social lion-hunter. Her older prey included Arnold Bennett, Bernard Shaw and Somerset Maugham, and the younger men she took up included Cecil Beaton, Rex Whistler and John Gielgud. When she died Harold Nicolson concluded that 'the disappearance of society means that young men have no opportunity of meeting the great men of their age'.[7] It was at one of her parties at Argyll House that Gladys met the celebrated Irish novelist George Moore, and they became friends. George Moore, though now in his middle seventies, enjoyed to the full the attention of London society. Physically he was a type well-known to Gladys, with a high forehead, a long nose, a white walrus moustache and the dignity of an aging sage.

Gladys was a kind friend to him at a time when illness and old age was closing in on him and he was struggling to complete his last work, *Aphrodite in Aulis*. A regular flow of game arrived at Ebury Street from Blenheim to sustain the writer in his work. 'Two pheasants in splendid plumage announced to me that I was not forgotten and I preened my feathers for a while',[8] he wrote.

Moore had expressed a wish to see Blenheim and Gladys often invited him. He thought she never quite appreciated that he was not well enough to come; but instead, as his cook Clara Warville remembered, Gladys was for a time a frequent caller at 121 Ebury Street. George Moore was always eager to see Gladys 'and the Duke who often appears in my imagination', but they never progressed to more intimate terms than 'My dear Duchess . . . always affectionately yours G.M.'

In the late 1920s he fell seriously ill with prostate trouble, but pressed on with his book, after which, he told Gladys, 'I shall become a spectator of life, asthetising the day away in some village by the sea'. In June 1929 Gladys sent him flowers, which he believed had come as a result of his wish to see her: 'Paeonies, anemonies, tulips are never very far from my thoughts, and they bloom in all their insidiousness, attractiveness when they come from a friend I wish to see.'[9]

His forthcoming operation prevented him from visiting

Blenheim, though he still worked five or six hours a day on his book. In July 1929 he wrote to Gladys:

> I should be the most unnatural man that ever walked on this earth if I didn't wish to pay you a visit at Blenheim. Everything attracts me thither, your companionship, the walks round the garden, the pictures, the Palace itself, everything.[10]

On 1 November *Aphrodite in Aulis* was completed. 'Today is my day of days', he declared. 'She's gone to the printer.'

Though he survived the operation, he fell victim to sciatica and travel was again restricted. His last letters to Gladys in 1930 show him in a state of depression which he hoped her 'gay voice' would dispel. In June 1930, he confessed: 'I can compose no longer. For the moment at least composition and Ebury Street terrify me like a nightmare.'[11] After that their correspondence ceased. The increasing burdens of ill-health and advancing years confined George Moore to Ebury Street, while Gladys had her own nightmares to contend with. He survived until 21 January 1933, a month before his eighty-first birthday.

In the last years of the 1920s Gladys became increasingly miserable, and relations with Sunny deteriorated steadily. He became bitter and disillusioned after years spent with two wives who denied him the affection he did not know how to seek. One of his friends said: 'Someone should have put their arms round him. That's what he needed.' It was in this spirit of dismay that he sold some of his papers to the Americans, enclosing a letter which Ambassador Houghton sincerely hoped would never see the light of day. 'I fear it would expose the donor to comments or remarks that would be, to say the least, most unfortunate',[12] wrote the Ambassador. In the letter Marlborough gave his opinion on social relations between England and the United States:

> It was a period when many of the daughters of America elected to marry and identify their lives with Europeans and notably Englishmen – They exchanged the home life of America for that of England and the new angles of vision with which they perceived the old world enabled them to leave an imprint on the customs of a society which hitherto had grown up sheltered in its insular traditions.

This period of social intercourse, this period of inter-national relation is not likely to recur because Europe and its traditions no longer appeals with the same force and vigour to the American feminine mind as it did in the closing years of the Victorian era.[13]

Gladys and Sunny continued to travel together in the late Twenties. They visited France, Italy and Capri where they saw the Duke and Duchess of Camastra, and they stayed with the Westminsters for the Grand National. At Eaton Hall Gladys photographed 'Bendor's' dachshund wandering happily about on the dining-room table. Soon after the General Election of March 1929 they both attended a party given by Lord Birken-head to mark the completion of some work at Charlton. Their old friend was nearing the end of his days. Now, when he attended parties at Blenheim, he had to be helped up the steps. He often sat for hours staring into space and once found his way to the dining-room where he ordered one bottle of champagne after another. Finally his wife and his daughter, Lady Eleanor Smith, found him and steered him home.

When he died, on 30 September 1930, the Marlboroughs lost a good friend, and they went to see his purple-draped coffin laid to rest at Charlton in a huge congregation which included such diverse figures as the exiled King George of Greece and Maundy Gregory.

About the only other interest which linked Gladys and Sunny was the work in progress of the Water Terraces. Gladys spent hours watching and photographing as trees arrived in carts drawn by three horses, and Venuses were hauled down from motor-trucks and put in place. One day she went down to the rock garden after it had been pouring with rain, fearing that the sluice had not been opened and that the lake would be over-flowing. Her suspicion was correct and she ran to the estate office to give the alarm. Then she 'grabbed' her camera and returned to the scene. The bank at this point of the lake was very unsound, but fortunately a quantity of clay was at hand. The damage was repaired and a disaster averted. Had the bank given way, Bladon would have been submerged in twenty feet of water in less than four minutes.

Gladys's contribution to the decoration of Blenheim was marked in two ways. In August 1928, the decorative and portrait painter Colin Gill came to paint her eyes on the ceiling of the portico. There are six panels with three blue eyes and three brown ones. Gladys is said to have mounted the scaffold and given Colin Gill a blue scarf the same colour as her eyes for him to work from. The brown eyes are said to be Consuelo's, for Sunny's eyes were also blue. These eyes still gaze down mysteriously on tourists waiting to enter the palace. When the Water Terraces were completed in 1930, two lead sphinxes were placed opposite each other on the first terrace. These are signed as the work of W. Ward Willis and bear Gladys's features. With the eyes, they remain today the only images of Gladys at the palace, for no portraits of her adorn the walls nor is there so much as a photograph to be seen of the woman who was mistress of the palace for twelve years.

In the early 1930s Abbé Mugnier reported to Bernard Berenson that Gladys was a prisoner of the grandeur of Blenheim. He was sure that she wanted to escape back to her little flat in Paris. The great palace seemed a forbiddingly grand place where two disillusioned and unhappy people lived uneasily together. Visitors at this time took away strange recollections. When André Maurois arrived at the main entrance in 1929, a servant directed him to a side door a considerable distance away. When Maurois enquired how he would know, the door-keeper replied: 'I don't know, I've never been there.'[14]

Maurice Ashley spent some time at the palace researching the first Duke's life for Winston Churchill. He worked in the archives, making copies in longhand, and the daily lunch he was offered never materialized. Arriving by car each morning he had to remember a hump in the drive placed there by the Duke to ensure that visitors observed a funereal speed limit. Ashley learnt when to slow down and did not therefore suffer the fate of Lady Ottoline Morrell. Her chauffeur took the hump so fast that she fainted. On arrival at the palace she had to be carried in and revived on Churchillian brandy.

Maurice Ashley was horrified by the Duke, 'an inspissated little man', who announced one day that he hoped the unemployment figures would rise to two million. The Duke was paranoid about being robbed and talked as disparagingly as ever about the lower classes. Though much taken by the beauty of Blenheim, Ashley dismissed it as 'a disappearing world, an aristocratic oasis, an eighteenth-century relic'. One day he took tea with Gladys at a small table in the middle of the Long Gallery. Noting that she was 'not without taste', he recalled: 'All I can remember now is being overawed both by her and by the statue of Queen Anne and swallowing the smallest sandwiches I have ever seen.'[15]

In 1930 Gladys made a final effort to be sociable. She thought the new society of 'Bright Young Things' compared ill with the days of the Belle Epoque. This was the era of the Prince of Wales and Mrs Simpson, on whom Gladys had strong views. 'Queen Mary', she said, 'had George v by the ear and the Prince of Wales did not really want to be king. He was attracted by the newness of America and hoped by marrying Simpson he would be free.' As for Mrs Simpson, 'she was just a common American making her way in the world. She was amusing and she had a good sense of fashion. Nothing more.' Gladys was a believer in two popular theories about the Prince. 'He was *impuissant*', she said, and went on to explain how he benefited from Mrs Simpson's prowess in intimate matters. Furthermore she recalled the inaccurate story: 'Her mother ran a boarding-house in New York. Not an hotel, a boarding-house. Well, you can imagine what that was ... !'[16]

A young acquaintance, Patrick Balfour, admired Gladys's 'amused aloofness from society'. She was forever surrounded by people such as 'Chips' Channon, who never left her alone and were all fearful gossips. 'People in society gossip', said Gladys, 'because it's the only thing they have in common.' When asked whether or not 'Chips' was a homosexual, she replied enthusiastically: 'Oh! yes they all were. Men with men, women with women, and dogs too, I shouldn't wonder!'[17]

Gladys's flurry of entertaining in 1930 began with a dinner-party at Carlton House Terrace on 6 March to which Arnold Bennett was invited by Sunny. They had met at the Other Club in 1917, but Bennett was surprised since all he knew of the Duke besides his august ancestry was that he was 'a very nice, ignorant chap, and an ardent Roman Catholic'.[18] Twenty-two sat down to a dinner of soup and fish off silver plate. Bennett and Gladys took to each other at once, and he admired her French pictures. She told him he was the first person to have done so. Later he fell to discussing one of them with Sunny. Sunny assured him it was a Van Gogh, Bennett was convinced it was a Cézanne, and Gladys confirmed this. Bennett concluded that he had enjoyed talking to her, 'but the bulk of the 20 guests seemed to me to have no interest whatever except sexual. I mean there were a few beautiful creatures.'[19]

A few days later Gladys invited Arnold Bennett to be part of a conversation piece she was having photographed at Carlton House Terrace. But Bennett was grappling with life in a large hotel (the Savoy) for his last novel *Imperial Palace*. 'I should have loved to come', he replied, 'but for months now I have maintained an iron rule against all lunches and teas. I am completely absorbed & enslaved by my terrible novel.'[20]

The idea for the photograph emerged following the success of a similar venture at Sir Philip Sassoon's house. Frankie Birrell assisted Gladys in gathering together a group of leading writers. Lytton Strachey looked forward to coming 'with some terror and more excitement';[21] Frankie's distinguished old father, Augustine Birrell, promised that 'with fear and trembling I will obey your summons for Thursday at 4'.[22] Siegfried Sassoon regretted he would be absent as he was in Sicily 'drudging away at my unfinished book',[23] and George Moore was not well enough to venture out. Other subjects included Raymond Mortimer, Harold Nicolson, David Garnett and Edith Sitwell.

The session was a fiasco from the start. Arriving guests were assailed by Gladys's spaniels and then condemned to a long wait while the American photographer wrestled with the Duke's complaints and restraints. First he forbade the use of a spiked tripod on the parquet floor. The spikes were removed and the tripod collapsed and had to be fitted with india-rubber bases. Flashlight bulbs were vetoed for fear that the smoke would dirty the ceiling or damage the paintings. This problem was solved by the photographer going in search of a transparent balloon into which the bulbs could explode and from which the gases could be released on the balcony outside. Meanwhile, David Garnett's eye was caught by a 'ravishingly beautiful Chinese woman'. Lytton Strachey did not know who she was and Raymond Mortimer misinformed him that she was the actress Anna May Wong. David Garnett was extremely disappointed to learn that she was not the celebrated actress but the daughter of the Chinese Ambassador in Washington. Worse than this she turned out to be married to the American photographer. Garnett confessed later: 'For a day or two I felt slightly sick from the violence of my attraction and the bitterness of my disappointment.'[24]

After the lengthy séance, the Duke served sherry downstairs. He asked Garnett whether he seriously thought any writer was a genius and worth immortalizing in a conversation piece. This led to a discussion about D. H. Lawrence. Lytton Strachey went home and complained: 'The exhaustion was terrific, the idiocy intense. Oh dear, Oh dear, Oh dear!'[25] But David Garnett thoroughly enjoyed himself, thanked Gladys for an afternoon 'unlike any afternoon I've spent in my life',[26] and recommended that she invite Henry Lamb, John Banting or Vanessa Bell to paint a picture from one of the photographs.

Gladys went to Eaton Hall again for the Grand National and astonished the Duchess of Westminster's guests by calling for housemaid's steps and perching on them to photograph the guests at table. From there she went to Yorkshire to stay with Lady Serena James at St Nicholas, Richmond, where she met Lady Serena's extraordinary cousin, Eve Fairfax.* Ten years older than Gladys, Eve had left Yorkshire as a young girl and lived in Rodin's house in Paris. At the behest of her one-time fiancé, Lord Grimthorpe, Rodin sculpted a bust of her. He admired the 'Englishness' of her character and declared to Jacques-Emile Blanche: 'Mademoiselle Fairfax? A Diana and a satyr in one: how flat-chested they are – oh, those planes and the bony structure of these Englishwomen!'[27] Thereafter she became one of Yorkshire's most celebrated figures, travelling from country house to country house, accompanied by a 'visiting' book, given her by Lady Diana Manners in 1911. Gladys signed it twice.

The parties continued in Oxfordshire and London. Lady Keeble played Ephigenia in the open air at Blenheim. Rain poured down but the crowd remained motionless throughout the performance, sheltering as best they could. Afterwards everyone flocked round the actors whom Gladys was encouraging to sink into hot baths. On 30 June she gave a dinner-party in London at which Edith Sitwell and Evelyn Waugh were present. Edith Sitwell liked Gladys and used to send her poetry. On one occasion she sent her a book which included *Gold Coast*

---

* Eve Fairfax died at the Retreat, York on 27 May 1978, aged 106. The present author had a long conversation with her in March 1977.

Customs, adding 'I set store by it. And you will understand it. Hardly anyone does.'[28] Evelyn Waugh recorded that at the dinner there were two ambassadors and 'about 40 hard-faced middle-aged peers and peeresses'. Gladys looked 'very battered with fine diamonds', while Sunny wore his Garter riband and a silk turban over a bandaged eye. As Waugh left, Gladys turned to him and declared: 'Ah, you are like Marlborough. He has such a mundane mind. He will go to any party for which he is sent a printed invitation.'[29]

That insult was a mild one compared to others to which Gladys subjected Marlborough. There had been an occasion on which he had struck Gladys on the way to a luncheon party, causing her to arrive with a black eye. There were rows about servants, Marlborough claiming that Gladys upset them and they left, and an atmosphere soon reigned in which neither party could do anything right. In her misery, Gladys responded by kicking out. One night Sunny was talking about politics. From the other end of the table Gladys suddenly shouted at him 'Shut up! You know nothing about politics. I've slept with every prime minister in Europe and most kings. You are not qualified to speak.' Sunny dug nervously into his dinner. On another occasion she instigated a conversation about communism, ingeniously involving the footmen in the conversation and creating general discomfort. And at one dinner she produced a revolver and placed it beside her. A rather startled guest at her side inquired: 'Duchess, what are you going to do with that?' to which she replied: 'Oh! I don't know, I might just shoot Marlborough!'

There was one final festivity before the collapse. Gladys organized a 'coming-of-age party' to celebrate the Duke's sixtieth birthday. In fact a mistake was made and the ball, held on 13 November 1930, fell just after his fifty-ninth birthday. The guests included old friends and neighbours such as Lord Berners, the Earl and Countess of Carnarvon, Sir Frederick and Lady Keeble, Mr and Mrs John Masefield, Colonel and Mrs Maurice Wingfield, Frank Pakenham (now Lord Longford) and Lord David Cecil. One guest recalled Sunny wearing a gold and yellow coat and the Garter and whirling round the dance floor with Constance FitzRoy, who became so giddy that she fainted. Winston Churchill and the new Lord Birkenhead surveyed the scene from the side, smoking enormous cigars. The celebrations included a bonfire 100 feet high, which took three weeks to construct, a torchlight procession and dancing in the open air. The courtyard at the front of the palace was filled with glittering fairy lights, which Sunny and Gladys watched from the steps. Gladys paid a local major £10.9.0 for eggs for the party and employed Ambrose's band at a cost of £116.5.0. It was the last public occasion where Sunny and Gladys shared any happiness, for by June 1931 their marriage had deteriorated to a state of hostility, pending the declaration of open warfare.

Chapter Twenty

THE UNUSUAL LIFE

The Duke of Marlborough left Gladys living alone at Blenheim in 1931. Now that the terraces were completed, he lost interest in the estate and was diverted by an unfulfilled romantic interest in the glamorous Canadian actress 'Bunny' Doble, wife of Sir Anthony Lindsay-Hogg. He spent more and more time in London and renewed his interest in racing. He purchased the racehorse Andrea which carried his colours in the Derby of 1932, won the St James's Palace Stakes at Ascot and, at Newbury, dead-heated in the Lingfield Park Plate and won the Norwich Handicap.

Now in his early sixties, he bore numerous grievances against Gladys. The first major cause of dissent was her Blenheim spaniels. Sunny's objection to these dogs was that Gladys devoted all her time to them, allowed them to live in the palace and create squalor everywhere. She was also accused of ordering doors to be cut between the state rooms to facilitate their peregrinations. Sunny used to curse and swear at them and search out new stains on the carpets to show his guests. Gladys loved dogs and had always owned at least one since her early days. When she found herself too weak to continue shifting rocks in the rock garden, she went to Crufts and saw how much her friends Lorna, Countess Howe, and Lady Mainwaring enjoyed showing their animals. Her uncle, Charlie Baldwin, visited her and gave her some money to restart the Blenheim spaniels in 1930.

Gladys, whose agile mind had tackled art, literature and politics, now turned to the exacting task of breeding a champion. She entered into the business methodically and diligently, listing long neat pedigrees, buying and selling dogs all over the country and in consequence making endless new friends, often unseen, of all classes and ages. The world of dogs broke down the barriers, and letters poured in from diverse places such as Exmouth, Wilmslow, Brighton and Colwyn Bay, reporting the safe arrival of a 'pup', and the happy wagging of tails in new homes. Many of the letters veer close to illiteracy, but all of them reflect membership of the mysterious club of the world of dogs which enables a housewife in Hove to discuss distemper with a Duchess. Gladys solicitously organized for the dogs to set off on their journeys to be met at the appropriate station at the right time, and sometimes astonished an owner with a Christmas card from Blenheim. She was assisted in her task by Agnes Grylls, who came to run the kennels at Blenheim, and in December 1932 she became Patron of the King Charles Spaniel Club.

At this time Gladys's diary, previously the record of social engagements, weekend parties and delighted trips to France, was devoted almost exclusively to breeding matters and the health of dogs. All the spaniels were documented at birth – for example, Babylas at 12.30 on 30 April – light 3 blotches – and all had romantic and imaginative names: Benita, Ghandi, Rita, Dragée, Daffodil, Zona, Aloma, Bacchus, Bettysan and her favourite, Snowflake.

Certainly there existed a contrast between the efficiency of the breeding and the domestic arrangements. Lady Gwendoline Churchill's daughter, Clarissa (now the Countess of Avon), remembers a visit to Blenheim when she was about nine. Gladys and Lady Gwendoline sat opposite each other on the train, deep in conversation. When they arrived at the palace, Clarissa Churchill was amazed to find the Great Hall divided into dog coops and reeking most terribly. The Duke's absence was dismissed in one of those brisk excuses given by adults to children. Gradually the pens spread to other rooms, partly because Gladys wanted the dogs round her and partly in the same spirit of spite that caused her on another occasion to point to Sunny's favourite topiary and command the gardener to 'savage it'.

Another problem was money. Gladys had enjoyed the benefit of a good income from the Deacon trust which at one point ensured the surviving sisters an income of $30,000 a year. It suffered badly in the crash of 1929 and Gladys found that she had lost her own means. Forced to rely on the Duke for funds which were seldom forthcoming, she took to wearing old court-dresses held up with safety pins, which gave her a somewhat bizarre appearance. She wore a nineteen-year-old musquash, which she had remodelled, and a worn, patched and faded squirrel coat made for her in 1925. She complained bitterly about Sunny's meanness, claiming to have made 150 small silk lampshades, pin-cushions for the bedrooms, and with exemplary efficiency to have mended, renovated, repaired and patched the furniture, saving him, as he freely admitted, £600 a year.

Sunny levelled at Gladys a general accusation of insanity and made play of the fact that she harboured a revolver. He used to tell neighbours that she chased him around the palace with it. Gladys once took a young friend, Sir Shane Leslie's daughter, Anita, to her bedroom and showed her this revolver, explaining merrily that it was to shoot Sunny in case he ever came to her room. Anita Leslie remembered Gladys looking like 'a beautiful frog' and admired her 'wicked astringent wit'. As Gladys's troubles grew worse Anita Leslie wrote to her: 'I never met anyone before who could think like you. . . . I just long to be with a real person.'[1] Clare Sheridan told her she thought Gladys had 'the brain of a man', and Anita Leslie wondered if this was a compliment.[2]

As ever Gladys remained many-faceted. She looked extraordinary now and behaved eccentrically, but her clear, logical mind grasped the situation that was enveloping her; and when she hit back at Marlborough, she did so with biting venom. She accused him of unkindness, an ungovernable temper, and of being 'a very frightened rabbit where public exposure is possible'. Frustrated in his attempts to woo Lady Lindsay-Hogg, who was more favourably disposed to the young Lord Birkenhead (often observed leaving her house in the small hours of the night), the Duke passed his time in the night-clubs, thus making himself vulnerable to the most obvious and sordid comments. Perhaps the harshest description of him was one that Gladys intended to make public in the course of litigation:

The keynote of the Duke of Marlborough's character I found in Brodie in 'Hatter's Castle'[3] and his mood towards me is — 'I'll wipe them out as I destroy all who offend me. I'll smash everybody that interferes with me. Let them try to do it.

Whatever comes I am still myself.'

A black, vicious personal pride like a disease that gets worse and worse.[4]

While Gladys corresponded eagerly with dog-lovers she cut herself off from society and to a large extent from Paris friends. In the spring of 1931 Albert Flament sent her an article about Madame Potocka. He wondered if Gladys would ever receive it. 'When I write to you at Blenheim I have the impression that letters do not reach you. Your "edifice" is so vast. . . . So many Duchesses of Marlborough have lived there before you!'[5]

The article arrived just before some more distracting news from France. Gladys's old nurse Irma was gravely ill. She immediately went to Paris, moved Irma to a nursing home and stayed with her for ten days until she died. Thus Gladys lost her last link with childhood.

A sorrow of a different kind befell Gladys in the summer. She had a spaniel called Snowflake who resembled Charlie Windfall in *Lady Wentworth's Book of Toy Dogs*. Snowflake was mated twice in June and then taken back to Blenheim. At the end of July Gladys could feel the puppies and very early on 8 August they began to drop. Gladys stayed while a puppy 'of unequalled beauty' was still-born and a second born by Caesarean section the following day. But Snowflake never recovered from the operation. Her temperature rose and then she fell quiet. She did not respond to a brandy and water injection, nor to a drop of pure brandy on the tongue. To Gladys's everlasting sorrow Snowflake died at one o'clock – 'passed away like a breath of air'.

On the day of the spaniel's death Gladys wrote 'My snuzzles! My Danduzenu! The pain, the agony of it all!' Three months later she was still writing about 'Little Danduzenu – never never will I forget you or lose the pain of your death, my snow, little dear Snu!' In her unhappiness there was a feeling of guilt that she had caused the death by mating Snowflake too soon, and she never forgave herself. She went twice to London to persuade Marlborough to have the spaniel stuffed. He agreed, but when she collected the result, she was further saddened as the reproduction was totally unlike the original.

Marlborough stayed away from Blenheim as much as possible.

If he had to come to the palace, he stayed in a hotel and lunched at the Bear in Woodstock. Gladys had him watched by detectives and gathered evidence for litigation. When his mother Albertha, Lady Blandford, died in January 1932, she joined him for the funeral but by the end of that year, the final stage of their long relationship had begun. Gladys was very hurt when the Duke yelled at her at lunch one day: 'Bah! I have no consideration for you and never have had.'

Marlborough had offered to have the reception for Diana Churchill's* wedding at Carlton House Terrace on 12 December. Gladys refused to attend the service, not wishing to appear in public with him, but went to the reception, skilfully avoiding playing the charade of 'united husband and wife'. A fortnight later, around Christmas, there was a series of fierce rows at Blenheim, after which Marlborough forbade Gladys to come to Carlton House Terrace and declared he never wanted to see her again. Needless to say when the Duke left the luncheon table to depart for London he patted Gladys on the shoulder to look well before his guests; and then walked out, taking the butler, under-butler, valet, chef and a kitchen-maid with him. It was the last time Gladys ever saw him, a pitiful conclusion to a romance of thirty-five years.

Thus Gladys remained alone at the palace with a handful of servants, many of whom took maximum advantage out of her plight to cause additional misery and mischief. Rumours spread that she took drugs and swore at servants from the bedroom window; stories of her sorrow wended their way to Florence.

Bernard Berenson in his villa at Settignano was now, by his own confession, 'more concerned with constipation than sex'. In *Sketch for a Self Portrait*, he said: 'It can get to be at least as much of a preoccupation, an obsession; and intestinal relief as eagerly awaited as ever sex relief in earlier years.'[6] In this disenchanted state he gave his last verdict on Gladys, on whom he had doted so much so many years before. He pronounced her ruined:

By now all people have deserted her, and nothing remains of her but a myth – she was, in former days, like Venus' cat –

* Diana Churchill (1904–63), daughter of Winston Churchill. Married John Milner Bailey in 1932. Divorced 1935. Later married to Duncan Sandys.

that cat who, made into a beautiful woman by the grace of the goddess, but could not remain in the company of women because she would suddenly spring and devour any little mouse that appeared. Gladys Deacon's mouse was the need to dominate, to crush under her heel the heads of those who were weaker than she. Thus no sooner would she see a possible victim than she forgot everything else, even her deepest interests, and would set out to pursue him until she had led him to his end. This is what ruined her.[7]

In December 1932 Gladys appealed for help to Father Martindale, but found the priest anxious not to get involved. He replied that he hardly ever saw the Duke and knew nothing of his private life. He suggested that Gladys should go away but hoped there would be no separation or divorce. The thought of further publicity made him 'seasick'. Gladys also turned to her stepson, Ivor. He too preferred not to get involved as the situation was a delicate one for him. 'My present difficulty is to show my friendliness to you which I want to do without being actively disloyal to my father', he wrote on 23 March 1933. 'I don't want to take any sides.'

In April Gladys made it quite clear that she 'would not under any circumstances bear to live with him again'. Her solicitors proposed that she should be granted an annuity of £10,000 and provided with a suitable residence, furnished 'in a way suitable to the needs of our client'. The proposal was rejected; but Gladys waited, advised that a divorce petition might not be successful, and could be disadvantageous financially.

Gladys was still at Blenheim in May 1933, claiming to have but £9 in her bank account. One weekend she expected nine guests, but at the last minute she received a telegram from Marlborough forbidding her to receive them. Rather than have them turned away at the gate, she cancelled the invitations. At the same time a letter from Marlborough's solicitors informed her that Blenheim was to be closed down at the end of the month and the cook, butler and kitchen-maid dismissed. Her solicitors protested that no suitable provision had been made for Gladys, nor had she anywhere to go, since the Duke had made it clear that if she arrived at Carlton House Terrace she would be thrown out. 'The action of the Duke in this matter is most humiliating to the Duchess, harsh and cruel', they wrote.

Nevertheless on 29 May Gladys summoned a van and a motor to remove her possessions and her dogs. The agent, who had for some time shared with the solicitors the role of spokesman for Marlborough, questioned the authority of Mrs Grylls, who was supervising the loading. Gladys was obliged to call for a young solicitor from Withers & Co to come down to see that 'no further insolences' were done to her. After his arrival, the agent, secretary and housekeeper went to ground and no sign of their presence was seen until the van and the motor had sped on their way to a friend's house in Buckingham. Gladys, nothing if not formidable in the face of adversity, stood on the steps of the palace photographing the scene. 'Goodbye to all that!' she wrote on one of the pictures, and noted: 'It was a lovely day.'

The following afternoon Princess Lida Thurn und Taxis arrived at Blenheim and Gladys left in a car with her. She went to Seaford House, Southampton, to recover, and never crossed the threshold of Blenheim Palace again. Quiet days followed as she braced herself for the further horrors of battle with Marlborough.

The Duke, meanwhile, was swift to return to Blenheim where he gleefully reclaimed the rooms so recently occupied by spaniels. One guest recalled having to leave the room hurriedly for fear of being asphyxiated by the smell. The bad state of the palace assisted the Churchills and their friends in condemning Gladys for her behaviour, and they circulated the story that she had gone mad. The Duke, for example, told Dorothy Hilton-Green,* wife of the Master of the Cottesmore Hounds, that Gladys was impossible, and would 'certainly be locked up within a year'; to which Mrs Hilton-Green laughed and replied that, on the contrary, Gladys was an extremely intelligent woman and far more intelligent than he or any of his family had ever been. But the sad truth was that such accusations reduced Gladys in three years from 'a woman full of life' to 'a broken woman, in health and spirits'.[8]

The Duke was anxious to find out who had been invited to Blenheim by Gladys. For this reason she took the precaution of removing the Visitors Book. When eventually it was returned, the Duke had it engraved 'Family Heirloom' to prevent its

---

* Dorothy Hilton-Green (1890–1966), daughter of Lord Henry Grosvenor.

further travels as and when future Duchesses departed.

Throughout June and July Gladys occupied a room at the Carlton Hotel in the Haymarket. On 1 June Marlborough's solicitors informed Gladys that the Duke would no longer be responsible for any of her bills. 'We shall be glad to hear that your client will observe this request', they concluded, 'as our client does not wish to take other steps to make this fact generally known.' A so-called voluntary allowance of £250 a month was paid to her.

Support came to Gladys from many friends. Lily de Clermont-Tonnerre declared Marlborough's behaviour 'scandalous'. She urged Gladys to hold firm to her rights and hoped that she would not forget Paris or her Paris friends. Gladys began to move in society once more to prove she was quite normal. In June she found time to discuss Proust with Harold Nicolson; she attended Wimbledon, and on 14 July she went alone to the wedding of 'Chips' Channon to Lady Honor Guinness.

Eventually her solicitors insisted that she should take up residence in 7 Carlton House Terrace to protect her valuable possessions there, and so at the end of July she began a vigil which lasted nearly ten days, during which time her friends, including Diana Guinness, Patrick Balfour and the Duchess of Hamilton and Brandon, came to call on her. She was visited by her doctor, and fruit, eggs and the *Daily Telegraph* were delivered regularly to the house.

Events took a sinister turn on the morning of Saturday 5 August, in the midst of an uncomfortably hot Bank Holiday weekend. The butler knocked on Gladys's door to inform her that the head housemaid, who was apparently in the habit of entertaining a lover at the house, had obeyed secret instructions from Marlborough and admitted three men. These individuals, smoking pipes and cigarettes as they went about their business, proceeded to lock up the linen closets, the glass and china closet, to cut off the electric light, throw the food out of the larder and lock that too.

Gladys rang the police and then succeeded in contacting some friends, who promptly came to join her at the house. One of them was Herbert Pell, an American friend of her family, who used to take her and her sisters out driving in Italy in happier days. He gave up a holiday at Cowes with his family to come to her rescue. Here is Gladys's account of her altercation with the men:

> I then went downstairs & found the 3 men with their hats & caps on their heads, smoking & laughing loudly together in the inner hall. I asked them who they were and they answered 'Is Gryce the dook of Marlborough' had given the whole house into their hands. I said I did not believe them & they must leave at once. One said 'No we won't, we've a right down here & you can only have the use of the bedroom.'
>
> He had a pipe in his mouth as he spoke. I said 'Please take that pipe out of your mouth & you others put your cigarettes out.' He turned away & spoke the following words to me over his shoulder with the pipe still between his teeth, he said 'you have no right in this house. We are here with the Dook's orders.' I then reached for the pipe & knocked it out of his mouth & the others threw their cigarettes behind the stove in the lobby!⁹

Gladys telephoned Blenheim and spoke to one of the weekend guests, Madame de Janzé. She asked her to 'felicitate Marlborough on his procedure'. Over the next few days the telephone, the gas, and the lift ceased to operate, and the surly detectives began to wedge the basement door to prevent Gladys and her friends coming down. Meanwhile Gladys ate cold dinners by candlelight, water for baths was heated by coal, water for tea and coffee was boiled in a saucepan over a coal-fire and, after the gas was cut off, all food came from cans smuggled in by a kind neighbour.

At length the situation became intolerable. Vans arrived to take away Gladys's possessions on 8 August, lawyers talked furtively outside, and a journalist from the *Daily Express* loitered for a story. At 10.15 that night Gladys and her friends left the house, while the butler made a last-minute check to see nothing further was amiss. Gladys went back to the Carlton Hotel.

Two days later with a vicious flourish of the pen Marlborough made a new will, cutting Gladys out for once and all. The solicitors resumed their flow of letters with renewed enthusiasm, each 'regretting' the action of the other's clients, failing to 'understand' the accusations made, and refusing to budge on any matter. Gladys was forbidden to take anything more from

Blenheim without a prior appointment. Methodically she listed her claims which included the stuffed remains of poor Snowflake, still in dispute as late as May 1938.

Support poured in from her friends. The Duchess of Hamilton and Brandon offered to have her dogs in Scotland and the Princesse de Polignac hoped that 'satisfactory arrangements may be made to ensure' her future comfort. Lily de Clermont-Tonnerre was horrified to read an account of what had happened and urged Gladys to 'try and stand the nasty circumstances for a time' as she was in the right. 'I think M has lost his head and all sense of decency', she declared. 'Mais quelle aventure chère Gladys!!' wrote Edith de Beaumont; and Ida Matthews, who ran a nursing-home for cats and dogs, offered any help she could give: 'Your Grace, remember the happiest time of my life was with you. And how I have regretted ever leaving "Your Grace's" service. . . .'

But the best letter came from the extraordinary Viscountess Churchill in Paris. Verena Churchill was a sister of the 'Yellow' Earl of Lonsdale; she had survived a sensational marital feud with her husband, which had involved gun play, the hiring of Arabs to kidnap the children, threats of disinheritance and the scattering of virtually all their material possessions, only to become a disciple of the Theosophists and a close friend of a creature called Kathleen Ellis, a woman with grey hypnotic eyes who practised automatic writing. Verena Churchill obliged her son to marry 'K' Ellis, and then the two women went to live in Paris together. 'K' committed suicide and Verena Churchill spent her last years alone and deserted.*

In this crisis, Verena Churchill was Gladys's keenest ally :

I feel full of sympathy for you . . . Both [Kathleen Spencer] and I know all the ungentleman like tricks that the family we both had the misfortune to marry into can do – the lies and spite – are you now called a lunatic as I was? – such an easy thing to say & such an unchivalrous lie to start. . . . I feel so deeply for you for it is so horrible to see one's name in all the papers & unless anyone knows the ways of the Churchill family AS I DO how could anyone know the truth – I do not even have to ask about it all – for I know Churchills only

*For an account of these dramas see *All my Sins Remembered* by Viscount Churchill.

fight women and children & persecute them – but never men in any position to retaliate. . . . Why not leave it all & come to Paris later on – one gets so tired of all their lies and malice – But in time of course lies are shown up – It is all a question of time 'For the wheel of God grinds slowly but it grinds exceeding small'.*. . . I wonder if your letters are opened as mine were. If so I hope they will like this one.[10]

News of Gladys's precipitous departure from Carlton House Terrace travelled to Florence where Berenson heard the story from Dorothy Palffy. Nicky Mariano, Berenson's secretary, gathered that Marlborough wanted to re-marry. But the hoped-for bride, 'Bunny' Doble, remained married to Sir Anthony Lindsay-Hogg until the following year, and neither the Duke of Marlborough nor her more welcome suitor, Lord Birkenhead, was a successful aspirant to her hand. Marlborough stayed married to Gladys until his death, while Birkenhead married Lord Camrose's daughter in May 1935.

Solicitors' letters continued throughout 1934, and Gladys pressed for a court case to 'let a little air into the stuffy atmosphere prevalent about my affairs & possessions'. One picture in dispute was an Israels. Gladys was furious that Marlborough would not hand it over:

I cannot imagine why you did this thing except as another general exhibition of your unwarranted ungrateful & terrifying hatred of me who have served you during my whole life with such unselfish & absolute devotion & love.[11]

Gladys stayed either at the Carlton Hotel or with friends. Mrs Stobart Whetherly often invited her to Ebrington Manor, and in March 1934, she visited York where she wrote in Eve Fairfax's book a quotation from Baudelaire: 'Conseil d'un poète – soyez toujours ivre, de vin, de vertu ou de poésie, à votre guise.'[12]

Siegfried Sassoon offered words of encouragement: 'I am dreadfully sorry that you are unhappy, but I have an idea that

*A misquotation from Longfellow's *Retribution. From the Sinngedichte of Friedrich von Logau*:
>Though the mills of God grind slowly, yet they
>>grind exceeding small;
>Though with patience He stands waiting, with
>>exactness grinds He all.

you are a courageous person, so you have that to help you.'[13] By and large, Gladys adopted a philosophical acceptance of her plight, writing in an album: 'After the foregoing horrors – life went on – it always does!' She still made an occasional sortie into society. Dressed in pale pink, she attended Lady London-derry's Eve of Session party and the next day took her place at the Opening of Parliament. Worries included writs from department stores and, in November 1933, a libellous cartoon in a magazine called *Hooey*.

The cartoon showed two rose trees intertwined and kissing. On one side a gardener was talking to a stout lady and in the background was a large house. The caption read: 'I guess we shouldn't have planted the Duchess of Marlborough and the Rev. H. Robertson Page in the same bed.' Though the choice of her name had clearly been a random one and Mr Page had been president of the National Rose Society in the United States and had never met Gladys, she sued the distributors in an attempt to have her name cleared. The action was not heard until January 1935, which meant she endured a further fourteen months of legal correspondence.

In May 1934 Gladys took a much-needed rest-cure, while the Duke of Marlborough gave a last dinner-party at Carlton House Terrace. The Duke was ill with a cancer, which originated near the liver and was inoperable. He was a difficult patient to treat and would cut his doctor short with the words, 'I know I have a filthy inside and my tongue is always dirty but that is nothing to worry about, look at me. I am a much better man than most people of my age.' Gladys was aware of his condition and heard regular reports from her faithful spy Enoch, the electrician at Blenheim. On 25 May Enoch wrote to say:

> He is in a very poor way now – looks as though he might die any day. We all think that he won't last very much longer. We understand that he is going to town for a few weeks & then going abroad, but his plans are so quickly changed.

Soon after this the Duke chanced to meet Lord Castlerosse in the street. 'I am feeling seedy', he said. Castlerosse said he hoped the warm weather would do him good, but forgetting his advice to Proust, the Duke merely shook his head. Castlerosse was inte-rested in the Duke's obsession with his health: he never immersed himself fully in a hot bath for fear of cardiac arrest, he danced for exercise, seldom smiled and ate and drank in moderation. 'Valetudinarians seem to die young', commented Castlerosse, 'and the Duke was no exception.'[14]

Shortly before his death Marlborough was visited by his sister, Lady Lilian Grenfell, and said he still hoped to recover. But his strength ebbed away. On the last night of his life he gave a tea-party for close friends including Winston Churchill. Father Martindale has testified that he took the sacraments seriously:

> ... after his confessions he would be like an old man; he would lean upon one's arm; and after his Communions he would be as it were dazed with the magnitude of the mystery to which he had been admitted.[15]

Because he believed suffering to be part of a Christian's life, the Duke refused morphia. Only when he was unconscious was it administered. A maid at the house telegraphed Gladys regularly with news of his condition.

Marlborough passed away painlessly on 30 June 1934 at the age of sixty-two. Blandford succeeded to the title and in accordance with the statutes of the Order, Marlborough's Garter banner was removed from over his stall in St George's Chapel.

Long obituaries were published in the newspapers, listing his accomplishments. Winston Churchill wrote some lines about his 'oldest and dearest friend' for *The Times*, and Castlerosse noted perceptively:

> To me he was a pathetic figure like a lonely peacock struggling through deserted gardens. . . . The Duke of Marlborough was the last duke who firmly believed that strawberry leaves could effectively cover a multitude of sins.
>
> I for one shall miss him, and it is a sadness for me to think that this man of brains spent his life sowing seed after seed where none can ever grow.[16]

Marlborough's funeral was held at Farm Street with Churchills present in force. King George v was represented by the Marquess of Salisbury, an honour the Duke would have much appreciated. Hovering at the portal of the church was Father Martindale, dreading that Gladys, or even Consuelo, might suddenly appear, draped in widow's weeds; but neither came.

Inside the Protestant mourners were confused by the candles they were given to hold and some burnt their fingers, not daring to extinguish the flickering symbols. Father Martindale gave an address.

After the service the coffin was conveyed to Blenheim for burial in the chapel that had confused Epstein when he saw it. Shane Leslie was one of those present and was much moved as he followed the hearse through the long avenues Marlborough had planted. He walked beside Winston Churchill and they discussed the survival of the spirit. Later Churchill greeted Blandford and addressed him sonorously: 'Le Duc est mort. Vive le Duc.' Meanwhile Enoch reported to Gladys, 'The attendance at the funeral was very small and there were only 56 wreaths altogether.'

Lady Edward Spencer-Churchill, Marlborough's great-aunt by marriage, who was one of several people intelligent and sensitive enough to realize that, despite recent bitterness, Marlborough's death would upset Gladys, wrote to her:

> I know you will feel deeply the termination of a life that for many years has been closely connected with yours. Blenheim looked very lovely yesterday in bright sunshine when it gave its last welcome to the owner who loved it so well.[17]

Lily de Clermont-Tonnerre also wrote to Gladys:

> Of course you must feel it and only remember the best period of your life ... you shall no more be upset by him – and stay for ever the one who adorned his home for many years.[18]

Nancy Mitford and her sister Diana Guinness noticed the sadness that fell over Gladys after the death. Many people wrote to her, some aware of the separation, others not. Gladys acknowledged all the letters, even the remote ones, and the task helped her through a difficult time. Inadvertently she had become Marlborough's widow. Meanwhile she remained quietly in the country.

PART FOUR

Renunciation

And finally the renunciation of all that

(Renunciation, it says, is the most
rewarding stage)*

*From notes in Gladys's diary, 1962

Chapter Twenty-one

MIXBURY

On 2 August 1934 Consuelo returned to Blenheim, one of the palace's first visitors under the new regime. She saw the completion of Marlborough's constructions, made possible by Vanderbilt finance, and for the rest of her life enjoyed the role of Duke's mother and paid many happy visits there to her son and grandchildren.

Gladys, the real Dowager Duchess of Marlborough, seemed to the world to have disappeared into smoke. She adopted the name of Mrs Spencer, 'half of "Spencer-Churchill" as a joke name I took for use in the derelict hamlet of Chacombe for fun'. And sometimes she signed herself 'The widow Marlborough', explaining 'I like that way of appellation better than the meaningless & slightly absurd "Duchess".' She was anxious to sever all connexions with Blenheim and was, of course, at liberty to adopt any name she liked: 'I loathe & detest that of M. & I am sure I spent enough money to try and get rid of it.'[1]

When Gladys remained hidden during Marlborough's obsequies, journalists began to sense a story and went in search of her. They traced her to Mixbury, a tiny village near Brackley in Northamptonshire. They sniffed around for a while and then investigated Town Farm, officially occupied by Mrs Grylls, who was still looking after dogs, some of which were hers and some Gladys's. The journalists discovered that Gladys did her own shopping in the village stores wearing a smocked overall. When one of them attempted to enter Town Farm, an upper window opened and Gladys tipped a jug of water on to his head. Presently, security guards took up position around the house until the furore died down. Reports about the incident appeared in the papers, stories of a hermit's life and a hundred spaniels, unfortunately becoming a well-remembered and often exaggerated tale, which ended by implying that Gladys had gone crazy and greeted all visitors in this fashion. In Paris the worst conclusions were formed, as the Abbé Mugnier reported to Berenson on 31 December 1934:

> Yesterday the old Princesse de Polignac informed me that the ex-Gladys Deacon and now also ex-Duchess of Marlborough has lost her head. She lives near London and when a visitor presents himself, she tips water from a window to invite him to take his leave. Poor woman! She no longer has her much vaunted beauty and now the rest is taken from her without pity. It makes one think of a famous myth by Ovid or the like.[2]

This story certainly had the qualities of a myth, for Gladys's own account of the incident presents a somewhat different picture. She wrote to her lawyer in August 1934:

> Three creatures, a burly bully, a camera man among others formed a party who pestered Mrs Grylls all day. They put a chauffeur at the gate to warn them when Mrs Grylls was not in the house & getting over a fence, she found them *battering* (I mean literally *battering*) at the front door which was locked. She said 'What you again? Please leave my premises' (she holds the lease by the bye in her name.) The bully, furious, replied shouting 'No I refuse to go until I see who is in this house' & pounded at the door again, as one wd not a barn. She was ½ hour trying to get them out. Finally the woman said to the bully who said he wd stay there all night 'Come on Ronnie it's no use' – They had a hearty tea at the village shop talking & laughing trying to make a scandal. They went to Finmere to phone their stuff which I have not seen. They took photos from over the wall.
>
> Some others were prowling around all day, questioning all the villagers breaking into their premises DEMANDING as if it were by divine gift to see me.
>
> You note the 'with a hundred dogs'. I have 3 of mine, the rest belong to Mrs Grylls. She is up in the air now abt dog licences for her 20. . . . You never saw outside of a film, the bullying, trespassing, impudence, insolence of these creatures. More will come.[3]

The Princess de Navaro, a friend of Gladys's, came to support her in the siege, and Mrs Grylls proved admirable. For some years, Mrs Agnes Evelyn Innocent Gerveys-Grylls was Gladys's staunch friend and companion. She came from Launceston and was the eldest daughter of Canon Townend, later Vicar of St Peter's, Fulham. About the same age as Gladys, she had married Mr Grylls in the early 1900s. She was widowed in the 1920s and left somewhat short of money. Always an ardent dog breeder, she took it up professionally and in 1930 was employed by Gladys as manageress of the kennels at Blenheim. She always called Gladys 'Your Grace' though she signed herself 'Yours affectionately' or 'Yours with love'. Besides looking after the dogs, she also wrote letters to the agent at Blenheim on Gladys's behalf demanding the return of certain outstanding possessions.

When dealing with Blenheim they were greatly assisted by the electrician Enoch, who went diligently about his business, saying nothing, but noting the whereabouts of Gladys's things, passing on lists of guests, dates of sales of the late Duke's possessions, and news of modernizations at the palace. He 'cultivated the Queen', which meant he kept in with the house-keeper, and he proved a splendid actor: 'The Queen informed me today you were staying at Hethe near Bicester. Imagine my astonishment!!' On another occasion he was asked if he knew where Gladys was; 'Of course I was quite ignorant', he assured her. Sometimes he slipped away to see her in person, but he had to be extremely careful. Not long afterwards he went to work for Lord Leconfield at Petworth, where for some years Gladys rewarded his loyalty with small Christmas gifts.

More than anything Gladys wanted to be free to start a new life, quite unconnected with Blenheim and the Marlboroughs. She was disgusted by the attitude of the new Duchess, who opened letters sent to Gladys at Blenheim, and then forwarded them, writing in a disguised hand 'opened in error' as though they were redirected by a servant. Gladys regretted that she had not cultivated powerful allies to help her:

> I quite see how I need them myself now. I know the strength
> of social opinion very well, I know what curs these in-laws
> are – what a one the late duke was! ... Blandford & Ivor are
> very rich – that will always gild with sunshine every mean
> thing they do, for everyone.[4]

As she began to create a new life, Gladys was entertaining and philosophical about her fall from society:

> I say to myself 'Horatio, to what base uses art thou re-
> turned!'* But of course it's all my fault for being the only
> one who ever believed the late duke of M. was other than
> what the world called him all his life![5]

On Gladys's last visit to Eaton to stay with the Westminsters in March 1934, before Marlborough's death, the guests who had previously posed eagerly for her camera took on a distant air, and in some pictures ignore the photographer completely. Gladys became aware very fast that they were no longer interested in her after the loss of Blenheim. But Lady Serena James remained a kind friend and invited her for Christmas in 1934. In January 1935 she was back at Mixbury, where she and Mrs Grylls pulled a solitary cracker on Twelfth Night.

At the end of January 1935, the *Hooey* court case was heard in London. For the last time she reverted to being the Dowager Duchess, and a pressman snapped her in the law courts, dressed in a black coat with a fur collar and an elegant little hat. It is the last public photograph of her. Gladys stepped into the witness box in an atmosphere described as 'a mixture of distaste and embarrassment'. She told the court that the cartoon suggested her adultery with a clergyman, and she had come to clear her name:

> I am in no way bringing this action for money not being in
> the least interested in whether damages are given or not but
> I do care about the good name of the House of Marlborough
> and I bring this action purely to clear the vile reflection on
> my character and that name.

The Lord Chief Justice, Lord Hewart, was convinced that nobody was attempting to assail Gladys's reputation and asked: 'Is this lamentable action really to go on?' Gladys was asked if it would have made any difference if the various newsagents and distributors sued had apologized. She replied that circumstances necessitated full publicity to clear her name. Lord Hewart commented, 'I take a very serious view of this case –

---

* A mild misquotation from Hamlet in the churchyard: 'To what base uses we may return, Horatio!' (Act v, scene 1).

25 Gladys in Eugene Higgins's garden on her wedding day, 25 June 1921 –
a photograph dedicated to her nurse Irma.

26 Blenheim Palace photographed from the air. 'The crooked lawn' can be seen to the left, leading down to the lake.

27 The Italian Garden at Blenheim, photographed by Gladys from the private apartments.

28 Epstein, 'un génie qui est jeune', working on his second bust of Gladys at Blenheim in 1923.

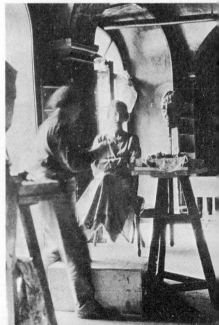

29 'Himself' – The Duke of Marlborough outside his Palace.

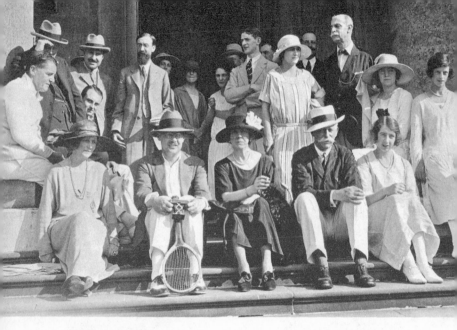

30 A house party at Blenheim 8 July 1923, photographed by Gladys.
Left to right (standing): Winston Churchill, M. Adrien Thierry (1st Secretary French Embassy), Lytton Strachey, Mrs Maurice Wingfield, Mrs L. de Rothschild, Lady Eleanor Smith, Edward Marjoribanks, Mme Thierry, Earl Fitzwilliam, Don Alfonso Merry del Val (Spanish Ambassador), 'Shelagh' Duchess of Westminster, and Viscountess Carlton. Seated: The Earl of Birkenhead, Lady Holford, Prince Paul of Serbia, Prince Christopher of Greece, Lady Sarah Wilson, Sir George Holford and Lady Joan Fitzwilliam.

31 Gladys in the 1920s.

32 The Duke of Marlborough feeling less than well.

33 and 34 Two Conversation Pieces at Carlton House Terrace in 1930.
Above (seated) : Harold Nicolson, Lord Berners, Edith Sitwell, Gladys and
Raymond Mortimer. *Below:* Gladys dispensing tea to a group including
Lytton Strachey (*left*), Raymond Mortimer (standing), and the Chinese wife of
the photographer.

35 Gladys's Blenheim spaniels enjoying life on a silk cover. *Left to right:* Daffodil, Betty, Snowflake, Corina, Dragée and Airmaid, watched by the maid, Paxton.

36 Colin Gill and his assistant painting Gladys's eye on the portico at Blenheim in August 1928.

37 Mrs Grylls with one of her prize-winning dogs.

38 The Noble Duke of Marlborough's 'Ignoble Antics' – an artist's impression during the siege in August 1933. '... the American Duchess of Marlborough was forced to cook meagre meals on a cheap oil stove smuggled in by her friends ...'

39 The weary figure of the Duke of Marlborough turning away from Gladys's sphinx on the West Water Terrace.

40 The last public photograph of Gladys, caught by a press-man waiting in the Law Courts in January 1935.

41 The Pole. Andrei Kwiatkowsky photographed by the author at Chacombe Grange a few months after Gladys's death.

very', and adjourned it until the following day. The case resulted in full apologies being offered and a fixed sum handed over; the court retained 'the foul emanation from the printing press', and Lord Hewart said he hoped the publication would not discredit the profession of journalism which, he added, 'as everyone knows contains a great number of able and conscientious gentlemen'.

Gladys retreated to the country, where she found a letter of congratulations from a certain Edgar East of Fulham:

> Pardon me Your Grace taking the liberty but I felt I must drop you a line to say how glad I was to see you exposed those despicable people, as one never knows who are at the back of scandalion [sic] literature. You was far to [sic] lenient. I should have made them pay full penalty that is the only way to make them realize. . . .[6]

Gladys never again entered the public eye, though she was often in London, lunching at Simpsons, the Berkeley or the Ritz. In the country she went to the Bicester meet, the National Hunt Festival at Cheltenham, a point-to-point in Worcestershire, Sandown, the Grand National and the Richmond Show. In February a local man stole a photograph of Marius Michel from her, which required more legal action. He was arrested and found guilty at Bicester, telling a pack of lies in court.

The Blenheim Estate Company was compulsorily wound up, since Marlborough had left many bad and unnecessary debts. On 8 April Robert Bruce Lockhart heard talk of the new Duke having 'compounded with his father's creditors'.[7] As late as 1938 Gladys was advised that it would be useless to make further claims against Marlborough's estate as it was insolvent. Meanwhile items such as kennels and pictures continued to arrive from Blenheim, and polite if somewhat reserved letters were exchanged between Gladys and her step-son.

1935 was the year of the Silver Jubilee but Gladys ignored the festivities. She spent her time planting antirrhinums and sweet peas, burning dead grass and blackberrying, according to the season. In September she noted that she was 'becoming quite a carpenter'. Edward VIII came and went, and she remained at Mixbury.

When the time came for King George VI to be crowned, Gladys became interested in the possibility of taking her seat in the Abbey, and in June 1936 applied to the Earl Marshal for a letter of summons to attend. The request was granted and in due course, the summons, the tickets and the instructions arrived. Gladys began to search for a Duchess's robe, 'the cape to be powdered with four Rows of Ermine, the edging five inches in breadth, the Train two yards . . .'. It was no easy matter, and the Army & Navy Stores reported that all known sources of supply had been explored without success. Finally N. Clarkson of Wardour Street, who advertised 'Every requisite for stage and film', offered the hire of a robe for thirty-five guineas.

At the very last minute Gladys lost her nerve and decided she could not face the ceremony. She telegraphed the Earl Marshal, pleading 'sudden indisposition' and seat number 23 in the Duchesses' block was therefore left empty. Once again it was the cause of some chatter in the long wait before the service, and of the acquiescent nodding of tiara-crested heads.

Chapter Twenty-two

CHACOMBE

In 1938 Gladys's lease on Town Farm, Mixbury, expired. She liked the area she was living in and began 'an appalling hunt' for a new home. On 5 October she paid Gertrude Mabel Railton £1,400 for Grange Farm at Chacombe. The house is built of Hornton stone in a small village two and a half miles north-east of Banbury on the road to Northampton. Gladys's new home occupied the entire central island of the village, with a yard in front, a garden beside it, and a big orchard behind. This was to be her home until 1962 and she settled in happily. Here is her description of it, written to the artist Jean Marchand:

> It is charming with a thatched roof, its stone walls covered with roses, an apricot tree and an old pear tree. There is a small but very pretty garden with three large asparagus patches and around the yard are the small farm buildings. Behind – an orchard which must be ravishing when in flower.
>
> Inside everything is very small but pretty and peaceful – a very small library and drawing-room, a dining-room, a kitchen and dairy, three bedrooms full of light, electricity and a pretty apple-green bathroom.
>
> In short all that we did not have in Mixbury.[1]

Gladys built an annex to the library to house her books including the fine collection of Marius Michels and Rodin's *Faunesse*. Boldini's portrait of Mrs Baldwin dominated the dining-room. There were also works by Jean Marchand, one of them a landscape:

> You have no idea how much it has improved. The colour

seems to me to have become more profound, and in its entirety it gives off a force and harmony which delights me at every hour.[2]

As she spread her collection of pictures about the little cottage, she was happy again:

Just imagine, how I leap from one to other, admiring them, saying good morning to them – I owe money on many but too bad, one mustn't think of that.[3]

Gladys was delighted to find that Chacombe was only ten minutes from the cinema in Banbury. The disadvantages were that water was scarce in summer, all the local girls worked in cloth manufacturers' – not as maids – and the house was very close to the factories and would be in danger in wartime. As early as January 1939, Gladys was convinced that war would come.

As at Mixbury, so now at Chacombe, Gladys and Mrs Grylls set themselves to work. They painted the house, pruned the roses and had the dairy ceiling mended. The house was re-thatched and a pergola constructed from the front door to the gate. In their early days there, friends were invited to dinner from time to time and a Mr Draper would come over from a nearby village to act as butler.

Gladys now dressed in a very eccentric manner, largely in an attempt to look poor so as to discourage burglars. One of the villagers was chatting to Mrs Grylls over the gate one day when she spotted what she thought was the farm-hand beckoning from the yard. Mrs Grylls informed her swiftly 'That's not a farm-hand. That's the Duchess.' Gladys took to wearing old wellington boots and a straw hat, which in winter she exchanged for a sou'wester. She applied paint to her legs to keep the flies out of her boots when she was working. This attracted a certain amount of local comment as it looked as if she was wearing garters. Her eating habits were also odd. She ate a lot of mashed potatoes which she liked, but refused to touch cow's milk. An unpopular feature in the village was a flock of geese, accidentally knocked down to Gladys at a local auction. These proved admirable guards for the cottage, attacking all comers without discrimination.

From time to time Gladys employed some of the villagers for

odd jobs or gardening. Some found her too strict a task-master, but others were fascinated by her and she won their loyalty and affection. One man was set happily to work knocking together coffins for her spaniels when they died. If she trusted a servant she gave him the freedom of the house, let him read her old diaries and related hair-raising tales of her past life. The Duke of Marlborough never emerged very well from these stories. Another strange hazard of living at Chacombe was that Gladys used to walk her dogs late at night, wandering around the village with an oil-lamp in her hand. If she saw a light on, she was quite likely to drop in for a chat which would extend into the small hours.

The Second World War was declared on 3 September 1939 and Gladys remained at Chacombe for the duration. She made no contribution to the 'war effort', and was at times something of a menace. She refused to black out her windows, and when the constabulary complained she referred them to Winston Churchill, whose recent rise to power had left her unimpressed. 'He was the right man for the time because he was showy and that's what they wanted.'[4] He compared badly in her eyes with his Nazi opponent. Gladys expressed her sympathy with the German war leader by naming one of her cats 'Itler'. It turned out to be an appropriate name, as the cat was inclined to steal the chickens' food.

Gladys continued to pass her time working on the farm, caring for her dogs and reading, Emile Ollivier one day, Schlumberger on Byzantium another. Books arrived regularly from the Times Book Club and Gladys scoured several daily newspapers and magazines. During these years she added substantially to her collection of Sitwells and acquired books by Berenson and Consuelo Vanderbilt Balsan. She also became a poultry farmer, which increased the daily work load.

The war made life difficult and relations between Gladys and Mrs Grylls became strained. They ceased to speak to one another, and one day Gladys said angrily that she hated the sight of her. In November 1941 Mrs Grylls could bear the strain no more; she made a precipitous departure, pleading that she was ill and worn, her nerves were at breaking-point and her spirit broken. 'I simply went to pieces and couldn't get on with anything', she wrote soon afterwards. Feeling let down, Gladys reacted by retorting that she was glad she had gone.

Gladys assumed the reins and, alone now, took on the running of the hens, the cooking, the farm-work, and the care of the dogs. Mrs Grylls kept in regular contact from afar, but never felt well enough to come back again. She was full of admiration for Gladys's strength of mind, as she coped not only with the burden of work, but also with a car accident, a sprained foot, later a scalded foot and a general state of loneliness.

It was in October 1942 that Mrs Grylls wrote to her about the fortune-teller, who, she claimed, had so much influenced Gladys's life. The letter was inspired by a dream:

> Last night I had a dream about you and the dogs. You were at a house – all comfortably furnished. I was with you & the dogs & you were very busy writing a book – you looked so well again and happy – I wish it were true.

Mrs Grylls urged Gladys to give up her present way of life in favour of 'a little rest & comfort'. But Gladys was determined to continue her gallant fight for survival in her own way and would not give in. She took on an extra responsibility, the keeping of bees, and survived the intense misery of watching a number of spaniels die one after another from insufficient food.

After the departure of Mrs Grylls, Gladys was helped in the house by May Hobbs, an evacuee from London who had come to live in Chacombe. Mrs Hobbs was very interested in the enigmatic personality of her new employer. While she found Gladys a shrewd judge of character and a very capable woman, all her ability seemed to be going to waste. Gladys claimed that she wrote books under a *nom de plume* which she refused to reveal; but this story, first tried on Berenson in St Moritz in 1908, was untrue and merely an excuse for the long hours of solitude. Gladys also spoke of a cut to her face and informed Mrs Hobbs that she had stitched the wound herself in front of the mirror. She seemed to care more for her books, which were kept warm by electric stoves twenty-four hours a day, than for her own well-being. Sometimes Mrs Hobbs cooked dinner for her and left it in an out-house for Gladys to collect in the night.

As an employer, Gladys was exacting and mean. She obliged Mrs Hobbs to pay for eggs from the farm, though Gladys had plenty of money in the bank. She once sent her to work in the attic where possessions were stored and then stole up on her to see if she was doing her work. Mrs Hobbs's attention had been caught by some albums and she had begun to look through some pictures of Blenheim about which Gladys never spoke. Just as her eye rested on a picture of the Duke of Marlborough, captioned 'Himself', instinct warned her of Gladys's approach and she closed the book. A second later Gladys was in the room.

Yet Gladys did not mind at all when Mrs Hobbs inadvertently burned a pullover she was cleaning. And once after Mrs Hobbs walked all the way from Banbury to Chacombe, Gladys was so sorry for her that she accompanied her to the well and helped her draw the water. For Mrs Hobbs was also treated as a friend. Some evenings she sat talking late into the night to Gladys at the Grange Farm, and at other times Gladys visited her cottage. The villagers were convinced that she was in great danger and that Gladys would murder her one day, but Mrs Hobbs was not at all afraid and listened to the stories with great pleasure. One night as Gladys left the cottage, the moon shone down on the strange figure in wellington boots and raincoat, and Mrs Hobbs noticed that Gladys's eyes even shone blue in that silvery light. The villagers did not believe that Gladys was a Duchess, and great confusion was caused in the post office when Gladys sent Mrs Hobbs down with a telegram addressed to Winston Churchill.

After a number of years Mrs Hobbs felt she should leave Chacombe for a better job in London. She and her husband went together to tell Gladys and the three talked for four hours before Mrs Hobbs summoned the courage to say she was leaving. Gladys revealed that she had known this would happen and that that was why they had come. 'Everyone I love lets me down', she said.

Several times in the ensuing years the need for news of Gladys drew Mrs Hobbs back to Chacombe. On one visit Gladys was so thrilled to see her that she threw her arms round her. Gladys met her son and talked to him. She pronounced him very bright and said he would go far. Not long afterwards he won a scholarship to Cambridge.

Gladys's early enthusiasm for her home had worn off by June

1943; though she was still in touch with the outside world, as this letter indicates:

> I am still in this hole of a house. I have broken my left arm, trying to do the work I can find no one to undertake & am fed up & will have to do the housework as well. . . . I went to London 10 days ago about my arm – I did nothing but sleep & eat while I was there with intervals at the dentist & having my hair 'permed' for tidiness. I hate country life. One becomes brutalized with work or for the rich with boredom & it is no wonder that all those that achieve anything must live in towns where live what 'brain' is abt. One wdn't know a war was on even, in the country. . . . Marlborough is hanging abt nightclubs at present, too much champagne & very fat. Mary haggard & lined was a general or something like that but is now expecting a miracle child in August. At her age not only an undertaking, poor thing. . . .
>
> I suppose the Americans are too busy trying on gas-masks. How utterly absurd they are with their terror of invasion. I think they think it is being fashionable to which end they'd sell their soul I always think.[5]

Gladys visited London again in August 1943, staying at the Ritz, and in December that year 'Chips' Channon had his strange meeting with her in a Bond Street jeweller's shop. She often visited jewellers to buy and sell jewels to supplement her income. After her death her collection fetched over £452,000. 'Chips' described Gladys as she examined a ruby clip:

> I saw an extraordinary marionette of a woman – or was it a man? It wore grey flannel trousers, a wide leather belt, masculine overcoat, and a man's brown felt hat, and had a really frightening appearance, but the hair was golden dyed and long: what is wrongly known as platinum; the mouth was a scarlet scar. . . .

'Chips' recognized Gladys and went over to greet her. She took his hand nervously. To her question 'Est-ce que je vous connais, Monsieur?' he wrote that he replied, 'Yes, I am Chips.' Since he did not know her as well as he liked to imply, it is more probable that he said 'Henry Channon'. Whatever he did say, he got a strange reaction:

She looked at me, stared vacantly with those famous turquoise eyes that once drove men insane with desire and muttered 'Je n'ai jamais entendu ce nom-là.'[6]

In an instant Gladys had thrown down the clip and bolted from the shop, leaving the M.P. in a state of confusion. In fact she had taken him in very cleverly because she was perfectly well aware who he was. The vacant stare was part of her acting repertoire and a good way of avoiding communication with those she sought to avoid. In 1976 Gladys discussed 'Chips', and to the question 'If he came up to you would you talk to him?' she replied, 'Certainly not! I can be very stiff – completely oblivious if I want to be!'[7] and then laughed. Her ruse was not entirely to her advantage, however, for 'Chips' concluded that she had gone totally mad, and his tongue was by no means a still one.

The war raged on into 1944, while Gladys continued her labours, cutting roses, mending chicken gates, attacking nettles, sweeping and constructing wire frames in the garden. Enemy aeroplanes flew overhead in February and the next month there was a local crisis. 'Allotment frenzy seizes thick, eating Chacombe', noted Gladys. In June a fox got into her chicken pen and killed all the chickens but two. The long awaited Anglo-American invasion began in Europe, and hordes of Londoners, who told Gladys they had not slept for fifteen days, arrived in the Banbury area.

At sixty-three, Gladys was finding life very hard. She was often unwell, slept with difficulty and was forever losing beloved animals following one or another crisis. She burned her feet and ankles so badly that they took eleven weeks to heal. The sheets on the bed began to fall to pieces and she could not replace them. In October Mrs Grylls came to see her, and was appalled by the squalor into which the house was descending and the bad state of Gladys herself. She left 'distracted with worry'.

In February 1945 some German prisoners of war came to help Gladys prune the apple trees. Gladys found them 'at once knowledgeable quick and well behaved'. She wrote for more to come and afterwards kept up a correspondence with them as they settled back into their former lives. She was depressed when friends died – Lady Lansdowne's two sons, Tom Mitford, and Elizabeth Bibesco – but continued to follow the war with keen curiosity. A typical diary entry (13 March 1945) reads

> What is depression? Is it only fatigue? Lovely day, frost last night. Is the war ending or not? Rumania & Bulgaria mysteries.

She heard the news of Hitler's fall on the 10.45 Foreign Service news on 1 May, and was appalled by revolting photographs of Mussolini and Clara Petacci hanging by the feet, and later lying on the ground 'with brutes spitting on them'.

Mrs Grylls remained concerned about her, wishing she was 'in some comfortable place with people to look after you & surrounded by love & affection'. Instead Gladys constructed elaborate fortifications around Chacombe to keep out intruders. Gradually the farmhouse became like a fort. One of the reasons for this was to deter the village boys from annoying her. Chacombe was remote from the modern world and several young inhabitants believed she was a witch. Some reacted to this by pelting the house with stones. And Gladys once came out with her shot-gun, though she assured Mrs Hobbs that it was not loaded.

On 4 April 1946 Hermann Keyserling wrote to her from Upper Bavaria, where, following a bad war, he had fallen on hard times:

> Dear Gladys – in case you still are alive as I hope you are, please answer personally to the adress [*sic*] on the other side of this letter; if not, please suggest to some heir of yours to do so. How have you passed this awful decade. I have lost everything, all my books, ms etc. But now I am living a new life, my real life; the one I anticipated even when I knew you first, at Innsbruck in 1908. . . .[8]

For many years Keyserling had been active with the School of Wisdom at Darmstadt. Now he invited Gladys to come and address the school as an important woman. 'Men have wrought such havoc, have concentrated entirely on the destructive side of life, so it is up to you . . . to build up a better world.' Having been out of touch with Gladys since 1928, and knowing her for a bad correspondent, he ended on a note both pessimistic and optimistic. 'In case there is no answer I will consider you dead

& look forward to a meeting in a better place than this world is.' The letter passed the Censor and arrived at Blenheim, from where it was eventually forwarded to Chacombe. But the philosopher was iller than he realized and by the time the letter arrived he was dead. He went to that 'better place' on 26 April, aged sixty-five.

As the 1940s progressed, so Gladys retreated further and further into her own world. Her brain continued to digest the world's problems and her own; she divided her time between reading and the most exacting physical work. Letters were still written in ink in a scrupulously neat hand. But disillusioned with her former life, she cared nothing for the conventions of normal dress or personal hygiene. Her hair became matted, her fingernails were uncut, her teeth taken out. She wore boots even in the house and looked more like a tramp than a Duchess. The house deteriorated around her.

In extreme old age she said once: 'Sometimes something happens that is so awful that it cuts you off and after that you don't care.'[9] The 'awful' thing was not her ruined face, but her ruined marriage, with its accompanying horrors and insults and its harrowing aftermath. Her dream had proved an illusion and she realized that she had spent her life in an unworthy cause.

Four years before marrying Marlborough Gladys gave enormous moral aid to a new friend of hers, Ethel Boileau,* who, though married, had fallen desperately in love with someone else, who made her so unhappy that she contemplated suicide. Gladys exhorted her with the words 'Tenez votre courage à deux mains et votre coeur haut.' Many years later Ethel Boileau reminded Gladys of her help:

> The mental and spiritual stiffening you gave me then I cannot explain to you, because it wasn't done deliberately by you but was the result of your own nature – so radiant and detached and serene which threw a mysterious charm over everything you touched, and reconciled one to life in a queer way....[10]

Ethel Boileau was convinced that Gladys had taught her 'the

* Ethel Boileau (*d.* 1942). A successful novelist. Only child of Rev. James Foster Young. Married Sir Raymond Boileau, 4th Bt.

greatest of all values in life – that of detachment, that sure and certain core in oneself which left one above the chances and bitterness of life'. She prayed that the cruelty Gladys suffered at Marlborough's hands would never result in her losing that detachment. But unfortunately too much had happened – first at Blenheim, then later in the struggles with solicitors, court cases and writs, the fight to regain possessions, the rumours and allegations, and the lack of ready money. On 19 May 1947, Gladys glanced at her diary of 1924:

> Look it's today – 23 years later – 1947 – again Monday the 19th! Well the existence of 1924 passed away 9 years later like a black heavy cloud leaving such a disgusted pain that for years & even now I cannot bear to even brush by it in thought. I had then no idea of how 'dirty' are so many people. Marlborough stealing the one nice thing I had the Corot . . .* in another place his son's doings – Ivor unwilling to make a statement the picture was mine, that his father had said so to & before him over & over again & before Blandford too. Well I feel cleaner not being in such contact & certainly happier.

Gladys now preferred the occasional company of village people, and was grateful for any kindness shown her. Mrs Speed, who lived at Chacombe and had worked in the house, cooked her a hearty meal for Christmas in 1946. Gladys wrote in her diary:

> England's presents continue innumerous in 1946 but given by needy people are most gratifying. A pair of bedsocks, a bottle of bathsalts, a good dinner, a basket of fruit.
> The rich guests of yesteryear – nothing.

But most of all she loved animals. Two years after her little dog Coronie died, she wrote:

> It is so hard to love cruel, calculating, selfish human beings who bring only pain to one – & it is so easy to love the defenceless & devoted like you.

Gladys fed the animals on healthy meat from the butcher, while she lived on boiled cabbage, drawing on an iron determination to survive. The house was not without alcohol and at times, when she felt really depressed, she took drugs.

* The Corot was never returned to Gladys.

Visitors to the Grange Farm were not usually made welcome. Mrs Grylls, who found that life since leaving Gladys's world had been nothing but a series of dull episodes, came back to see her several times and stayed for two months at the end of 1947. When she came to collect some things in 1948, Gladys obliged her to wait three-quarters of an hour before admitting her to the house. Nevertheless Mrs Grylls kept in touch with Gladys until 1951. The following year, on 28 September, Mrs Grylls's body was found in the Thames off County Hall. The inquest produced insufficient evidence to show how she had come to be in the water. She was aged seventy-five.

Gladys was not often seen about the village, but her rare appearances were not forgotten. Lady Sophia Schilizzi,* who moved to Chacombe House in 1947, met her, wearing dirty wellington boots, a black Molyneux gown, and a hat which resembled a witch's peaked hat. Gladys immediately said: 'You look like something out of a book!', but Lady Sophia was too nonplussed to ask which one. Gladys called on her one evening when she saw the light on and related strange tales. Subsequently she telephoned Lady Sophia several times between midnight and 3 a.m. to ask if she knew how to make strawberry jam. Finally Lady Sophia had to say that she preferred to make it by daylight.

Relations who attempted to visit Gladys had gruelling experiences. One of them came to see her in November 1946 and knocked several times at the door. Nothing happened so she went away and made enquiries at the local pub. During a final attempt to stir Gladys, the front door suddenly opened slightly. The visitor pushed it and to her considerable astonishment came face to face with Gladys. Simultaneously a dozen cats flew out from the darkness within and scuttled out through her legs into the daylight. Gladys yelled at her 'Get out! Leave me alone.' Then just as suddenly, she made a complete volte-face and said in a well modulated voice: 'If you would be so kind as to wait outside, I will join you.' True to her word, she emerged a few minutes later, wrapped in a shawl, and chatted for twenty minutes or so in a mixture of English and German.

She knew who her visitor was, but little of the minutiae of her life. Nevertheless she asked no questions. For all she cared

* Daughter of 11th Earl Waldegrave.

the visitor could have dropped from the sky. But she clearly liked her, because she spontaneously gave her a present of £25. Then just as suddenly as before, she darted back into the house, slammed the door and was gone.

Chapter Twenty-three

THE POLE

One day in 1951 a young man was bicycling through Chacombe on his way home from work. Gladys was in her garden, trying to mend the front gate. She spotted him and cried out, commanding him to help her. He promptly dismounted and came over. The two fell into conversation and she discovered that he was Polish, a 'D.P.' (Displaced Person) who had settled in the area. Because Gladys was an exacting task-master she had never retained an English servant for long, nor had she really taken the English to heart. But here was a man who knew how to obey. Moments later she was ordering him to come and work for her. He protested that he had a job, to which Gladys replied, 'Very well, you will come at weekends.' She would pay him £1 for half a day's work.

The young man was Andrei Kwiatkowsky, then in his twenties, whose father had, by coincidence, worked at Mankiewicze, the estates of Charles Radziwill, brother of Prince 'Aba' Radziwill, the first husband of Gladys's sister Dorothy. During the war Andrei had been a victim of the Russian pressgangs and had been forced to assist in building their army's route through the Finnish marshes to Mannerheim. He escaped in Persia and made his way to England. On his arrival he secured a job in a factory and married a girl from Liverpool. She produced two sons, who have since made their father proud by finding excellent jobs.

Gladys inspired total loyalty in Andrei, an unceasing service which continued until the day she died. He spoke five languages, so they often conversed in German and were thus not understood by the villagers. He tended the garden and did a number of odd jobs around the farm buildings. Gladys did not allow him into the house for two years, and so there were days when she would open an upper-storey window and lower the garden implements to him on a string. At the end of the day the process was reversed. She had adopted Proustian hours, sleeping during the day and rising at about five in the afternoon. Andrei started work at midday and pottered about the garden quietly at his work.

Gladys liked to steal up on him to see if she could catch him idling, but Andrei always knew when she was about to appear. She would unbolt the kitchen door, which was a lengthy matter, due to the profusion of locks and chains. Meanwhile the cats would scamper out and perch on the walls. The sight of a cat heralded Gladys's arrival as clearly as white smoke from the Vatican heralds the election of a new Pope. Thereafter Gladys would accompany Andrei around the garden giving him very specific instructions as to what was to be done. At other times she might summon him from the upper window, her cry ringing out over the neighbourhood: 'Andrei! Come here!'

One of his duties was to turn the wheels of two Austin 7s that stood on blocks in one of the barns. One day she asked him if he had performed this duty. He replied that he had. 'No you haven't', she snapped, 'I marked them with a crayon!' She would get him to inject the thistles with wax, which surprised him – she never told him the effect it had had on her face, passing that off as a result of a car accident.

Once she wanted to go for a walk around the village. She tied a sack around her middle, over her boiler suit, put a fisherman's hat on her head, and being somewhat lame, took his arm and they set off. This extraordinary pair were in the middle of their excursion when a red Midland bus passed by. The driver was so astonished by the sight that met him that he nearly drove the bus and passengers into the ditch.

The fortuitous arrival of Andrei meant that Gladys could retire indoors and need never come out again. Meat, milk, newspapers, and other essentials were delivered to the house. Instructions to tradesmen were written on a blackboard which was placed outside the house in the small hours of night. Business affairs were dealt with by her bank manager, Mr S. B. Cooper of Lloyds Bank, St James's. Though she was often out of contact for months and refused to sign forms or pay her taxes, he remained a patient and loyal friend; he unquestionably had a soft spot for his strange and difficult client. To a letter from

Gladys in 1953, in which she expressed mistrust of the tax authorities and others in classical terms, he replied with the concluding paragraph:

> We can well understand your feelings of mistrust but are hopeful that you could perhaps, to continue the excursion into Greek mythology, look upon us as a modern Olympus, offering you all possible protection from Scylla and Charybdis.[1]

Andrei attended to all other external matters, and in time he was admitted to Gladys's strange domain.

The drawing-room of the house was in good condition. Here were the pictures and the books, and the stove was still alight twenty-four hours a day to keep everything at a constant temperature. Sometimes Gladys sat in a chair in this room, with her feet up, smoking a pipe and with cats clambering all over her. Gladys had had all her teeth out in 1948. Andrei was astonished when she dropped her false teeth on the floor, picked them up at once and put them straight back into her mouth. Near her chair stood a refrigerator, delivered in good condition, but never connected. Any cat that died was put inside it to await solemn burial in a corner of the garden.

The dining-room was piled high with newspapers and periodicals. Upstairs her bed had collapsed and the broken mattress she lay on was filled with old books. Her famous revolver lay nearby, and it was not unknown for Gladys to take pot-shots from the upper windows with a shot-gun. The plumbing of the house had been a thing of the past for some time. The main area of occupation was the kitchen where Gladys would stand over a huge cauldron, providing food for the cats and eating from it herself. Joints of meat from the butcher were stored in one corner and invariably went bad before they were touched, or Gladys would attempt to cook a herring, forget about it, and let it burn to a frazzle. Medicine of one kind and another lived in a cupboard outside her bedroom, everything clearly marked.

The house was thoroughly fortified. Heavy black curtains covered all the windows, and once a year Andrei was ordered to drench them in oil to prevent the moths from eating them. All the doors were bolted, and a small chopper stood by the main door lest some too persistent visitor should present himself. Outside, the house was surrounded by miles of chicken-wire and pig-wire.

Andrei remembered several attempts made by friends to visit her. If they left a visiting card Gladys threw it into the fire, but if they succeeded in catching a glimpse of her, they invariably scurried away on their own accord. One visitor, who was allowed in after a long period of waiting, was astounded by Gladys's physical strength. Seeing her about to pick up some poultry boxes, he offered to help. But it was useless, they were far too heavy. During his attempt, she watched him with her piercing blue eyes, then casually picked both up without effort and carried them across the room. The same visitor listened fascinated to her stories, for in her solitary state she had become something of a sage, observing the outside world with the disillusioned perception of a cynic. But as her visitor sat there, night began to fall and he became increasingly uncomfortable. He was well aware that Gladys had detected this and was enjoying the situation.

Gladys did not celebrate Christmas, but she excused Andrei his duties during the holiday, and observed the ritual of Christmas cheer by offering him some fine white Burgundy. To Andrei's horror she poured it into two plastic tumblers from Woolworth's which did little to enhance its taste.

In the 1950s Sir Shane Leslie began to wonder what had happened to Gladys, and was delighted to hear news of her from the local Catholic priest, Father John Maunsell. He urged him to visit her and armed him with a letter of introduction:

I cannot forget old days when staying with you and Sonny [*sic*]. Time passes but the memory of your beauty descends the ages. I am sure you will find Father Maunsell a sympathetic friend.[2]

Chacombe lay in Father Maunsell's parish. For about six years he called on her once every two months. He experienced some difficulty in getting her to admit she was a Catholic. She told him she had undergone two baptismal ceremonies in the same day, one at a Protestant church in the morning and another at a Catholic one in the late afternoon, the latter unbeknown to her father. Finally she announced: 'Yes, I am a Catholic, but a bad one.' Father Maunsell contacted Father Martindale, now living in retirement at Petworth. Martindale regretted that he was too ill to visit Gladys, nor did he think it would do much good. He urged Father Maunsell to keep in touch with her and at the end to give her the sacraments and a Catholic burial.

In 1960 Sir Shane went to stay with Mr and Mrs Edward Courage at Edgcote House. Mr Courage drove him and Father Maunsell to Chacombe, and Gladys admitted Sir Shane to the house. He spent half an hour with her and came away very upset by the state of his old friend. His verdict was that she was very poor, full of grievances, but certainly not insane. He contacted the Most Reverend Gerald P. O'Hara, Apostolic Delegate in Great Britain, and urged him to pay Gladys a visit. The Apostolic Delegate made plans to do this, the purpose of which was to persuade Gladys to receive the sacraments in the hope that this would bring her 'consolation that at the present time she knows nothing about'.[3] The visit never took place as the Apostolic Delegate was too busy.

As Gladys approached her eightieth year, the rate of domestic accidents increased. She broke her shoulder in a fall and did nothing about it. In time it set on its own. She believed that one germ could take care of another germ and thus ignored all ailments. On a few occasions she hurt herself so badly that the doctor had to drive her to hospital. She refused to stay in overnight, and was strong enough and determined enough to ensure her immediate return to the sanctuary of Chacombe.

When movement became a serious problem due to a bad foot, Andrei took closer charge of Gladys. He dressed her wounds and he carried her up and down stairs. Her day ended as his began. Each morning he came to the house, carried her upstairs and put her to bed. The process for locking the house was executed to a rigidly established formula. When Gladys was safely installed in the bedroom, Andrei lowered the key to the front door from the upper window on a string. He let himself out and locked the door from the outside. Then he called up and Gladys pulled the key into the bedroom window. At the end of his day, the business was reversed, but only after Gladys was quite sure that it really was Andrei outside.

Theirs was an extraordinary friendship. She used to say to him: 'You were born a peasant and you'll die a peasant, but me – I'm a Duchess.' And she told him to trust nobody: 'Friendship doesn't last', she said. On a good day she would regale him with stories about Russian Grand Dukes kissing first the tips of her fingers, then her hand, then all up her arm. When they reached the shoulder, they were firmly halted. Though he did not have an easy time, Andrei loved working for Gladys and when later he visited her in hospital he used to recall with nostalgia 'the good old days at Chacombe'.

Gladys never lost the sense of time, nor her ability to digest news from the world outside. If an item interested her she cut it from the newspaper and found a home for it. For example, a cock robin was killed when he flew into a store window in Wisconsin. Beside his dead body stood his mate on solitary guard until the evening traffic frightened her away. Gladys folded the photograph into a book by Berenson. She dated it, correctly, '17 April 1961 (Budget Day)'. Almost the only entry in her diary for the same year concerned an event in the outer world in October: 'Day the great bomb was sailed into space.'

In August 1961, Gladys's niece, Mrs Austen T. Gray, daughter of Edith Gray, came to England for the first time. She telephoned Gladys and made an appointment to visit her. In Chacombe she underwent the time-honoured ritual of finding the house and waiting in the farmyard for a sign of life within. But the house stayed silent and the door did not open. Yet Milo Gray had an uncanny feeling that from one of the upper windows those blue eyes were watching and her presence had not gone unobserved. Nevertheless she was obliged to retreat without a direct confrontation. Annoyed, she wrote to Gladys, complaining of her unfriendliness to one who had come a long way to see how she was. Promptly Gladys sent Andrei out to despatch a telegram which read 'Dear Heart, Don't be a silly-bill. Of course I wanted to see you but I was ill.'

The winter of 1961 was very bad for Gladys. Her fear of intruders increased, and the sight of a village boy stealing an apple from the orchard was invested with sinister significance. She called the police in the middle of the night complaining of strange happenings. Concern for her condition now grew apace. Andrei's devotion never failed and he continued to see she was fed and cared for. Though her constitution was remarkable, the human frame can only stand so much. Without Andrei's care, Gladys would surely have been found dead somewhere in that house that winter.

One night sitting in the darkness, she wrote in an old diary:

I am left alone in this house!! Unable to move!!

None of such a monstrous abandoning of a completely helpless wounded woman unable to move cd happen except in England.

Yet there remained one thing that meant more to her than anything else – something she had valued all her life – her freedom. For this reason she refused to have anyone living with her or to move from the house. For her there was no compromise, despite the entreaties of Andrei and others.

The irony of the date on which the worst happened will not have escaped Gladys. On the night of 15 March 1962, the Ides of March about which the soothsayer warned Shakespeare's Caesar in vain, cars drew up outside the house; people moved about in the yard. Pressure was put on Andrei to help gain admission to the house. Four men in white coats took hold of Gladys, who fought like a wild animal cornered in its lair, and dragged her from the house. She cried out to Andrei, who stood petrified and helpless in a corner of the farmyard. Gladys was marched to a waiting Rolls-Royce and driven away from Chacombe for ever.

Chapter Twenty-four

ST ANDREW'S

I have long been ill since I was dragged out of my room by
force only partly dressed in not even a dressing-gown & stockings or slippers – the kidnappers refused to give any information or even speak & dragged me after a gallant fight by me
down the stairs by 3 men grabbing my feet & making me lose
my balance into their hands which I was lugged out to a
waiting [car] pushed into it & quickly taken away, frozen to
the bone (15th of March) & brought here – No doctors, 2
women tore my clothes off, put me to bed.[1]

Thus begins Gladys's account of her transfer to St Andrew's
Hospital, Northampton. She was eighty-one years old and
destined to stay there for the rest of her life. St Andrew's
describes itself as 'a private psychiatric hospital independent of
the National Health Service'. Gladys called it 'a vast lunatic
asylum'. The hospital was opened by the third Earl Spencer in
1838 to accommodate fifty-two paupers and thirty private
patients in an imposing Georgian mansion set in 100 acres of the
Nene Valley. Since then the inevitable numerous extensions
have been added, a golf course and tennis courts as well as
facilities such as a gymnasium, a swimming-pool, occupational
therapy units, dental clinics, a physiotherapy department and
even a beauty salon. There is a chapel built of Northamptonshire stone to the design of Sir Gilbert Scott.

St Andrew's is one of the leading psychiatric establishments
in the country and patients come to it from all over the world.
It still retains a reputation as the repository for members of the
British aristocracy unable to cope with everyday life. Walking

266

along its network of endless corridors one sees on the doors the names of unknown members of well-known families, patients from the peerage, from distant branches of royal families and from the upper echelon of the professional classes. One of its most famous inmates was the poet, John Clare, who was admitted in 1837 and died there in 1864.

Gladys began her sojourn in The Cedars, a villa in the grounds some distance from the central unit of the hospital. For some months she suffered from a respiratory tract infection, which nearly cost her her life. Her physical condition horrified the matron, who declared she could not remember ever having seen a patient admitted in such a dirty state. As Gladys recovered, she began to enjoy a regular bath, even to demand one.

Gladys found it impossible to adjust to her new surroundings. She demanded continually to be set free and to be allowed to return to Chacombe. Unfortunately the persistence of her demands earned her a reputation as a difficult and aggressive patient; it was felt that her discharge was not in her best interests. She was suspicious by nature and refused to sign any documents, and she was without friends to advise her or present the alternatives. She made attempts to escape and had to be restrained, none of which helped her cause. Her sole ally was Andrei, and she even blamed him for letting her be taken from her home. She said to him: 'I forgive but I don't forget.' In the confusing world in which she found herself, Gladys decided to revert from being Mrs Spencer to her ducal status. Since the tenth Duke's wife, Mary, had died in May 1961, Gladys felt within her rights to call herself 'The Duchess of Marlborough' without qualifications such as 'Gladys' or 'Dowager'.

Soon after her removal from Chacombe, the extent of its squalor was determined. The chicken- and pig-wire was removed and a massive cleaning operation began. Two five-ton trucks took away loads of newspapers, poultry-feed bags, tins full and empty, and hundreds of pots of jam, some of which were nearly ten years old. A tomato sauce carton, discovered in a long deserted cat's bed, revealed an exquisite silver snuff box. A sapphire pin and a necklace of pinkish pearls were found in a pigskin case in the attic. A Kelmscott Chaucer, cited as 'one of the great books of the world' and destined to sell at Christie's for £32,000 in 1978, came to light as did a book of sexually explicit drawings by D. H. Lawrence and a 1526 Erasmus. The ground floor alone produced thousands of pounds of valuables lurking in the muck.

As soon as she was well enough Gladys resumed the writing of a diary, an account for posterity of what she was suffering. From this little pink book emerges a picture of a woman convinced that she was being wronged, complaining frequently about the inadequacy of the food and the service and occasionally revealing a sense of humour in surprising contrast to the general bitterness of her lot. Her handwriting had changed considerably since the age of forty. According to a graphologist, at the time of her marriage it showed confidence, leadership and drive. She was self-sufficient and a logical thinker with an ability to administrate and common sense. There was a certain controlled sensitivity. His examination suggested that at eighty-one her writing revealed mental initiative, alertness, confidence, leadership and a confused thought pattern. She was spontaneous but irrational, her moods changed quickly and she was very energetic. Gladys's mind was more active and more interesting at eighty-one than forty years previously.

Gladys wrote numerous letters from the hospital, most of them concerned with the issue of her release. She approached relations, friends, some of those who had tried to visit her at Chacombe, and high officers of state. Nobody was willing to assist her and so in St Andrew's she remained. To one written request for release sent to the Superintendent, the Sister replied that he would send a reply in due course: 'Sounds quite Macmillan-like!' commented Gladys.

The nurses were a constant source of aggravation and she made their lives as difficult as possible. One nurse was accused of having removed some papers from her chest of drawers. In the midst of the harangue, Matron entered the room. Gladys related what happened:

> At that moment the *Arch Yapper* walked in, evidently been listening outside the door secretly & starts a loud & constant flow of un-understandable yapp. Finally my heart thumping my ribs, I yelled at her 'The Dess. of Marlborough to Miss Anderson get out of my room *at once*' & out she went still yapping.

Any normal hospital activity such as hair-washing or inspections were treated as a regular comedy and an assault on the rights of the individual. Matron brought health visitors in one day. According to Gladys, they marched in 'to see beef on a Duchess'.

Gladys detested her fellow inmates and, by and large, ignored them. 'Oh dear what a dead set of people', she wrote. The diary is full of references to 'the mads'. Like her father in Boston, she found their behaviour irritating. From time to time she was pleased to note 'quiet of all lunatics, not a sound'. When Princess Alexandra was married in April 1963, she observed 'all these women in the English state of excitement over "Royal Marriages" '. She did not bother to inform them that she sat in the South Lantern of the Abbey for the bride's uncle's wedding forty years before. Unlike that occasion, this wedding occurred on a very hot day; 'in the sun 82', noted Gladys. 'Poor wedding guests – no wonder they looked furious.'

Gladys followed the news with deep interest – the Argyll divorce case, the Profumo affair, the H Bomb, the actions of President Kennedy and even the fluctuations of the New York Stock Exchange. This is what she wrote about Cuba: 'I think Cuba may be a teeth showing by Kennedy'; and, later, 'Cuba still looks like electioneering.' She was pleased to find her political judgment still sound: 'As I surmised last Tuesday, Cuba was nothing but cold war & so it is continuing.' She felt sorry for Stephen Ward but reckoned that he would be 'got off by the faceless ones at his trial'. When he committed suicide, she was deeply moved by Cassandra's article in the *Daily Mail*, though later depressed by the Denning Report.

When Pope Paul VI was elected, Gladys emerged from despondency to send him 'a telegram of real joy'. She followed with interest his visit to Jerusalem, the first ever aeroplane flight by a reigning Pope and the first meeting between the Roman Catholic leader and the head of the Orthodox Church for over 500 years:

> The Pope's journey – its terrific fatigue, his cheerful endurance of it, that part of his journey finished today – King Hussein has been splendid through it. . . . I feel my heart uplifted & yet like a gaffed fish.

Andrei remained a faithful visitor to the end of her life, bringing news of Chacombe, flowers from the garden and food. He did not tell her that her cats had been destroyed by order as this would have upset her. Loyal Andrei put on his Sunday best for these visits and announced proudly, 'I go there on my wheels.'

As at Chacombe, visitors were not, as a rule, made welcome. When her niece Milo Gray came to the hospital, Gladys was at her worst. Mrs Gray brought her scent. 'Don't you know you only give scent to whores?' cried Gladys, pushing it away. She then launched into a vicious attack on America and the Americans, after which her visitor retreated in disarray.

Besides reading, Gladys's greatest interest was the birds. She encouraged the pigeons to fly to the window-sill, where she gave them food. Sometimes they flew right into the room and the nurses got used to seeing Gladys, sitting in bed, surrounded by them. She would get upset when accidents occurred. One day a bird flew from a plinth and killed itself by hitting a table – 'a half-grown starling so pretty and so hurt'. The deaths of old friends upset her too – 'depressed to read Vita Sackville died over the weekend'. But she was buoyed up by an interest in racing. 'Gold Cup day for the free', she wrote and proudly recorded that she had had several winners. She was amused by one nurse whose knowledge of history was somewhat slight. The nurse was convinced that Gladys had spent her early life in the French Revolution.

Christmas remained a sad time as always, but Gladys was entertained by the picture of the superintendent and matron making a 'whistle stop with good wishes', and then 'speeding away in a large grey car'. There were sad entries too: 'Feel so unhappy here, wish me dead.' But the saddest of all was on 29 July 1963, when she realized her long battle for freedom was lost forever:

> Food continues awful but it seems these 10 old people gobble any & everything. Am getting more depressed especially as Home News are that my side has been *roulé en grand* so I will be imprisoned here all my life.

In 1964 Gladys gave up keeping a diary. At her own request her affairs were put under the Court of Protection. Unbeknown to her, the Grange at Chacombe was put on the market in March 1965 and sold a year later.

Reports from St Andrew's in 1968 indicated that Gladys was in good health. She could still converse 'brilliantly' on current events, was reading several daily newspapers from cover to cover and was considered likely to live for a number of years. She broke her hip in January 1971 and spent her ninetieth birthday in Northampton General Hospital. There was no celebration, not even a card. She made a remarkable recovery from this and was soon walking the corridors of St Andrew's again with the use of a frame.

Gladys had been moved from her villa to a psycho-geriatric ward in the main block as old age advanced upon her. She had her own room there and often stayed in it all day. She told one health visitor that the food was inadequate and that she could tell her enough stories about the hospital 'to fill a book'. The visitor reported that Gladys was very demanding, expected the staff to be at her beck and call, but that, despite this, the nurses were very fond of her and she was 'a very likeable character'.

And so, in O'Connell Ward at St Andrew's Hospital, Gladys lived on into her nineties. She took to a wheel-chair as her official mode of transport along the corridors, although she could still walk a bit if she wanted to; she spent her days either in her room or in her chair to the right of the door in the 'Green Room'.

The world she had known changed dramatically. Blenheim, formerly a family home, transformed itself into a major enterprise of tourism. One night in 1975 the floodlit palace opened its doors to entertain merry-making American salesmen to a sumptuous banquet in the Long Library, complete with fanfares at appropriate moments. A reporter from the *New York Times* scampered about, overhearing the goggle-eyed guests in rented tuxedos: 'There are no broken windows or graffiti here', and 'Two weeks ago I was on the run, eating a cheeseburger at McDonalds – talk about contrasts!' Meanwhile Sunny's grandson, the eleventh Duke, emerged briefly and was heard to mutter: 'Remarkable, remarkable.'[2]

Far removed from all that, Gladys sat in the clinical abyss of a hospital ward, kept alive by a phenomenal appetite, an extraordinary will to live, yet with nothing to live for, and a superhuman resistance to illness and accidents. She rose like a phoenix from a series of breakages, influenzas and comas, to the astonishment of all. Many times the doctors brought out the death certificate book and she confounded them; many times were the last rites said, and she survived them. She lived on and on, seemingly indestructible, into her ninety-seventh year.

Chapter Twenty-five

LAST ENCOUNTER

O'Connell Ward marked the end of Gladys's long journey through life, a voyage that began in Paris, raised her to the heights of fame as a radiant beauty in vestal white, took her to Blenheim and then allowed her to drop into the black squalor of an Augean stable at Chacombe. Throughout her life she was content to be alone, and in old age her spirit was unbroken. Looking at illustrations of works of art, she would say: 'Look at that! Despair! Artists always despair because they never attain. But I'm not like that.'

Yet it is not in solitude that she will be remembered. The name of Gladys Deacon evokes the picture of a beautiful girl with a devastating sense of humour, abundant charm and that quick conversation which enabled her to monopolize great men at the dinner-table. Charm is a dangerous quality and it is hard to keep the champagne sparkling twenty-four hours a day. Eventually most of those whom Gladys charmed became suspicious and searched for what lay behind the façade, and they turned away from her. She survived the ghastly drama of her face, but she did not weather her Pyrrhic victory in winning Marlborough. How sad that she did not wed someone who might have fulfilled the demands for which Marlborough was so inadequate. She paid a high price for her coronet.

Of course, Gladys failed in the wife's duty to make her husband happy; her marriage failed as so many of those Anglo-American matches failed. And when she lost her own income and had to rely on him, Marlborough threw her to the lions. She ended her days disillusioned, but not despairing.

Gladys was ninety-four when I met her and thirteen years of hospital life had seen to it that her principal concerns were now her routine and her food. She said once: 'I seem to have had two lives, the past and the present.' She did her best to put the former out of her mind. For years Andrei had been her only regular visitor and friend, though some of the nurses were special favourites. She nicknamed Sister Dillon 'Mrs England' or 'the English nurse', and Staff Nurse Battle was called 'Franka'. Less politely, one of the male staff was dubbed 'Fat Doctor' or '*Le Gros*'. In the twilight of her life she allowed me to become a friend because, I believe, I was too young to have any connexion with her past life.

She was a difficult patient because she was a born actress. One of her routines involved pretending to be asleep. She had brought this to such an art that more than once the doctors reported her comatose only to find her sitting up wide awake two minutes later. Andrei regularly endured this charade. He would sit beside her watching television. From the corner of his eye he could observe Gladys watching him secretly. After about half an hour she would 'wake up' and greet him with the words: 'Goodness me! How long have you been sitting there?' I once sat beside her so long that I fell asleep myself.

When I visited Gladys, she would normally be found in the Green Room. When she recognized me, she took hold of my hand and without seeming to exert any pressure on it, held me in a vice-like grip. She would hold on to me until she was certain that I would not suddenly disappear. We used to talk in the doctor's office, and after she was seated comfortably there, I would hand over the '*nonnettes*' (two packets of currant buns) and After Eights, which were stored in her basket for nocturnal consumption. Conversation often began with a strange tale about the iniquities of the hospital or the fate of the old ladies in the ward. Once she told me: 'They're all in the kissing halls, you know.' I said: 'You mean like the women of the Pigalle?' 'Heavens no!' she replied. 'Not even as good as that!' We both laughed; this was my cue to produce a book. She would concentrate on it, insist on seeing every photograph, and on a good day, talk at length about what she saw. The favourite books were about artists. She enjoyed a good conversation, and stipulated: 'I don't like fools. Fools rub off on you like bad dye.'

A source of particular fascination and of distress was the Prince Imperial. Shaking with emotion and with tears in her eyes, she told me: 'That poor young man lost everything, his brave spirit – and was killed, all because he was Napoleon's son and the French had no place for him. All that was left of him was bones. . . . Oh! The French can be brutes!' She used to dream a lot, sometimes good dreams, sometimes bad ones. 'I wake up panting', she said, 'and find myself *here* – in this hospital!'

Gladys was a surreptitious reader of newspapers in the night. She knew about Concorde, the Italian earthquake in 1976, the Snowdon separation and the demise of Mao. If she had missed something, she was not lost for an answer. In May 1976 my father asked her who the next President of the United States would be. She replied: 'To be honest I haven't been following the campaign, but you can be sure it will be the worst possible man.' Some weeks later I told her that Harold Wilson was about to be installed a Knight of the Garter at Windsor. She commented:

> Well he had been Prime Minister for ten years. Of course he is of very common birth, but I like him. He does his best, which is more than can be said for the rest of them. He's a good liberal.
> 'You mean Labour by name, Liberal by politics?' I asked.
> 'Well, of course, he had to get the votes, didn't he?'

Gladys hated going into the garden, but one hot Sunday afternoon she was wheeled out there with the other inmates and we sat in the sun, eating chocolate ice-creams. I asked her: 'What is the highest form of knowledge?' She thought for a moment and then said: 'Knowledge of science is the most important thing. But don't be a scientist. It's all new discoveries. The newest thing is held. You be a banker. Bankers have a finger in every pie. They can do anything.'

I protested that I did not have a good head for figures. 'That's perhaps because you don't like them much', she said. 'It is a passion that can be very profitable, I'm told.'

I tried another line by saying that City men seemed to take little interest in art, that my father had never been in the National Gallery. 'That's because he's never made the effort', she went on. 'Now take my friends the Rothschilds in Paris. He owned lovely pictures and he understood them. And he went to all the exhibitions.'

'Well, what would a banker say to Epstein?' I asked. 'They would have nothing in common.'

'Epstein!' she cried. 'Honestly! Epstein was pained and unhappy. He used to cry over me. He was never happy doing what he did. He always wanted to do something else. You know, I think that's why he veered so much towards ugliness in his work. . . . No, you be a banker. That way you'll always have a good dinner every night. I worry about that sometimes. Otherwise you'll end up in a place like this!'

Gladys remained preoccupied with the idea of escaping from St Andrew's, and hoped that I would help her. She said once: 'You take me downstairs and put me in your car.' I asked where we would go. 'Out into the world', she answered.

After a bad fall in September 1976 she was transferred to Northampton General Hospital and underwent an operation. She was ninety-five at the time, but survived it with no anxiety to herself. Finding that she was in different surroundings, she thought I had pulled off a miraculous coup. When she returned to St Andrew's she was disappointed and cross.

I was always afraid that something might occur to cause her to break off her friendship with me as she had done with so many others in the course of her life. I survived an occasion when – claiming not to have recognized me – she tipped a glass of water over me; but on 1 May 1977, a terrible scene occurred when I showed her a Helleu drawing of Helena Rubinstein. She threw it across the room and then engaged me in a game similar to that inflicted on the Duke of Norfolk in 1903. She was to be Napoleon and I was to be a peasant. My imitation was a poor one, not least because it was undertaken in French. She saw that I was becoming self-conscious and asked: 'Do you need wine? Do you need gin? Do you need hashish?' She then launched into one of the most fluent onslaughts on my character that I have had the misfortune to endure. She folded her arms and 'went to sleep'.

I had no alternative but to leave and so went into the garden. Here by good fortune I met an eighty-six-year-old patient who decided to be friendly to me. When I had finished pouring out my story, he said: 'Oh! Don't break it off, don't give up. Women are all the same. They're very difficult. You arrive next week with some flowers and you'll be all right.' His advice was sound, for when I returned five weeks later, Gladys said simply:

'I am glad to see you. I thought you'd given me up.' To which I replied 'No'.

Late that summer she suffered a bad fever and the last rites were said. A message reached me on holiday to say that Gladys was 'not expected to last out the day'. Yet, when I telephoned, the Sister told me the crisis was over. 'She must have twenty-one lives', she said.

9 October 1977 was a Sunday and Gladys was in the same chair in which I had first met her two and a half years earlier. I asked her how she was and instead of her habitual answer: 'Oh, I'm all right', she replied: 'I'm very far from well.' She tried to eat an After Eight, but even half a chocolate was too much; she looked at a bust of Conrad in an Epstein book, but soon lost interest. She spoke, but her normally powerful voice had sunk to a whisper and she was hard to understand. I did hear her say: 'I don't want to die.' Finally she asked for my hands and took them in hers, squeezing them tightly. When I got up to leave, she looked at me and smiled. Then she turned to look towards the window. Her hair was very white in the morning sun, her skin very pale and her eyes still a blue that baffles description. As she sat there silently, I was struck by how much she resembled the bust by Epstein in 1923. That night I wrote: 'Gladys sat mellow in the chair . . . and I had the distinct feeling that it was our last meeting. If this is the beginning of the end, then Gladys is peaceful and untroubled. She is, as it were, just slowly going to sleep as at the end of a very long day.'

Four days later, on Thursday 13 October, at eleven o'clock at night, Gladys died peacefully in her sleep. The cause of death was given as broncho-pneumonia. A requiem mass was said in St Gregory's Church, Northampton, in the presence of a tiny group of mourners. Then they took her to Chacombe church-yard, where Father Maunsell officiated at the interment. Only six wreaths lay upon the coffin, one of them from Blenheim, 'with deepest sympathy from the Marlborough family'. Andrei stood sadly by the grave. Also present were Mr John Schilizzi, a church warden, and his wife, Lady Sophia, and Joan Rees, a London solicitor, who was to be one of the administrators of the estate. A small crowd of villagers gathered outside the church-yard to witness the return of the lady of the Grange. It was a wet and gloomy day and the mourners did not linger long at the graveside.

In 1978, Gladys's possessions were sent to Christie's and fell to the auctioneer's hammer. Jewellery raised £452,755 in one hour, a sapphire single-stone ring of 12.86 carats fetching £105,000 (about £8,165 per carat); Rodin's *Faunesse* fetched £17,000, and an unrecorded Toulouse-Lautrec £58,000. By the end of the season the total stood at £784,000.

A stone was placed in Chacombe Churchyard to mark the grave. The inscription reads: GLADYS MARIE DEACON DOWAGER DUCHESS OF MARLBOROUGH 1881–1977. Above the name the stonemason carved a representation of Gladys's eye, a copy of that painted by Colin Gill on the portico at Blenheim fifty years before.

In one of the suitcases in which Gladys kept her letters there is a poem apparently written in 1901. It is impossible to know who wrote it, but the author knew the young girl, to whom he gave it, very well and he understood her. The poem is by no means a masterpiece but it is written with love and inspired by the radiance of a personality that influenced the lives and works of great and gifted men.

Sweet and Twenty

Bright, sweet and fair, with a head that's sometimes level,
A wit most rare, with more than a spice of devil.
And large round eyes that appear so intent and true,
She looks so wise while she inwardly laughs at you.
Sometimes she affects a look like a madonna;
Then one quite expects a halo to grow on her:
Inconsequent – in every succeeding minute
Her mind is bent on something and how to win it;
Withal, such charm, you'll forget she's sometimes selfish,
Your rage she'll calm with a sweetness almost elfish;
Young men and old men lie down and bow before her;
Young girls and old dames all equally adore her;
All things that bore her are wished by her in Hades,
You won't want more now to guess her name is Gladys.

Bibliography

ASHLEY, MAURICE, *Churchill as Historian*, Secker & Warburg, 1968.

ASQUITH, LADY CYNTHIA, *Diaries 1915–18*, Hutchinson, 1968.

BALDWIN, C. C., *Baldwin Genealogy Supplement*, Cleveland, 1881 & 1889.

BALSAN, CONSUELO VANDERBILT, *The Glitter and the Gold*, Heinemann, 1953.

BARING-GOULD, S., *A Book of the Riviera*, Methuen, 1905.

BARKER, H., *Marcel Proust – A Biography*, Faber & Faber, 1959.

BATAILLE, A., *Causes Criminelles et Mondaines 1892*, Paris, 1893.

BATCHELLOR, T. B., *Glimpses of Italian Court Life*, Doubleday, 1905.

BEEBE, LUCIUS, *The Big Spenders*, Doubleday, NY, 1966.

BENNETT, ARNOLD, *Letters to his Nephew*, Heinemann, 1936.

BERENSON, BERNARD, *Sketch for a Self Portrait*, Constable, 1949.
The Passionate Sightseer, Thames & Hudson, 1960.

BERTIE OF THAME, LORD, *The Diary of Lord Bertie of Thame, 1914–18*, Hodder & Stoughton, 1924.

BIBESCO, MARTHE, *La Vie d'une Amitié (Vol 1)*, Plon, Paris, 1951–57.

BIRKENHEAD, EARL OF, *F. E. The Life of F. E. Smith*, Eyre & Spottiswoode, 1959.
The Prof in Two Worlds, Collins, 1961.

BITHELL, JETHRO, *Modern German Literature 1880–1950*, Methuen, 1959.

BLANCHE, JACQUES–EMILE, *Portraits of a Lifetime*, Dent, 1937.

BONNET, HENRI, *Marcel Proust de 1907 à 1914*, A. G. Nizet, Paris, 1971.

BONVICINI, O. F., *Caprarola, Il Palazzo e la Villa Farnese*, Roma, 1973.

BUCKLE, RICHARD S., *Jacob Epstein Sculptor*, Faber & Faber, 1963.

BUNTING, BAINBRIDGE, *Houses of Boston's Back Bay*, Harvard Paperbacks, 1967.

BURNS, EDWARD, *Staying on Alone – The Letters of Alice B. Toklas*, Angus & Robertson, 1974.

CAMERON, RODERICK, *The Golden Riviera*, Weidenfeld & Nicolson, 1975.

CARAMAN, PHILIP, *C. C. Martindale*, Longmans, 1967.

CARDONA, *Vie de Jean Boldini*, Eugéne Figuière, Paris, 1931.

CARNARVON, EARL OF, *No Regrets*, Weidenfeld & Nicolson, 1976.

CASTELLANE, BONI DE, *Comment j'ai découvert l'Amerique*, Cres, Paris, 1925.

CHAPMAN-HUSTON, D. (ED.), *The Private Diaries of Daisy, Princess of Pless 1873–1914*, John Murray Albemarle Library, 1950.
Daisy, Princess of Pless, by Herself.

CHURCHILL, RANDOLPH S., *Winston S. Churchill Companion Volume II*, Houghton Mifflin, Boston, 1969.

CHURCHILL, VISCOUNT, *All my Sins Remembered*, Heinemann, 1964.

CHURCHILL, W. S. & MARTINDALE, C. C., *Charles ix Duke of Marlborough Tributes*, Burns & Oates, 1934.

CLARK, ALAN (ED.), *A Good Innings – The Private Papers of Viscount Lee of Fareham*, John Murray, 1974.

CLERMONT-TONNERRE, E. DE (GRAMONT, E. DE), *Marcel Proust*, Flammarion, Paris, 1948.
Memoires, Vol II, Bernard Grasset, Paris, 1929.
Pomp & Circumstance, Jonathan Cape, 1929.
Robert de Montesquiou et Marcel Proust, Flammarion, Paris, 1925.

COOLIDGE, T. JEFFERSON, *Autobiography 1857–1900*, privately printed, Boston, 1902.

CRONIN, A. J., *Hatter's Castle*, Victor Gollancz, 1936.

CURTIS, CAROLINE GARDINER, *Memories of Fifty Years in the Last Century*, Boston, 1947.

CURZON OF KEDLESTON, MARCHIONESS, *Reminiscences*, Hutchinson, 1955.

DAVIE, MICHAEL (ED.), *The Diaries of Evelyn Waugh*, Weidenfeld & Nicolson, 1976.

DE STOEKL, AGNES, *My Dear Marquis*, John Murray, 1952.

DODGE LUHAN, MABEL, *European Experiences*, Harcourt, NY, 1935.

ELLIOTT, MAUD HOWE, *This was my Newport*, The Mythology Co– A. Marshall Jones, 1944.

EPSTEIN, JACOB, *An Autobiography*, Art Treasures Book Club (Vista Books), 1963.

FIELD, J. O. (ANON), *Uncensored Recollections*, Lippincott, Philadelphia, 1924.

FOUQUIERES, ANDRE DE, *Mon Paris et Ses Parisiens Vol I*, Horay, Paris, 1953.

Fantômes du Faubourg St Honoré, Oeuvres Libres, no 353, December 1956.

GARNETT, DAVID, *The Familiar Faces*, Chatto & Windus, 1962.
GARTEN, H. F., *Modern German Drama*, Methuen, 1959.
GIRAUDOUX, JEAN, *Souvenir de Deux Existences*, Bernard Grasset, Paris, 1975.
GRAMONT (see CLERMONT-TONNERRE).
GRAVES, CHARLES, *Royal Riviera*, Heinemann, 1957.
GREEN, DAVID, *Blenheim Palace*, Country Life, 1951.
Blenheim Palace, Blenheim Estate Office, 1973.
Blenheim Park and Gardens, Blenheim Estate Office, 1972.
GRINDEA, MIRON, *Adam International Review*, no 260, 1957.

HAMILTON, EDITH, *Mythology*, Mentor (New American Library), 1969.
HARRISON, MICHAEL, *Lord of London*, W. H. Allen, 1966.
HOFMANNSTHAL, HUGO VON, *Briefe 1900–09*, Bermann–Fischer Verlag, Vienna, 1937.
HOFMANNSTHAL, HUGO VON, & NOSTITZ, HELENE VON, *Briefwechsel*, S. Fischer Verlag, Vienna, 1965.
HOLROYD, MICHAEL, *Lytton Strachey Vol II*, Heinemann, 1969.
HONE, JOSEPH, *The Life of George Moore*, Victor Gollancz, 1936.
HOYT, EDWIN P., *The Vanderbilts and their Fortunes*, Frederick Muller, 1963.

JOBSON DARROCH, SANDRA, *Ottoline*, Chatto & Windus, 1976.
JONAS, KLAUS W., *The Life of Crown Prince William*, Routledge & Kegan Paul, 1961.
JULLIAN, PHILIPPE, *D'Annunzio*, Pall Mall, 1972.
Robert de Montesquiou – un Prince 1900, Librairie Academique Perrin, Paris, 1965.

KEYSERLING, HERMANN VON, *The World in the Making*, Jonathan Cape, 1927.
KIEL, HANNA, *Looking at Pictures with Bernard Berenson*, Harry N. Abrams, NY, 1974.
KILHAM, WALTER H., *Boston After Bulfinch*, Cambridge, Mass., 1946.
KOLB, PHILIP (ED.), *Lettres à Reynaldo Hahn*, Gallimard, Paris, 1956.

LEES-MILNE, JAMES, *Ancestral Voices*, Chatto & Windus, 1975.
LESLIE, ANITA, *Edwardians in Love*, Hutchinson, 1972.
LESLIE, SIR SHANE, *Long Shadows*, John Murray, 1966.
LEWIS, R. W. B., *Edith Wharton*, Constable, 1975.
LINZEE, JOHN WILLIAM, *History of Peter Parker and Sarah Ruggles of Roxbury, Mass.*, privately printed, Boston, 1913.

MCCARTHY, LILLAH, *Myself & My Friends*, Thornton Butterworth, 1933.

MACLAY, E. S., *A History of the United States Navy 1775–1893* (3 Vols), Bliss, Sands & Foster, London, 1894.

MAGNUS, PHILIP, *King Edward VII*, E. P. Dutton, NY, 1964.

MARIANO, NICKY, *Forty Years with Berenson*, Hamish Hamilton, 1966.

MASSON, GEORGINA, *Italian Gardens*, Thames & Hudson, 1961.
Italian Villas and Palaces, Thames & Hudson, 1959.

MATTHIESSEN, F. O. & MURDOCK, KENNETH B., *The Notebooks of Henry James*, Oxford University Press, 1947.

MAUROIS, ANDRE, *The Chelsea Way*, Weidenfeld & Nicolson, 1966.

MONTESQUIOU, ROBERT DE, *Le Chancelier de Fleurs*, privately printed, 1908.

MORAND, PAUL, *Le Visiteur du Soir*, Palatine, Geneva, 1947.

MORRA, UMBERTO, *Colloqui con Berenson*, Garzanti, Milan, 1963.

MOSLEY, SIR OSWALD, *My Life*, Nelson, 1968.

NICOLSON, HAROLD, *Diaries and Letters 1930–39*, Collins, 1966.
Diaries and Letters, 1945–62, Collins, 1968.
The Peace-Making, Constable 1933.

NICOLSON, NIGEL, *The Question of Things Happening – The Letters of Virginia Woolf Vol II 1919–22*, Hogarth Press, 1976.

OTIS-SKINNER, CORNELIA, *Elegant Wits and Grand Horizontals*, Michael Joseph, 1962.

PAINTER, GEORGE D., *Marcel Proust – A Biography Vol II*, Chatto & Windus, 1967.

PARKS, MERCEDES GALLAGHER, *Introduction to Keyserling*, Jonathan Cape, 1934.

PONIATOWSKI, PRINCE, *D'un Siècle à l'Autre*, Presses de la Cité, Paris, 1948.

PRINGLE, HENRY F., *Theodore Roosevelt,* Jonathan Cape, 1932.

PROUST, MARCEL, *The Guermantes Way Part II*, Chatto & Windus, 1973.

RECUPERO, JACOPO, *Il Palazzo Farnesse di Caprarola*, Bonechi Edizione 'Il Turismo', Florence, 1977.

RHODES, JAMES, ROBERT (Ed.), *Chips – The Diaries of Sir Henry Channon*, Weidenfeld & Nicolson, 1967.

ROUMANIA, QUEEN MARIE OF, *The Story of My Life* (Vols I & II), Cassell, 1934.

ROWSE, A. L., *The Later Churchills*, Macmillan, 1958.

SAMS, WILLIAM, *Court Anecdotes*, London, 1825.

SCHLUMBERGER, GUSTAVE, *Mes Souvenirs Vol II*, Plon, Paris, 1934.

Bibliography

SECREST, MERYLE, *Between Me and Life*, Macdonald & Jane's, 1976.

SERMONETA, DUCHESS OF, *Things Past*, Hutchinson, 1929.

SPARKS, EDWARD I., *The Riviera*, J. & A. Churchill, 1879.

STEIN, GERTRUDE, *The Autobiography of Alice B. Toklas*, John Lane : The Bodley Head, 1933.

TREVELYAN, RALEIGH, *Princes Under the Volcano*, William Morrow & Co, NY, 1973.

WADDINGTON, MARY KING, *Letters of a Diplomat's Wife 1883–1900*, Smith Elder & Co, 1904.

WECHTER, DIXON, *The Saga of American Society*, Charles Scribner, NY, 1970.

WESTMINSTER, LOELIA DUCHESS OF, *Grace and Favour*, Weidenfeld & Nicolson, 1961.

WHARTON, EDITH, *Italian Villas and their Gardens*, John Lane : The Bodley Head, 1904.

WHITEHILL, WALTER MUIR, *Boston – A Topographical History*, Harvard, Mass. 1968.

YOUNG, KENNETH B. (ED.), *The Diaries of Robert Bruce Lockhart 1915–38 Vol I*, Macmillan, 1973.

Magazines

THE MONTH, *April 1953* (New Series Vol IX no 4).

Sources

1 GLADYS DEACON PAPERS (GDP)

The collection includes letters addressed to Gladys from the 1890s to 1962 and her diaries, account books, legal documents, photographs, invitation cards and receipts. It also includes letters she wrote to her mother between 1892 and 1918. None of the material has previously been published. At present it is in the care of the Administrators of the Estate.

2 MRS AUSTEN T. GRAY PAPERS (ATG)

Mrs Gray, who is Gladys's niece, inherited letters from various Deacon ancestors. She also owns Admiral Baldwin's diary, which contains a detailed account of the Coronation of Czar Alexander III of Russia in 1883.

3 VILLA I TATTI, SETTIGNANO, ITALY (VIT)

The correspondence between Berenson and his wife are in the library at I Tatti. So are Mary Berenson's diaries. Of particular importance are twenty-five letters from Gladys written at the turn of the century and three from Mrs Baldwin. Other letters contain references to Gladys, notably those of Walter Berry, Roffredo Caetani, Hugo von Hofmannsthal, Robert de Montesquiou, Abbé Mugnier, Carlo Placci, Count Rembrelinski and Edith Wharton.

4 BIBLIOTHEQUE NATIONALE, PARIS (BNP)

The Montesquiou papers contain several letters addressed by Gladys and Mrs Baldwin to the Count and to Yturri. There are notes on both Gladys and Mrs Baldwin written by the Count and letters of relevance from Helleu and Count Alexandre de Gabrieux.

There is one letter from Gladys to Anatole France in the Anatole France Collection.

5 MUSEE RODIN, HOTEL BIRON, PARIS (MR)

Letters written by Gladys and Mrs Baldwin to the sculptor towards the end of his life can be found in the Musée Rodin archives.

6 HUMANITIES RESEARCH CENTER, THE UNIVERSITY OF TEXAS AT AUSTIN (HRC)

Five letters and one card written by Gladys to Lady Ottoline Morrell in 1922 are in the Morrell collection.

7 ATHENAEUM, BOSTON (AB)

This library has a number of rare books relevant to the Deacons, the Parkers, and Deacon House, Mr David McKibbin had some private notes and references to the Deacon family.

8 LIBRARY OF CONGRESS, WASHINGTON (LCW)

The Duke of Marlborough sold some papers to the United States in 1929, including letters from Winston Churchill, invitation cards and thank-you letters. Among this collection are a few letters from the Prince of Wales (later the Duke of Windsor), and the Duke of York (later King George VI). The letters are in the manuscript division.

9 AUTHOR COLLECTION (HRV)

The author has a few letters of importance and retains all the notes relevant to this biography.

Source References

KEY:

Florence Baldwin	FB
Bernard Berenson	BB
Mary Berenson	Mary
Duke of Connaught	HRH
Edward Parker Deacon	EPD
Daily Express	D Exp
Daily Mail	D Mail
Daily Telegraph	D Tel
New York Times	NYT

'Conversation with author' means conversations between Gladys and the author in St Andrew's Hospital between 1975 and 1977. For published sources the author's name only is given and should be cross-checked in the Bibliography.

INTRODUCTION

1 Rhodes James p 382.
2 Conversation with author.
3 Ibid.
4 Ibid.

CHAPTER ONE

Based on papers in ATG, notably the diary of Admiral Baldwin, also correspondence between Joseph W. Alsop and Sir Francis Watson on Deacon House June 1968.

1 Will of David Deacon Sept 1823 (ATG).
2 Edward Preble Deacon to David Deacon 27 July 1839 (ATG).
3 Curtis pp 20 & 25.
4 Ibid.
5 Ibid.
6 Conversation with author.
7 Elliott pp 243–244.
8 European Station General Order no 7, USS Lancaster – Smyrna, Turkey 30 April 1884 (ATG).
9 Report by Rear-Admiral Baldwin to Hon W. E. Chandler, Secretary of the Navy Washington DC 22 June 1883 (ATG).
10 Mr Wurtz, Legation Department of US, St Petersburg to Navy Department 9 Oct 1883 (ATG).
11 Waddington pp 137–138.
12 Conversation with author.

CHAPTER TWO

Based on newspaper accounts 1892, notably NYT 18 Nov 1892, L'Affaire Deacon in Bataille pp 161–186, and letters from BB to Mary 9 July 1904, 14 Aug 1908, & 19 Nov 1916 (VIT).

1 Dedication of photograph from Philippe Berthelot to Gladys March 1930 (private collection).
2 D Tel 23 Feb 1892.
3 BB to Mary 9 July 1904 (VIT).

CHAPTER THREE

Based on *Drame de Cannes* (246) *Note concernant Madame Deacon* – Montesquiou (BNP), and newspaper accounts in 1892, including:

The News, Newport, 19 Feb, 21 May; *Times* 19, 20, 23, 29 Feb, 11 March, 21 May; D Tel 20, 23, 29 Feb, 21, 23, 28 May; NYT 20, 25, 29 Feb, 21, 22 May.

1 Heartbreaks of Society – *American Weekly* 21 Aug 1949.
2 D Tel 23 Feb 1892.
3 NYT 21 Feb 1892.
4 Matthiessen & Murdock p 116.
5 Ibid p 308.
6 Dumas Statement 19 May 1892 D Tel 20 May 1892.
7 NYT 21 May 1892.

CHAPTER FOUR

Based on Gladys's letters to her parents 1892–96, and newspaper accounts : *Times* 14 Oct & 23 Nov 1892; NYT 24 & 26 July, 9 Aug, 24 Sept, 14 Oct, 4, 6, 17, 18, 23 Nov, 3 & 29 Dec 1892, 3 & 7 Feb, 2, 3, 17, 25 Oct 1893, 4 Jan & 30 Sept 1894, 9 June & 7 Nov 1895, 23 Aug 1897, & 7 July 1901.

1   EPD to Gladys 30 March 1892 (GDP).
2   Sister to FB 2 April 1892 (GDP).
3   EPD to Gladys 24 Sept 1892 (GDP).
4   Gladys to FB 14 March 1893 (GDP).
5   NYT 24 March 1893.
6   Reported in Gladys to FB 19 May 1893 (GDP).
7   Gladys to FB 19 Nov 1893 (GDP).
8   Gladys to FB 22 Oct 1894 (GDP).
9   Gladys diary 8 Feb 1894 (GDP).
10 Gladys to FB 23 April 1895 (GDP).
11 Gladys to FB 19 Sept 1895 (GDP).
12 Gladys to FB 16 Oct 1895 (GDP).
13 Gladys to FB (undated) 1896 (GDP).
14 Gladys to FB (undated) 1896 (GDP).
15 Henry James to EPD 6 June 1897 (copy) (GDP).
16 Conversation with author.
17 *The News*, Newport 24 Aug 1897
18 Edward Cowles to W. P. Blake 9 Sept 1897 (ATG).

CHAPTER FIVE

Based on letters in the Montesquiou papers (for example from Helleu) (BNP) and letters at I Tatti (VIT).

1 Balsan p 98.
2 Conversation with author.
3 Gladys to FB 17 Oct 1897 (GDP).
4 Gladys to FB 8 Dec 1898 (GDP).

5 Conversation with author.
6 Unidentified press cutting dated 11 Feb 1902 (ATG).
7 Sermoneta p 104.
8 Morra pp 88–89.
9 Unidentified press cutting dated 11 Feb 1902 (ATG).
10 Clermont-Tonnerre, *R. de Montesquiou & M. Proust* p 61.
11 Berenson *The Passionate Sightseer* p 167.
12 Conversation with author.
13 Kiel p 22.
14 Ibid p 40.
15 Mary to BB 31 Dec 1901 (VIT).
16 Mary to BB 1 Jan 1902 (VIT).
17 Gladys to BB (undated) (VIT).
18 Gladys to BB (undated but 1898) (VIT).
19 Gladys to BB (undated but 1898) (VIT).
20 Gladys to BB (undated but 1898) (VIT).
21 Secrest p 217.
22 Gladys to BB (undated but Spring 1899) (VIT).
23 FB to BB (undated but 1900) (VIT).
24 Gladys to BB (undated but a Saturday 1900) (VIT).

CHAPTER SIX

Based on letters in GDP and VIT, and on *The Lady* 1902.
1 Mariano pp 91–92.
2 BB to Mary 21 April 1901 (VIT).
3 Mary diary May 1902 (VIT).
4 Churchill to Marlborough 22 Dec 1898 (LCW).
5 Consuelo to Gladys 6 Jan 1901 (GDP).
6 Ibid.
7 Conversation with author.
8 Lady Lansdowne to Gladys (undated but *ca* Dec 1921) (GDP).
9 Consuelo to Gladys 6 Jan 1901 (GDP).
10 Marlborough to Gladys (undated) Aug 1901 (GDP).
11 Mary to BB 3 Sept 1901 (VIT).
12 Balsan p 116.
13 Ibid p 117.
14 Chapman-Huston – Daisy, Princess of Pless p 89.
15 Consuelo to Gladys (undated) (GDP).
16 Gladys to BB (undated but Oct 1901) (VIT).
17 Forbes to Gladys 23 Dec 1901 (GDP).
18 BB to Gladys 28 Dec 1901 (GDP).
19 Gladys to BB (undated) (VIT).
20 Gladys to BB (undated) (VIT).
21 Conversation with author.

22   Mary diary 13 March 1902 (VIT).
23   Ibid 26 March 1902.
24   Ibid 30 March 1902.
25   Ibid 8 May 1902.
26   Copy in Mary diary 9 May 1902 (VIT).
27   *The Lady* 24 May 1902.
28   Mary diary 19 June 1902 (VIT).
29   Leslie, Sir Shane p 237.
30   *Le Matin* 11–13 Aug 1902.
31   Ibid 14 Aug 1902.
32   La Revue de Paris – Tableaux de Paris – La Comtesse Potocka –
     par Albert Flament 1931, p 697.

CHAPTER SEVEN

Material from *The Lady* May to July 1903, and Chapman-Huston
(10 Aug 1903), p 115.
 1   Conversation with author.
 2   Gladys to BB 25 Nov 1902 (VIT).
 3   Copy of letter Gladys to Marlborough (GDP).
 4   Gladys to BB 25 Nov 1902 (VIT).
 5   Gladys to Montesquiou (undated but Dec 1902 or Jan 1903)
     (BNP).
 6   Conversation with author.
 7   Sermoneta p 103.
 8   Ibid pp 103–104.
 9   Gladys to BB (undated but 1903) (VIT).
10   Dodge pp 241–242.
11   Bibesco pp 8–16.
12   Notes et Reflexions inédites de Robert de Montesquiou 4e
     accueil – Ombres Portées – 229 note concernant Miss Gladys
     Deacon – *Americanisme* (BNP).
13   Mary to BB 4 April 1903 (VIT).
14   Mary to BB 5 April 1903 (VIT).
15   Mary to BB 8 April 1903 (VIT).
16   BB to Mary 7 April 1903 (VIT).
17   Copy of letter Logan Pearsall Smith to Mary in Mary diary 27
     May 1903 (VIT).
18   Gladys to BB (undated but summer 1903) (VIT).
19   Gladys to BB (undated but Aug–Oct 1903) (VIT).

CHAPTER EIGHT

Largely based on material in VIT & GDP.
 1   Placci to Mary 10 Jan 1904 (VIT).

2   Rhodes James p 382.
3   Conversation with author.
4   Account of Audrey's death by Hortense Rey 1904 (GDP).
5   Hortense Rey to Gladys undated 1904 (GDP).
6   Copy of letter Gladys to Consuelo (GDP).
7   Gladys to Montesquiou (quoted in *Le Chancelier de Fleurs* 1908) (written 1905) (BNP).
8   Gladys to Montesquiou (undated) (BNP).
9   BB to Mary 20 June 1904 (VIT).
10 Gladys to BB (letter folded in BB to Mary 20 June 1904) (VIT).
11 Gladys to Roffredo – copy (GDP).
12 BB to Mary Aug 1904 (VIT).
13 Mary to BB 30 Aug 1904 (VIT).
14 Gladys to BB (undated, but *ca* 3 July 1904) (VIT).
15 BB to Gladys 7 July 1904 (VIT).
16 Gladys to BB (undated but *ca* 3 July 1904) (VIT).
17 Camastra to Gladys 7 Sept 1933 (GDP).
18 Ibid (undated but July 1904) (GDP).
19 Gladys to BB (undated but Aug 1904) (VIT).
20 Gladys to BB (22) Aug 1904 (VIT).
21 Dodge pp 241–242.
22 BB to Mary 17 Dec 1904 (VIT).
23 Garnett to author 24 Nov 1975 (HRV).
24 Mariano p 24.
25 BB to Mary 18 Dec 1904 (VIT).
26 Mary diary 28 March 1905 (VIT).
27 Dodge pp 241–242.
28 Gladys to Montesquiou 1905 (BNP).
29 Gladys to BB Dec 1905 (VIT).
30 Trevelyan p 324.
31 Gladys to BB 24 June 1906 (VIT).
32 Stein p 60.
33 Conversation with author.
34 Burns pp 281–284.
35 Painter p 63.
36 Proust to Hahn 7 Jan 1907 – Ibid p 124.
37 Proust to Gladys (undated but July–Aug 1918) (GDP).

CHAPTER NINE

1   Mary to BB 22 Oct 1906 (VIT).
2   BB to Mary 23 Oct 1906 (VIT).
3   Stead to Gladys (GDP).
4   Chapman-Huston, Diary (13 Nov 1902) p 69.
5   Balsan p 136.

6 Churchill, Randolph S. (Companion Vol II) p 588.
7 Ibid pp 588–589.
8 Magnus pp 405–406.
9 Pringle p 117.
10 Chapman-Huston, Diary (15 April 1907) p 207.
11 Clermont-Tonnerre, Marcel Proust pp 38–42.
12 Clermont-Tonnerre, R. de Montesquiou & M. Proust p 137.
13 Conversation with author.
14 Gramont, E de, Memoires (II) p 54.
15 Gramont, E de, Pomp & Circumstance p 22.
16 Conversation with author.
17 Ibid.
18 Ibid.
19 Mary to BB 18 June 1909 (VIT).
20 Reported in BB to Mary 31 Aug 1907 (VIT).
21 Conversation with author.
22 Mary to BB 2 Sept 1907 (VIT).
23 Copy in GDP.
24 Churchill, Randolph S. (Companion Vol II) pp 679–680 (W. S. Churchill to Lady Lytton 19 Sept 1907).
25 Conversation with author.
26 Copy of Gladys letter (GDP).

CHAPTER TEN

Based on Keyserling's letters to Gladys (GDP), and VIT material.
1 BB to Mary 29 March 1908 (VIT).
2 Keyserling p 20.
3 Ibid p 22.
4 Keyserling to Gladys 12 May 1908 (GDP).
5 Ibid 24 May 1908 (GDP).
6 Ibid 3 June 1908 (GDP).
7 Ibid.
8 Keyserling to Gladys 12 June 1908 (GDP).
9 Hofmannsthal p 277.
10 Hofmannsthal & Nostitz p 173.
11 Hofmannsthal to Gladys (undated) (GDP).
12 BB to Gladys 19 Aug 1908 (GDP).
13 Keyserling to Gladys 29 June 1908 (GDP).
14 Keyserling to Gladys 20 Sept 1908 (GDP).

CHAPTER ELEVEN

Based on letters between Gladys and her mother and letters from Marlborough to Gladys (1912–1914) (GDP).
1 FB to Gladys (GDP).

2   Clermont-Tonnerre, Marcel Proust pp 38–42.
3   Gabrieux to Montesquiou (BNP).
4   FB to Gladys 22 Feb 1911 (GDP).
5   Copy in GDP.
6   Edith Wharton to BB 28 March 1911 (VIT).
7   Conversation with author.
8   Gladys to FB 11 Nov 1911 (GDP).
9   Gladys to Rodin (MR).
10 Conversation with author.
11 Ibid.
12 Rodin to Gladys (undated) (GDP).
13 Conversation with author.
14 FB to Gladys (undated) (GDP).
15 Gladys to FB (April 1912) (GDP).
16 Ibid.

CHAPTER TWELVE

Includes material from Marlborough to Gladys 1914–1915, FB to Gladys, and letters between Mary and BB June, Aug, Sept, & Dec 1915; also NYT 19 April & 26 July 1915.
1   Ralph Curtis to Mrs Gardner (Gardner Museum Boston).
2   Gladys to FB (dated only Tues 24th) (GDP).
3   Gladys to FB 30 Nov 1914 (GDP).
4   FB to Gladys 27 Jan 1915 (GDP).
5   BB to Mary 30 Aug 1915 (VIT).
6   Mary to BB 25 Sept 1915 (VIT).
7   Ibid.
8   Mary to BB 28 Sept 1915 (VIT).
9   Marlborough to Gladys (undated) (GDP).
10 Marlborough to Gladys (undated) (GDP).
11 FB to Gladys (undated, but early 1916) (GDP).
12 Mary to BB 22 Feb 1916 (VIT).
13 Bibesco, pp 8–16.
14 Giraudoux, Jean (dimanche 1916).
15 Marlborough to Gladys 29 May 1916 (GDP).
16 Ibid (undated but Dec 1916) (GDP).

CHAPTER THIRTEEN

Based on Marlborough to Gladys, FB to Gladys, Walter Berry to Gladys, material in *Edith Wharton* by R. W. B. Lewis, and NYT 18 July 1918.
1   Gladys to Rodin 17 Feb 1917 (MR).

2   Buckle p 88.
3   Epstein p 96.
4   Ibid pp 95–96.
5   Gladys note on letter from Marlborough 18 March 1917 (GDP).
6   Marlborough to Gladys 5 Feb 1918 (GDP).
7   Gladys to FB 15 May 1918 (GDP).
8   Ibid.
9   Conversation with author.
10 Gladys to FB 15 May 1918 (GDP).
11 FB to Mary 29 June 1918 (VIT).
12 Gladys to FB 15 May 1918 (GDP).
13 Proust to Gladys (undated but July-Aug 1918) (GDP).
14 Marlborough to Gladys 28 July 1918.

CHAPTER FOURTEEN

Based on 37 letters from HRH Duke of Connaught to Gladys 1919–1920, in GDP; also Daily Graphic 1 Jan, 19 & 20 March 1920, Times 19 March 1920, Painter pp 286–287, & Mariano pp 25–26.
1   Morra pp 58–59.
2   Leslie, Anita p 216.
3   HRH to Gladys 20 March 1919 (GDP).
4   Ibid 26 March 1919.
5   Ibid 2 April 1919.
6   Ibid 9 April 1919.
7   Ibid 11 April 1919.
8   Ibid 20 April 1919.
9   Nicolson, Harold – The Peacemaking 30 April 1919 pp 318–319.
10 HRH to Gladys 19 July 1919 (GDP).
11 Ibid 22 July 1919.
12 Julian Trevelyan to author 13 Dec 1975 (HRV).
13 Conversation with author.
14 David Garnett to author 24 Nov 1975 (HRV).
15 Birrell to Gladys 22 Sept 1919 (GDP).
16 Ibid 1 Oct 1919.
17 Fry to Gladys 25 Jan 1920 (GDP).
18 Jaloux to Gladys 20 June 1920 (GDP).
19 HRH to Gladys 18 Dec 1919 (GDP).
20 Ibid 29 Dec 1919.
21 Ibid (1st letter) 30 Dec 1919.
22 Ibid (2nd letter) 30 Dec 1919.
23 Ibid 17 April 1920.
24 Copy of Gladys to HRH 4 May 1920 (GDP).
25 Marlborough to Gladys 10 Nov 1920 (GDP).
26 Jaloux to Gladys (undated) (GDP).

27 Conversation with author.
28 Gladys diary 2 June 1922 (GDP).

CHAPTER FIFTEEN

Based on Barker p 347, Painter pp 322–323, Lees-Milne p 272, NYT 2, 10, 11, 20, 23, 24, 25, 26 June, D Exp 3, 24, 25 June, *Times* 2, 24, 25, 27 June, D Mail 2, 25, 27 June, The Lady 30 June, Sunday Express 26 June (all 1921).

1 Marlborough to Gladys 2 June 1921 (GDP).
2 Bibesco p 8.
3 Schlumberger p 183.
4 Proust, letter to M & Mme Sydney Schiff 17 Oct 1921 – Correspondence Generale (III) pp 27–29.
5 Morand, undated letter – probably 16 June 1921 – quoted in *Le Visiteur du Soir*.
6 Grindea p 34.
7 Maurois, p 61–64.
8 Revue Hebdomadaire June 1936 p 18; & Figaro Littéraire 15 Oct 1955.
9 NYT 25 June 1921.
10 D Exp 25 June 1921.
11 *Times* 27 June 1921.
12 NYT 26 June 1921.
13 Ibid.

CHAPTER SIXTEEN

Based on Gladys diaries, Birkenhead – F. E. The Life of F. E. Smith, & NYT 17 Nov 1921.

1 Author conversation with Lady Epstein.
2 Sams, p 134.
3 Green, Blenheim Palace Guide Book p 37.
4 Green, Blenheim Palace (Country Life) pp 205–206.
5 Clermont-Tonnerre, Pomp & Circumstance p 283.
6 Gladys diary 9 Oct 1922 (GDP).
7 Conversation with author.
8 Ibid.
9 Clark, pp 261–262.
10 Conversation with author.
11 Gladys to Ottoline 13 June 1922 (HRC).
12 Ibid.
13 Author conversation with Paul Maze.
14 Gladys to Ottoline 13 June 1922 (HRC).
15 Nicolson, Nigel p 494.
16 Ibid p 499.

17   Mariano pp 25–26.
18   Trevelyan, Lord, The Happy Man (Saturday Review) – *Times* 29 April 1978.
19   Birkenhead, The Prof in Two Worlds p 128.
20   Ibid p 29.
21   Gladys to Ottoline 2 Aug 1922 (HRC).
22   Ibid 27 Sept 1922.

CHAPTER SEVENTEEN

Based on Gladys diary & Times 4 Oct 1922.
1   Gladys to Ottoline 27 Sept 1922 (HRC).
2   Ibid 25 Oct 1922 (HRC).
3   Copy of letter dated 29 Oct 1922 (GDP).
4   Conversation with author.
5   Holroyd, p 469.
6   Strachey to Gladys 5 Nov 1929 (GDP).
7   Epstein pp 94–96.
8   Marlborough to Gladys 18 Jan 1926 (GDP).
9   Ibid (26) Jan 1926.
10   Gladys diary 8 Feb 1924 (GDP).
11   Walter Berry to Gladys (undated) (GDP).
12   McCarthy, pp 254–255.
13   Clark, pp 261–262.

CHAPTER EIGHTEEN

Based on NYT 11 Nov – 8 Dec 1926, & Times 2 Feb 1927.
1   Churchill & Martindale, pp 9–10.
2   Leslie, Shane, pp 236–238.
3   Churchill & Martindale, p 15.
4   Ibid p 13.
5   Caraman p 158.
6   Martindale to Father John V. F. Maunsell 11 May 1959 (Collection of Father Maunsell).
7   Caraman p 161.
8   Times 26 Nov 1926.
9   NYT 22 Nov 1926.
10   NYT 26 Nov 1926.
11   NYT 18 Nov 1926.
12   NYT 6 Dec 1926.
13   NYT 1 Dec 1926.
14   NYT 20 Nov 1926.
15   NYT 17 Nov 1926.

CHAPTER NINETEEN

Based on Gladys diary, the letters of George Moore to Gladys (GDP), & the *Times* 15 Nov 1930.

1 Mugnier to BB 10 Oct 1927 (VIT).
2 Mugnier to Gladys 8 Nov 1927 (GDP).
3 *The Lady* 8 March 1928.
4 Gladys to Maurice Alexander 1 Oct 1934 (copy) (GDP).
5 Keyserling to Gladys 21 Dec 1929 (GDP).
6 Clermont-Tonnerre, Pomp & Circumstance pp 280–285.
7 Nicolson, Harold, Diaries & Letters 1945–62 (15 Nov 1951), p 212.
8 Moore to Gladys 15 Dec (undated, but 1926–28) (GDP).
9 Ibid 6 June 1929.
10 Ibid 25 July 1929.
11 Ibid 28 June 1930.
12 Houghton to Hon Hubert Putnam 1929 (LCW).
13 Marlborough to Putnam 4 Jan 1929 (LCW).
14 Times 16 Oct 1929.
15 Ashley, pp 4–7.
16 Conversations with author.
17 Ibid.
18 Bennett, p 292.
19 Ibid (11 March 1930), pp 292–293.
20 Bennett to Gladys 12 March 1930 (GDP).
21 Strachey to Gladys 12 March 1930 (GDP).
22 Augustine Birrell to Gladys 11 March 1930 (GDP).
23 Sassoon to Gladys 10 March 1930 (GDP).
24 Garnett pp 24–26.
25 Holroyd, p 650.
26 Garnett to Gladys 15 March 1930 (GDP).
27 Blanche, J-E, p 114.
28 Sitwell to Gladys (undated) (GDP).
29 Davie, p 318.

CHAPTER TWENTY

Based on documents in GDP, D Exp 9 & 10 Aug 1933, & Times 2 May & 2 July 1934.

1 Leslie, Anita to Gladys 24 May 1933 (GDP).
2 Ibid 6 Aug 1933 (GDP).
3 Cronin.
4 Gladys statement to Withers & Co 1933 (GDP).
5 Flament to Gladys 12 March 1931 (private collection).
6 Berenson, Sketch for a Self Portrait p 47
7 Morra, pp 88–89.

8 Grylls, Agnes, statement to Withers & Co 1933 (GDP).
9 Notes in Gladys photograph album (GDP).
10 Viscountess Churchill to Gladys 10 Aug 1933 (GDP).
11 Gladys to Marlborough copy 20 Oct 1933 (GDP).
12 Book belonging to late Eve Fairfax.
13 Sassoon to Gladys 16 Nov 1933 (GDP).
14 Sunday Express 1 July 1934.
15 Churchill & Martindale, p 16.
16 Sunday Express 1 July 1934.
17 Lady Edward Spencer–Churchill to Gladys 4 July 1934 (GDP).
18 Lily to Gladys 1 July 1934 (GDP).

CHAPTER TWENTY-ONE

Based on Gladys diary, Press Association report 4 Sept 1934, *Times*
31 Jan & 1 Feb 1935, D Tel & D Exp 31 Jan 1935, NYT 26 Aug 1934.
1 Gladys to Maurice Alexander 27 Aug 1934 (copy) (GDP).
2 Mugnier to BB 31 Dec 1934 (VIT).
3 Gladys to Maurice Alexander 27 Aug 1934 (copy) (GDP).
4 Ibid 1 Oct 1934.
5 Ibid.
6 East to Gladys 3 Feb 1935 (GDP).
7 Young, p 318.

CHAPTER TWENTY-TWO

Based on a letter from Lady Sophia Schilizzi to author, talks with
Mrs May Hobbs and Mr & Mrs Simon Speed, Gladys diaries and
letters to Gladys from Agnes Grylls (GDP).
1 Gladys to Marchand 19 Jan 1939 (copy) (GDP).
2 Ibid.
3 Ibid.
4 Conversation with author.
5 Gladys to Countess Palffy 4 June 1943 (copy) (GDP).
6 Rhodes James p 382.
7 Conversation with author.
8 Keyserling to Gladys 4 April 1946 (GDP).
9 Conversation with author.
10 Ethel Boileau to Gladys 7 July 1933 (GDP).

CHAPTER TWENTY-THREE

Based on conversations with members of Gladys's family, & Andrei
Kwiatkowsky; letters in the collection of Father John V. F. Maunsell.
1 Cooper to Gladys 21 Jan 1953 (GDP).

2   Leslie, Shane to Gladys 15 May 1959 (GDP).
3   O'Hara to Maunsell 22 Sept 1960 (Father Maunsell collection).

CHAPTER TWENTY-FOUR

Based on Gladys's diary 1962–1964 (not in GDP), and various reports from visitors, *all* of which are in private collections.

1   Letter from Gladys 6 May 1962 (private collection).
2   NYT 8 Jan 1976.

CHAPTER TWENTY-FIVE

Based on conversations with author, conversations between Andrei Kwiatkowsky and author. 'Sweet & Twenty' is in GDP.

Index

Index

Bennett, Arnold (1867–1931), 216, 220–21

Berenson, Bernard (1865–1959), on G, 54; career, 58–9; marriage, 60–63; relationship with G, 60–63, 73, 94, 111; taken in by FB, 65; G fades out of his grasp, 66; tours Italy with G, 74–5; visits Oxford & London, 76; visits US, 89; invites FB & G to dinner, 93–4; visits Roffredo Caetani, 95; on Camastra, 98; amused by G, 98–9; visits Rome, 100–101, 116–17; FB questions over Lord Brooke, 102; in St Moritz, 102, 112–14, 122–4, 130; falls under G's spell again, 103; Caetani drama, 103–4; beguiled by G, 113–14; notes G failing to dazzle, 117; probes G's personality, 123; G visits in hotel, 124; G drifts out of friendship with, 128; meets Doria in Milan, 128; lured to Caprarola, 141–2; on FB, 142; last meeting with G, 162; conclusions on G, 162, 229–30; hears about G's separation from M, 235; mentioned, 20, 24, 57, 84, 86, 130, 149, 156, 213, 215, 219, 242, 249, 250, 264

Berenson, Mary (née Pearsall Smith) (1865–1945), marriage, 59–60, 60n, 63; meets G, 65; visits FB in Paris, 65; speculates over Ivor Guest, 69; tours Italy with G, 74–5; visits Oxford & London, 76; calls on G at Sollier's, 84–5; worries about G, 86, 95–6; visits US, 89; long talk with G, 100–101; meets G in Florence, 103; on G's relationship with M, 106; horrified, 110; adoration of G, 111; questions BB about feelings for G, 114; calls on FB & G in London, 121–2; on Caprarola, 127–8; G drifts out of friendship with, 128; on FB's character, 142; at Caprarola, 142; FB visits at I Tatti, 143; on G's face, 145; sad letter from FB, 159; diary notes, 66, 74–5, 76, 100–101, 103, 143; mentioned, 112

Bergson, Henri (1859–1941), 122, 149

Berners, 14th Lord (1883–1950), 206, 223

Bernhardt, Sarah (1844–1923), 40, 80

Berry, Walter (1859–1927), 130, 193, 194, 207; at Degas sale, 156; character, 156–7; friendship with G, 157–8; at G's wedding, 177, 179; attempts to de-blenheimize G, 205; death, 213

Berthelot, Philippe, 179

Bertie, Sir Francis (later 1st Viscount Bertie of Thame) (1844–1919), 138, 145

Beuret, Rose (Madame Rodin) (1844–1917), 133, 151, 152

Bibesco, Princess Marthe (1888–1973), 83, 145–7, 175

Birkenhead, (Margaret) Countess of (1878–1968), 187, 188, 191, 200, 204, 206, 218

Birkenhead, 1st Earl of (1872–1930), 144,

188, 191, 199, 200, 206, 214; death, 218

Birkenhead, 2nd Earl of (1907–75), 185, 223, 227, 235

Birrell, Rt Hon. Augustine (1850–1933), 167, 221

Birrell, Francis (1889–1935), 167–8, 189, 221

Blanche, Jacques-Emile (1862–1942), 56–7, 207, 222

Blandford, Albertha Lady (Sunny's mother) (1847–1932), 67, 78, 175, 186, 197, 229

Blandford, (Mary) Lady (wife of 'Bert', later 10th Duke of Marlborough) (1900–61), 171, 186, 190, 252, 267

Blandford, Lord (later 8th Duke of Marlborough, Sunny's father) (1844–92), 67, 184

Blandford, Lord (Bert, later 10th Duke of Marlborough) (1897–1972), birth, 51, 72, 143, 154, 161; marries, 171; 175, 186, 211; succeeds M as 10th Duke, 237, 238, 243, 245, 252, 256, 267

Blenheim Palace, Woodstock, description, 183–6; G's early visits to, 68–70, 75, 86–7, 88; passim 183–238; mentioned, 2, 3, 6, 41, 51, 66, 67, 68, 71, 78, 79, 81, 107, 114, 135, 143, 145, 146, 149, 154, 173, 176, 241, 243, 244, 245, 251, 255, 256, 278

Bliss, Mrs Robert Woods (Mildred), 156, 179

Boileau, Lady (Ethel) (d. 1942), 169, 197, 255 & n, 256

Boisrouvray, Christine du, 179

Boisrouvray, La Comtesse du, 177, 178, 179

Boldini, Giovanni (1845–1931), 20, 56, 57–8; his portrait of G, 144–5; 148–9, 162, 168, 247

Bonar Law see Law, Andrew Bonar

Borghese, Prince Giovanni, 102

Bourne, Cardinal Francis (Archbishop of Westminster) (1861–1935), 211–12

Bowes-Lyon, Lady Elizabeth (later HM Queen Elizabeth The Queen Mother) (b. 1900), 199

Broglie, Princess Jean de (Daisy Fellowes) (d. 1962), 136

Brooke, Lord (later 6th Earl of Warwick) (1882–1928), 102, 103, 107, 113, 174

Brooks, Romaine (1874–1970), 63, 110

Buckle, Richard, 152

Buckmaster, 1st Viscount (1861–1934), 151, 204

Cadogan, Hon. Mary see Blandford, (Mary) Lady

Caetani, Prince Roffredo, 94; letter from G, 95; 97, 100, 103–4, 112, 113; marries, 130–31; letter to G, 131

Camastra, Octave Duke of, 97–8, 100, 218

Index

Index

G. Gray) (1887–1965), 12, 24, 27, 28,
29, 31, 33, 34, 36, 37, 38, 39, 43, 44,
45, 56, 66, 82, 90, 93, 97, 98, 101, 122,
128; engagement, 129, 130, 136;
marries, 141; 160, 179, 226, 232, 264
Deacon, Edward Parker (G's brother)
(1883–87), 12, 20
Deacon, Edward Parker (G's father)
(1844–1901), in Paris, 11–12; ancestors,
12–18; birth, 14; career and marriage,
15, 18; differences with FB, 20–26; in
Cannes, 27–31; shoots Abeille, 30;
press opinion of, 32; trial and imprisonment, 33; release, 35; kidnap attempt
on G, 35; divorce, 36; in London with
G, 36; in USA, 36–47; visits G at school,
44; at Somerset Club, 44; letter from
Henry James, 45; insanity of, 45–6;
death, 47, 66; mentioned, 174, 269
Deacon, Edward Preble (G's grandfather)
(1813–51), 13–14
Deacon, Florence, see Baldwin, Florence
Deacon, Gladys (later Duchess of
Marlborough) (1881–1977), Part One:
author's early interest in, 1–4; Chips on,
1; author's 1st visit to, 4–6; author's
2nd visit to, 6–7; 95th birthday of, 11;
birth, 11; background, 11–12; ancestors of, 12–18; childhood, 20, 25;
illness, 23; visits Homburg with EPD,
24; in Cannes with FB, 27; at Hotel
Splendide on night of murder, 29; in
custody of Marraine Baldwin, 31, 34;
travels to Genoa, 34; at convent at
Auteuil, 34–5; kidnapped by FB, 35;
travels to London with EPD, 36; travels
to NY with EPD, 36; re-united with
sisters, 37; at Newport, 37–8; at
Howard Seminary, 38–44; developing
talents of, 39–40; battles to escape from
EPD, 40; comments on M's engagement
to CV, 41; & the fortune teller, 42;
faces NY gossips, 43; in dilemma over
parental fights, 44; returns to FB in
France, 44; Henry James's interest in,
45; EPD's letter forwarded to, 46
Part Two: meets the Marlboroughs, 51;
CV on, 51; at school in Bonn, 51–3;
studies at Sacré Coeur, 53; descriptions
of, 53–4; in world of Montesquiou,
55–8; Helleu paints, 56; Blanche pre-
pares to paint, 56–7; Boldini sketches,
57; meets BB, 58–61, 63–4; visits
California, 62; in Paris, 62; attends
Lady Anglesey's receptions, 63; visits
BB at I Tatti, 65; & her father's death,
66; early visits to Blenheim, 68–70, 75,
86–7, 88; involved with M & CV, 68–9;
Ivor Guest in love with, 69; Crown
Prince of Prussia in love with, 69–70;
visits Germany with CV, 70; gives
M presents for his sons, 72; Lord Francis
Hope in love with, 72–3, 85; in Paris for

Christmas (1901), 73; travels with the
Berensons, 74–5; Mary on, 74–5, 84–5,
100–101, 145; London season of
(1902), 75–8; visits Norfolk, 78; and
Crown Prince story published, 78–9; at
zenith of success & beauty, 79; at
Versailles (1902), 80; in Devon with
CV, 80–81; angry with M for attending
Durbar, 81; amused by Montesquiou's
visit to NY, 81–2; Marion Crawford on,
82; 1st wax injections, 83–4; at
Sollier's for cure, 84–5; condition of
nose of, 85; FB afraid of elopement with
M, 85; Mary tries to take to I Tatti, 86;
Duke of Norfolk in love with, 86;
London season with Audrey (1903),
86–8; at Cowes with Daisy of Pless, 88;
in London with Norman Forbes, 89;
meets d'Annunzio in Rome, 90–91;
nurses Audrey, 91; worries & rumours
over Audrey's death, 92; contacts
Montesquiou from Rome, 93; in
Florence with FB, 93–4, 99–100, 103;
Roffredo Caetani in love with, 94–5,
103–4; illness of (1904), 95–6; feelings
of, 96, 98; description of Vallombrosa,
96–7; Duke of Camastra in love with,
97–8; at Versailles with FB, 99; meets
Robert Trevelyan, 99; life in Rome,
100–101; problems over Doria & FB,
101; in Roncegno, 101–2; & Yturri's
death, 101; Lord Brooke 'broken
hearted' over, 102; in Rome (1906),
103; wins BB back, 106; meets
Gertrude Stein, 104; Proust fascinated
by, 104–5, 108–9; & the Marlborough
separation, 106; snubs Prince Gorchakov,
108; friendship with Lily de Gramont,
109–10; lesbianism gossip about, 110;
on physical love, 111; fascination of BB
& Mary, 111; fascination of M & CV,
111–12; in St Moritz (1907), 112–14;
BB on face of, 112–13; further Brooke
dramas, 113; beguiles BB, 113; in
Venice with M & Winston, 114–15;
failing to dazzle in Rome, 116–17;
Keyserling in love with, 117, 119–22,
124–5; Hofmannsthal fascinated by,
122–3; quarrels with Montesquiou,
123; further deterioration of face of,
123; BB spends time with, 123–4; at
Caprarola, 127; Proust's attempt to
engage to Loche Radziwill, 128–9; &
Dorothy's wedding, 129; takes rooms in
London (1911), 129; visits Norway,
129–30; reacts to Roffredo's wedding,
131; & FB's debts, 131–2, 160; friendship with Rodin, 132–3, 139; & Rilke,
133; close relationship with M begins,
134; visits Mont-Dore with M, 135;
invites M to Caprarola, 135; in London
(1913), 135–6; visits Monet, 136–7; &
the outbreak of war, 138–9; on war

Index

Index

Index